LAW, LOVE AND FREEDOM

How does one lead a life of law, love and freedom? This inquiry has very deep roots in the Judeo–Christian tradition. Indeed, the divergent answers to this inquiry mark the transition from Judeo to Christian. This book returns to those roots to trace the twists and turns that these ideas have taken as they move from the sacred to the secular. It relates our most important mode of social organization, *law*, to two of our most cherished values, *love* and *freedom*. In this book, Joshua Neoh sketches the moral vision that underlies our modern legal order and traces our secular legal ideas (constitutionalism versus anarchism) to their theological origins (monasticism versus antinomianism). *Law, Love and Freedom* brings together a diverse cast of characters, including Paul and Luther, Augustine and Aquinas, monks and Gnostics, and constitutionalists and anarchists. This book is valuable to all lawyers, philosophers, theologians and historians who are interested in law as a humanistic discipline.

Joshua Neoh is a tenured faculty member at the law school of the Australian National University (ANU). He completed his LLB at the ANU, LLM at Yale, and PhD at Cambridge, and held visiting research positions at Harvard and Oxford. He is committed to an interdisciplinary study of law, and he has published in the fields of law and religion, law and literature, law and culture, law and philosophy, and law and the humanities.

LAW AND CHRISTIANITY

Series Editor
John Witte, Jr., Emory University

Editorial Board
Nigel Biggar, University of Oxford
Marta Cartabia, Italian Constitutional Court / University of Milano-Bicocca
Sarah Coakley, University of Cambridge
Norman Doe, Cardiff University
Rafael Domingo, Emory University / University of Navarra
Brian Ferme, Marcianum, Venice
Richard W. Garnett, University of Notre Dame
Robert P. George, Princeton University
Mary Ann Glendon, Harvard University
Kent Greenawalt, Columbia University
Robin Griffith-Jones, Temple Church, London / King's College London
Gary S. Hauk, Emory University
R. H. Helmholz, University of Chicago
Mark Hill QC, Inner Temple, London / Cardiff University
Wolfgang Huber, Bishop Emeritus, United Protestant Church of Germany / Universities of Heidelberg, Berlin, and Stellenbosch
Michael W. McConnell, Stanford University
John McGuckin, Union Theological Seminary
Mark A. Noll, University of Notre Dame
Jeremy Waldron, New York University / University of Oxford
Michael Welker, University of Heidelberg

The Law and Christianity series publishes cutting-edge work on Catholic, Protestant, and Orthodox Christian contributions to public, private, penal, and procedural law and legal theory. The series aims to promote deep Christian reflection by leading scholars on the fundamentals of law and politics, to build further ecumenical legal understanding across Christian denominations, and to link and amplify the diverse and sometimes isolated Christian legal voices and visions at work in the academy. Works collected by the series include groundbreaking monographs, historical and thematic anthologies, and translations by leading scholars around the globe.

Books in the Series

Great Christian Jurists in French History Olivier Descamps and Rafael Domingo
Church Law in Modernity: Toward a Theory of Canon Law Between Nature and Culture Judith Hahn
Common Law and Natural Law in America: From the Puritans to the Legal Realists Andrew Forsyth
Care for the World: Laudato Si' and Catholic Social Thought in an Era of Climate Crisis Frank Pasquale
Church, State, and Family: Reconciling Traditional Teachings and Modern Liberties John Witte, Jr

Great Christian Jurists in Spanish History Rafael Domingo and Javier Martinez-Torron
Under Caesar's Sword: How Christians Respond to Persecution edited by Daniel Philpott and Timothy Samuel Shah
God and the Illegal Alien Robert W. Heimburger
Christianity and Family Law John Witte, Jr. and Gary S. Hauk
Christianity and Natural Law Norman Doe
Great Christian Jurists in English History Mark Hill, QC and R. H. Helmholz
Agape, Justice, and Law Robert F. Cochran, Jr and Zachary R. Calo
Calvin's Political Theology and the Public Engagement of the Church Matthew J. Tuininga
God and the Secular Legal System Rafael Domingo
How Marriage Became One of the Sacraments Philip Reynolds
Christianity and Freedom (Volume I: Historical Perspectives, Volume II: Contemporary Perspectives) edited by Timothy Samuel Shah and Allen D. Hertzke
The Western Case for Monogamy Over Polygamy John Witte, Jr.
The Distinctiveness of Religion in American Law Kathleen A. Brady
Pope Benedict XVI's Legal Thought Marta Cartabia and Andrea Simoncini

Law, Love and Freedom

FROM THE SACRED TO THE SECULAR

JOSHUA NEOH

Australian National University, Canberra

CAMBRIDGE
UNIVERSITY PRESS

University Printing House, Cambridge CB2 8BS, United Kingdom

One Liberty Plaza, 20th Floor, New York, NY 10006, USA

477 Williamstown Road, Port Melbourne, VIC 3207, Australia

314–321, 3rd Floor, Plot 3, Splendor Forum, Jasola District Centre, New Delhi – 110025, India

79 Anson Road, #06-04/06, Singapore 079906

Cambridge University Press is part of the University of Cambridge.

It furthers the University's mission by disseminating knowledge in the pursuit of education, learning, and research at the highest international levels of excellence.

www.cambridge.org
Information on this title: www.cambridge.org/9781108427654
DOI: 10.1017/9781108564939

© Joshua Neoh 2019

This publication is in copyright. Subject to statutory exception and to the provisions of relevant collective licensing agreements no reproduction of any part may take place without the written permission of Cambridge University Press.

First published 2019

Printed and bound in Great Britain by Clays Ltd, Elcograf S.p.A.

A catalogue record for this publication is available from the British Library.

ISBN 978-1-108-42765-4 Hardback

Cambridge University Press has no responsibility for the persistence or accuracy of URLs for external or third-party Internet websites referred to in this publication and does not guarantee that any content on such websites is, or will remain, accurate or appropriate.

To my first love.

Contents

Acknowledgments		*page* x
	Introduction	1
1	Cosmological Beginning, Eschatological End	9
2	Conceptual Bipolarities	42
3	Methodological Turn to Historical Narrative	78
4	Prior Narrative: From Monasticism to Constitutionalism	98
5	Counter Narrative: From Antinomianism to Anarchism	133
6	Value Pluralism and the Search for Coherence	166
	Conclusion	182
Bibliography		190
Index		203

Acknowledgments

The great delight of publication is the ability to thank people in print. I have been waiting to thank Nigel Simmonds and Peter Cane for being such exemplary role models of what a scholar should be. I could only wish to be half the kind of scholars that they are. If there is any intellectual rigor at all in this book, I have learned it all from them. Peter, who was my undergraduate thesis supervisor at the ANU, sent me to Nigel, who became my doctoral thesis supervisor at Cambridge.

It is often difficult to account for academic debts, but the following are easy cases, for the debt is huge. Tony Connolly and Leighton McDonald were my first teachers in jurisprudence at the ANU, where I did my LLB. Robert Burt and Paul Kahn were the first who taught me to see law from a theological perspective at that most lawless of places called the Yale Law School, where I did my LLM. Paul Babie blazed the trail for law and religion in Australia, and I have followed in his trail ever since. I would not have persisted in this field, but for Paul's encouragement, which kept me going.

This book started life as a PhD thesis at Cambridge. I would not have been able to get to Cambridge without the generous financial support of the Cambridge Australia Trust and the institutional support of the ANU Law School, which gave me three years' leave to complete the PhD. Stephen Bottomley and Don Rothwell, who were the Dean and Deputy Dean at that time, believed in me enough to let me go, and for that, I am truly grateful. Sally Wheeler, the current Dean, accepted the return of the prodigal son.

At Cambridge, Matthew Kramer convened the Cambridge Forum for Legal and Political Philosophy, which became my primary academic community. The graduate student community in legal philosophy at Cambridge – John Adenitire, Raffel Fasel, Visa Kurki, Jyr-Jong Lin and Yalan Zhang – made doing legal philosophy fun. Jan Anton van Zanten and Yan Zi Au, despite being nonlawyers and nonphilosophers, were patient enough to sit through countless Gonville & Caius College Formal Dinners, with me going on and on about legal philosophy. Nick McBride and Sean Coyle were the examiners of the thesis. At the viva, they were frank, yet gentle. They kept a cool head, with a warm heart.

Part of the thesis was written at Harvard Law School. At Harvard, Noah Feldman's seminars on Jewish Legal Theory introduced me to a whole new world and a whole new way of thinking about the world. Franz Bauer and Kelly Dhru kept me fed with food for thought, while Keitaro and Hitomi Hamada kept me fed with actual food. While I was at home in Malaysia, the Penang Institute provided me with the most conducive environment imaginable for a scholar to read and write. Ooi Kee Beng, Wong Yee Tuan, Lim Sok Swan, Koay Su Lyn and Pan Yi Chieh were kind enough to welcome me, a stranger, into their midst. In Kuala Lumpur, Kamal Fadzil provided me with a home away from home.

At the ANU, my colleagues continue to be a source of inspiration. As faculty mentors, Des Manderson and Tim Bonyhady taught me, a babe in the woods, the ways of the world, while Alex Bruce and Matthew Zagor taught me the ways of the Lord. Kim Rubenstein gave me a job when I was a student, and then her good counsel when I became her colleague. Dilan Thampapillai saved me, twice, from having to live on the streets. As a research assistant, Joe Dean helped in the preparation of this manuscript with great care and good cheer. As a friend, Ryan Goss proves that a faithful friend is a sturdy shelter.

Finally, I thank John Witte, the General Editor of this series and a pioneer in the field of law and religion, for showing an interest in my work when he was at Harvard for a conference, although I was then a lowly graduate student, which led to a conversation, which led to this book; and John Berger, Silvia Glick, Danielle Menz and Claire Sissen at Cambridge University Press for their excellent editorial teamwork.

I am forever grateful to my parents for the most precious gift: the gift of life.

Introduction

How does one lead a life of law, love and freedom? This inquiry has very deep roots in the Judeo–Christian tradition. Indeed, the divergent answers to this inquiry mark the transition from Judeo to Christian. This book returns to those roots to trace the routes that these ideas have taken as they move from the sacred to the secular. The life of the monk is the paradigm case of a form of life that seeks, systematically and methodically, to integrate the values of law, love and freedom. Reading the various monastic codes, one finds the recurrent themes of law, love and freedom being emphasized in the form of life that the code creates. The monks seek to realize these values in their lives, and thereby actualize them in the world. The story of the monks goes to the heart of this book, and hence, it is placed right in the middle of it. With the story of the monks in the middle, the inquiry will start before and end beyond the monks. The monks were neither the first nor the last to engage in this pursuit of law, love and freedom. The monastic ideal has pre-Christian origins and post-Christian manifestations.

Law, love and freedom occupy center stage in both the Hebrew Bible and the Christian Bible, also known as the Old Testament and the New Testament. Both testaments could be read as different attempts to realize the values of law, love and freedom in the lives of the protagonists in the respective narratives – the Israelites in the Hebrew Bible and the Christians in the Christian Bible. Just as the key event in the Christian Bible is the Resurrection of Christ, so the key event in the Hebrew Bible is the Exodus of the Israelites. The two events are so closely connected theologically that the Exodus is often treated as foreshadowing the Resurrection. Both events are connected through what theologians call typological correspondence. Both events are also connected through a continuous contestation over the values of law, love and freedom.

The Exodus narrative provides the template for the recurrent trope of liberation in Western political thought: the hope for deliverance from oppression, and the march of history toward the Promised Land.[1] The Exodus narrative was the template for the Puritans as they journeyed from the Old World to the New. Law, love and freedom are all implicated in this narrative. The Israelites rid themselves of one set of laws, only to be bound by another. They rid themselves of the law of Egypt, only to be bound by the law of God. The law of God is infinitely more demanding and intrusive than the law of Egypt, regulating as it does every minute detail of life. The new Lord is a jealous God. His demands are exacting, and his punishments harsh. The Lord God demands nothing less than total love: 'you shall love the Lord your God with all your heart, and with all your soul, and with all your might'.[2] This love is to be expressed through absolute submission and complete obedience to him and his laws.[3]

As a result of the Exodus, have the Israelites become more or less free? There is no straightforward answer to this question, though this book will attempt to inch toward an answer in the course of six chapters. Standing at the foot of Mount Sinai with Egypt behind them and the Promised Land ahead of them, the Israelites are crossing a threshold more significant than the crossing of the Red Sea. At that point, Spinoza suggests that the Israelites have returned momentarily to the natural liberty of the state of nature; however, 'since natural liberty is in practice unendurable, the covenant – one or another covenant anyway – necessarily follows'.[4] The formation of the covenant on Mount Sinai is accompanied by the promulgation of laws, laws and more laws. The Israelites, understandably, 'want laws but not too many'.[5] There is an old Jewish folk tale that tells the story that, on the day after the Sinai covenant, 'the Israelites rose early and marched at double speed away from the mountain so that they would not be given any more laws'.[6]

Both the Exodus and the Resurrection are stories about the crossing of thresholds: the crossing from the law of Egypt to the law of the Torah in the Exodus, and the crossing from death to life in the Resurrection. Upon being convinced of the reality of the Resurrection, Paul would renew the contestation over the values of law, love and freedom. In transitioning from the law of Egypt to the law of the Torah, have the Israelites merely substituted one yoke for another yoke? Again, there is no straightforward answer to this question.

---

[1] Walzer, *Exodus and Revolution*, 134.
[2] Book of Deuteronomy 6:5.
[3] May, *Love: A History*, 26–7.
[4] Walzer, *Exodus and Revolution*, 75; Spinoza, *Theologico-Political Treatise*, 1:218–19.
[5] Walzer, *Exodus and Revolution*, 73.
[6] Ginzberg, *The Legends of the Jews*, 3: 242, as quoted in Walzer, 'The Legal Codes of Ancient Israel', 335.

Paul's view on this matter is equivocal. Paul struggled mightily with this question, which haunted him throughout his entire missionary career. He kept returning to this question in his letters. Paul is convinced that Jesus is the long-awaited Messiah, who has finally arrived with the good news to set the captive people free. That much is clear. Less certain is what the people are held captive by, and correspondingly, what they have to be freed from. One possible answer is law: Law is that which holds them captive and from which they have to be freed.[7] On this reading of his letters, the gospel that Paul preaches is a gospel of freedom from the law, founded on love alone. Even if this reading is right, one should bear in mind that Paul did not get to this conclusion at one go. Paul got there with stops and starts. He equivocated at every step of the way. Paul renewed the inquiry into law, love and freedom without solving it once and for all. Just as Paul renewed the contestation over the values of law, love and freedom as he carved Christianity out of Judaism, so Luther would do the same many centuries later as he carved Protestantism out of Catholicism. During the Reformation, the same values became the subject of controversy, but this time, the target of attack had shifted from the Pharisee to the Pope, and the yoke of the law had shifted from the law of the Torah to canon law.

The contestation over the values of law, love and freedom is as much a political question as it is a religious question. Moving from religion to politics, there is a similar tension being played out. We could ask of a political community what Paul asks of his religious community: What would it take to create a people? On the religious side of the coin, the ancient Israelite answer is the covenant. The covenant creates the people of Israel as a people of God. Freedom is achieved through membership in the covenantal community; and membership in the covenantal community is achieved through the observance of the law. In contrast to the ancient Israelites, Paul proposes a different answer: not law, but love. Instead of law, love would unite the new Christian community. On the political side of the coin, one could give an analogous response. On the one hand, one could say that the constitution creates a people. The constitution founds a political community, invests it with authority, and creates its trans-temporality. On the other hand, like Paul, one could retort: not law, but love. That which ultimately sustains the nation and links the person to the nation is a love for the nation. A citizen needs to

---

[7] Letter to the Galatians 5:1–4: 'For freedom Christ has set us free; stand fast therefore, and do not submit again to a yoke of slavery. Now I, Paul, say to you that if you receive circumcision, Christ will be of no advantage to you. I testify again to every man who receives circumcision that he is bound to keep the whole law. You are severed from Christ, you who would be justified by the law; you have fallen away from grace'.

become one with the nation in the deep and affective way that only love can sustain.

The contestation over the values of law, love and freedom returns and recurs in legal theory debates in different guises every now and then. In the 'ethic of right versus ethic of care' debate and the 'liberalism versus communitarianism' debate, there is a truly felt and deeply held concern that the language of rights, which is the quintessential language of law, is an alienating and imprisoning form of discourse. The language of rights places us in a combative and antagonistic posture in relation to one another. It builds walls instead of bridges. This dissatisfaction and discontentment with the language of rights then triggers the search for an alternative paradigm, which will provide an alternative mode of relating to one another. The ethic of care presents itself as an alternative to the ethic of right, and communitarianism as an alternative to liberalism.[8] With the Black Eyed Peas, they are asking: 'Where is the love?'

This book will make a renewed attempt to address this question. For such an ancient question, to aim for a definitive solution is sheer hubris. Instead, this book aims to shed some light on the puzzle, by arranging ideas and events differently, with the hope that one could see them in a new light. The goal is not so much to effectuate a paradigm shift as to introduce a gentle reorientation of perspective. Its unique contribution is its unremitting interdisciplinarity. This book deploys a whole range of disciplinary tools. The book draws on analytic jurisprudence in its analysis of law; ethics and aesthetics in its analysis of love; political philosophy in its analysis of freedom; biblical scholarship in its interpretation of Paul; the history of ideas in its study of the formation and transformation of these ideas; and moral philosophy in concluding how one could lead a life of law, love and freedom.

THE ARGUMENT

The argument of this book is threefold. First, it argues that the concepts of law, love and freedom are each internally polarized. Each concept contains, within itself, conflicting values. Paul's equivocation in his letters is a striking manifestation of this internal polarization. Second, it argues that while values are many, my life is one. Hence, one needs to combine the plurality of values within a singular life. Values find their coherence within a form of life. There are, at least, two ways of leading a life of law, love and freedom: monastic versus antinomian. Third, it argues that the Reformation transformed these religious ideals into political ideologies. The monastic ideal is politically

---

[8] See Taylor, 'Cross-Purposes: The Liberal-Communitarian Debate'.

manifested as constitutionalism, and the antinomian ideal is politically manifested as anarchism. There are, at least, two ways of creating a polity of law, love and freedom: constitutional versus anarchic.

CHAPTER OUTLINE

The threefold argument will be elaborated and defended in six chapters.

Chapter 1 will begin by considering two views of human nature. It will do that through an extended meditation on the creation myth in the Book of Genesis. The two views of human nature emerge chronologically in the myth, before and after the Fall: prelapsarian and fallen. Chapter 1 will then map those two views of human nature onto the two dominant accounts of the state of nature provided by Rousseau and Hobbes, respectively. Paul struggles to mediate between these two opposing views of human nature in his letters. Paul seesaws between these two views. The seesaw is most evident in his equivocal treatment of the values of law, love and freedom.

In contrast to Chapter 1, which is a show-and-tell, Chapter 2 is more cut and dried. Chapter 2 will tackle the concepts of law, love and freedom directly, that is, analytically. Chapter 2 will argue that law, love and freedom are bipolar concepts. Each concept is structured by two opposing values. Law is polarized between authority and resistance. Love is polarized between union and attention. Freedom is polarized between identification and independence. Chapter 2 will leave us in a conceptual quandary. The subsequent chapters will try to get us out of this quagmire.

Chapter 3 is both the midpoint and the pivot point for the book. Chapter 3 suggests a methodological change of direction. Chapter 3 will be the explicitly methodological chapter. It will argue that the way forward, to get out of the maze, is not through further abstract conceptual analysis, but through a narrative and historical turn. It will explore the merits of a historical narrative approach to understanding the nature of values.

Chapters 4 and 5 will apply the historical narrative method to make sense of the multiplicity of values embedded in the concepts of law, love and freedom. Chapters 4 and 5 will provide two historical narratives: a prior narrative and a counter narrative. Paul will be the starting point and the Reformation the turning point for both narratives. The prior narrative charts the story from Paul, through monasticism, to the Reformation, ending in constitutionalism. The prior narrative will unite the values of law as authority, love as union and freedom as identification. The counter narrative charts the story from Paul, through antinomianism, to the Reformation, ending in anarchism. The counter narrative will unite the values of law as resistance, love as attention and freedom as independence. Schematically, the two narratives could be represented as follows:

Prior Narrative: Paul → Monasticism → Reformation → Constitutionalism
Counter Narrative: Paul → Antinomianism → Reformation → Anarchism

PRIOR NARRATIVE	COUNTER NARRATIVE
Law as Authority	Law as Resistance
Love as Union	Love as Attention
Freedom as Identification	Freedom as Independence

Chapter 6 will be the explicitly theoretical chapter. I have not begun the book with a theoretical framework. My reason for postponing the theory till the end is to allow the theory to emerge over time, or more specifically, over the course of the preceding five chapters. Chapters 1 and 2 unpack the values of law, love and freedom. Chapter 3 supplies the methodological apparatus to repack these values. Chapters 4 and 5 repack these values in two narratives. Finally, Chapter 6 will wrap them up into a theoretical package. The book will end on the high note of value pluralism. Chapter 6 concludes with an endorsement of value pluralism, but with a twist. Although values are plural, my life is singular. There are many values, but there is only one life. Hence, there is a search for coherence amidst a pluralism of values. The coherence of values is to be found within a form of life.

TARGET AUDIENCE

Ideally, a reader would read the book from cover to cover, in the order and sequence in which it is presented. However, time is precious and life is short. Some readers may wish to take the shortcut and go straight to the chapters that interest them. For readers who are so inclined, the following remarks will help them to cut to the chase. This book has three target audiences in mind.

First, it targets scholars who are interested in the intersection of law and religion, especially legal theory and theology, specifically Anglo-American legal theory and Judeo–Christian theology. Chapters 1, 4 and 5 would be of particular interest to this audience. Chapter 1 maps the prelapsarian and the fallen views of human nature in the Book of Genesis onto the Rousseauian and Hobbesian views of human nature, and links these opposing views of human nature to the Pauline equivocation on the values of law, love and freedom in human life. Chapter 4 continues where Chapter 1 left off and tells the story of the history of ideas from Paul to the emergence of monasticism to the Reformation, and finally, to the growth of constitutionalism. Chapter 5 takes up the counter narrative and tells the story of the history of ideas from Paul to the emergence of antinomianism to the Reformation, and finally, to the growth of anarchism.

Second, it targets analytic jurisprudes, philosophers of law and legal theorists. These three groups of scholars constitute three expanding concentric circles. The catchment area gets larger as we move from the former to the latter. Chapters 2 and 6 would be of particular interest to this audience. Chapter 2 presents a conceptual analysis of the ideas of law, love and freedom. It argues that law, love and freedom are bipolar concepts, each of which is structured by two opposing values. Law is polarized between authority and resistance, a division that draws on debates in analytic jurisprudence. Love is polarized between union and attention, a division that draws on debates in ethics and aesthetics. Freedom is polarized between identification and independence, a division that draws on debates in political philosophy. Chapter 6 concludes with a qualified endorsement of value pluralism, which draws on debates in moral philosophy.

Third, it targets legal theorists with a lively interest in history, especially the history of ideas. History can teach us something about theory. History can substantiate theory: It can add substance to abstract theory. This approach to history and theory is expounded and defended in Chapter 3, which is the methodological chapter. Chapters 4 and 5 apply the method to tell two historical narratives: the prior narrative in Chapter 4 and the counter narrative in Chapter 5. The two narratives tell the story of the transition of ideas from Judeo to Christian, from ancient to medieval, from medieval to modern, and finally, from the sacred to the secular.

A NOTE ABOUT TIME AND TENSE

The subject matter of this book – law, love and freedom – is, at once, timeless and time bound, which makes the choice of tense a difficult one. With the exception of quotes, which I have kept as they are, this book adopts the following rule of thumb. It uses the present tense when making a philosophical or theological point, or when narrating a literary plot, and the past tense when making an historical point, or when narrating an historical event, or when there is otherwise a need to indicate the passage of time. This distinction is not easy to draw and it is often artificial to make such a distinction, but the grammar of the English language requires it. The choice of tense is even more contentious in the case of the Bible, which contains a mix of historical fact and fiction. The fictional elements are best read as literature, while the factual elements could, with the appropriate caveat and caution, be read as history. Sometimes, it might be necessary to switch tense in midsentence. In general, I have tried to adhere to the rule of thumb as far as possible, while striking a balance between sense and tense.

1

Cosmological Beginning, Eschatological End

In the moral domain, the problem is not scarcity but surplus. There is a surplus of moral goods – more than could be realized in a single life. Hence, the challenge of moral reasoning is to reconcile the one and the many: the one life and the many moral goods. Moral reasoning is the process of coming to grips with how moral goods fit together in a whole and wholesome life. The 'diversity of goods' needs to be fitted within the 'unity of life'.[1] The diversity of goods creates a conflict of values, which may be partially reconcilable in my subjective life, but the conflict remains in its full force in the objective realm of values. In this chapter, I shall introduce three moral goods: law, love and freedom. The next chapter will provide an analytic account of these goods and show what is good about them. The question that will occupy the rest of the book is how one could lead a life of law, love and freedom. Note the word *lead*: a life well lived is a life well led. Ordinary language is especially illuminating here. One does not just live a life. One leads a life. The former could be done willy-nilly, while the latter requires a conscious effort. Leading a life requires giving it a certain direction and not just drifting hither and thither where the wind blows in the sea of values. To be sure, one may choose to lead a life that embraces the vagaries of fate, along the path of what Nietzsche calls amor fati, but even then, it is a choice. When Nietzsche posits amor fati as the 'formula for greatness', he is presenting it as a conscious and considered choice.[2] It is a choice to lead one's life in a particular way. Leading a life is simply the ordinary-language way of expressing the Socratic insight that an unexamined life is not worth living.

---

[1] Taylor, 'Leading a Life', 183.
[2] Nietzsche, 'Why I Am So Clever', §10.

Law, love and freedom are what Taylor calls 'life goods': they make life good.[3] To comprehend these 'life goods', we need to connect them to a higher level of analysis, 'where we try to clarify what it is about human beings' that makes those 'life goods' good for us: it requires us to paint 'a certain kind of picture of the universe, our capacities, and the possible stances toward this universe they make possible for us'.[4] The life goods only make sense within a certain picture of the universe, and that picture is sustained and passed on in a whole range of media: 'stories, legends, portraits of exemplary figures and their actions and passions, as well as in artistic works, music, dance, ritual, modes of worship, and so on'.[5] I will introduce the three 'life goods' of law, love and freedom by recounting a story. The story that I will recall is as old as the hills, or rather, as old as the world. It is a story of the beginning of the world.

Let's start from the beginning, from the very beginning. Let's begin with Eden. Eden is our cultural field site for the study of the state of nature. Geertz, the famous proponent of symbolic anthropology, defines culture as 'a system of inherited conceptions expressed in symbolic forms by means of which men [and women] communicate, perpetuate, and develop their knowledge about and their attitudes toward life'.[6] The story of Eden in the Book of Genesis is symbol laden. For centuries, thinkers in the West 'saw their own situations, their sufferings and their hopes mirrored in the story of the creation and the fall'; they 'read the story of Adam and Eve, and often projected themselves into it'.[7] Their 'conceptions of perfection and experiences of imperfection' were 'explicated in terms of the Genesis story'.[8] As a creation myth, the Edenic story provides neither a scientific account of the origin of the species nor a historical account of actual events; rather, it provides an imaginary and a highly imaginative account of human nature. As Rousseau says at the start of his Second Discourse: 'Let us begin by dispensing with the facts, for they are not relevant to the question. We must not take the investigations which one could enter into concerning this subject for historical truths, but only for hypothetical and conditional reasons, more suitable for illuminating the nature of things than for showing the true origin'.[9]

The Edenic narrative is a 'scenic imagination': it presents the scene of the origin of humanity. *Skene*, from which the word *scene* is derived, refers to the

---

[3] Taylor, 'Leading a Life', 173.
[4] Taylor, 'Leading a Life', 173.
[5] Taylor, 'Leading a Life', 179.
[6] Geertz, 'Religion as a Cultural System', 87, 89.
[7] Pagels, *Adam, Eve and the Serpent*, xx–xxi.
[8] Morris, 'A Walk in the Garden: Images of Eden', 21.
[9] Rousseau, *Discourse on Inequality*, [6].

background for the performance of ancient Greek theater. It is the background before which the human and divine drama is played. Likewise, the scenic imagination of a creation myth is the background before which the play of life unfolds. As the Bard tells us, 'all the world's a stage, and all the men and women merely players'.[10] The scenic imagination of origin 'generates the meaning and structure that characterize the human'.[11] At first, the scene of origin was invariably religious. However, over time, the scenic imagination morphed into 'a more or less rigorously controlled anthropological thought experiment, no longer concerned with what the gods have given humanity, but with what it has generated on its own'.[12] As a result, the thought experiment replaced the creation myth. Nonetheless, the purpose of a scenic imagination, whether in the form of a creation myth or a thought experiment, remains the same. Its purpose is not empirical validation, but ethical illumination. How we imagine our cosmological beginning has direct impact on how we perceive our eschatological end.

The two most prominent scenic imaginations of origin that are generated through thought experiments are those of Hobbes and Rousseau, both of whom aim to paint a picture of original humanity in the state of nature. This chapter will show that these two thought experiments about the state of nature are more continuous with the Edenic creation myth than they appear to be. Hobbes paints a picture of universal strife, while Rousseau paints a picture of perfect tranquility. Hobbes and Rousseau may be worlds apart, but both could be accommodated within the Edenic frame. Rousseau's world is prelapsarian, while Hobbes's world is fallen. The Edenic narrative, Rousseau's prelapsarian world and Hobbes's fallen world will set the background scene, or *skene*, for the initial investigation into the place of law, love and freedom in human nature. In this chapter, we will go back to Eden to find where law, love and freedom first arise in the story, based on my interpretation of the creation myth. This chapter will conclude with a turn to Paul: to look at how Paul the Apostle uses this story of cosmological beginning to construct a vision of the eschatological end, and how Paul situates the values of law, love and freedom within his eschatological vision. This chapter will be a show-and-tell: it will show the concepts by telling a story (in a more literary style). Chapter 2 will be more cut and dried: it will provide detailed accounts of these concepts (in a more analytic style).

---

[10] Shakespeare, *As You Like It*, 2.7.138–9.
[11] Gans, *The Scenic Imagination*, 4.
[12] Gans, *The Scenic Imagination*, 10.

I COSMOLOGICAL BEGINNING: THE STORY OF EDEN

The story of the Garden of Eden is a creation story that consists of two chronologies of creation. The first chronology runs from Genesis 1:1 to 2:3. The second chronology runs from Genesis 2:4 to 3.

In the first account of creation, God says, 'Let us make man in our image, after our likeness' (Genesis 1:26). 'God created man in his own image, in the image of God he created him, male and female he created them' (Genesis 1:27). At that point, God moves from solitude to society: a community of three – God, man and woman – comes into existence. Then God says, 'Be fruitful and multiply' (Genesis 1:28). This statement is not so much a commandment, but a statement of ontological fact. The nature of human beings is *to be* fruitful and multiply. That is the very nature of being human. Being fruitful is part of the natural condition of being alive, not only of human beings, but also of all living beings. Humans share this creative and procreative nature with the other creatures of the earth: a few verses earlier, the creatures of the seas are similarly called to 'be fruitful and multiply and fill the waters in the seas' (Genesis 1:22) and the earth is called to 'put forth vegetation' (Genesis 1:11) and 'bring forth living creatures' (Genesis 1:24).[13] Even if one were to read this statement as a commandment, it is an affirmative commandment with no prohibition or punishment attached, which is radically different from the commandment that we will encounter in the second creation account. In Genesis 1:29, God says, 'Behold, I have given you every plant … and every tree'. Note the word *every*. The gift by God is given in abundance, indeed in superabundance. The earth is lavish and plentiful for human dwelling. In Genesis 1:31, the final verse of the chapter, 'God saw everything that he had made, and behold, it was very good'. It is not just good, but very good. The image is one of goodness, overwhelming and overflowing goodness.

On the seventh day, God rests. But while God rests in Genesis 2:3, his creation unravels and his good work is undone, so much so that, in the next verse (Genesis 2:4), God has to recreate the world. In the second account, God has to exert some physical force to mold man out of clay. In contrast to the first account, man is not created with woman. Woman is created later, out of the ribs of man. Everything else in the world is created by an act of speech; only man and woman are created by the hand of God.[14]

In the first account, God says, 'Behold, I have given you every plant … and every tree'. In the second account, there is no such plenary grant. In Genesis 2:16–17, 'the

---

[13] Brett, *Genesis: Procreation and the Politics of Identity*, 27.
[14] Zornberg, *Genesis: The Beginning of Desire*, 18.

Lord God commanded the man, saying, "You may freely eat of every tree of the garden; but of the tree of the knowledge of good and evil you shall not eat, for in the day that you eat of it you shall die"'. This commandment is very significant, because in this statement lies the emergence of the logic of law in the Garden of Eden. The phrasing of the command consists of two clauses: the first clause ('you may freely eat of every tree of the garden') suggests that everything is permitted – only to, a moment later, take it back in the same breath with the second clause ('but of the tree of the knowledge of good and evil you shall not eat'). One's mind is teasingly brought to imagine total freedom only to be encaged immediately by the prohibition. The resulting image is not one of plenitude, but rather it is one of limitation. This prohibition is backed by the threat of punishment, capital punishment: 'in the day that you eat of it you shall die'. This is the first prohibition in the Bible, the first of many.

This prohibition is issued before humans have the capacity to exercise any private moral judgment – for they have not yet eaten the fruit of the tree of the knowledge of good and evil – which reinforces the point that 'what God commands must be obeyed, not weighed'.[15] This sole prelapsarian prohibition, in contrast to all other later prohibitions, derives all its obligatory force from its being commanded by God. Its obligatoriness comes purely from its positivity, not its morality. Later prohibitions could, in principle, derive their obligatory force from their moral quality, but not this prelapsarian prohibition, for at this point humans lack the knowledge of good and evil. Lacking the knowledge of good and evil, they cannot engage in moral reasoning. Without the capacity for moral reasoning, they cannot turn to morality to discern the obligatory force of the prelapsarian prohibition. This particular commandment is, literally, beyond good and evil.

The story then proceeds to the infamous transgression. The serpent confronts Eve to ask her to clarify God's command. The serpent is like a typical lawyer who is obsessed with clarifying the boundaries of the rule. Eve's reply is found in Genesis 3:2–3: 'And the woman said to the serpent, "We may eat of the fruit of the trees of the garden, but God said, you shall not eat of the fruit of the tree which is in the midst of the garden, neither shall you touch it, lest you die."' Eve's restatement of the rule is not entirely accurate. The prohibition is limited to the eating of the fruit. Eve has extended the prohibition to cover, not only the eating of the fruit, but also the touching of it. The serpent responds by saying, 'You will not die'. God's threat is that, *on the day* humans eat of the fruit, they shall die. However, as it turns out, after eating the fruit, Adam and Eve survive. The threat proves to be an empty threat. It is often said that the

[15] Kaplan, *Judaism as a Civilization*, 152.

cunning serpent tricked Adam and Eve into eating the fruit, but did it really? The serpent is, strictly speaking, truthful: Adam and Eve remain alive after eating the fruit. In fact, Adam will continue to live for another 930 years! One could only speculate as to why God does not carry out his threat. My own speculation is that he wants to continue to have a relationship with humans.[16] He wants to love and be loved by humans – he cannot love them if he kills them; they cannot love him if they are dead. The Book of Genesis never mentions the hereafter or the existence of life after death.[17] In fact, God tells Adam quite directly that 'you are dust and to dust you shall return' (Genesis 3:19).

Eve eats the fruit and gives it to Adam, who also eats it. The first thing that they realize after they eat the fruit and gain the knowledge of good and evil is that they are naked. So, they sew fig leaves to cover themselves. Up till this point, they were naked before God and they were not ashamed; they were in an intimate relationship with God, in which shame had no place. This linkage between nakedness and shame shows that the divine–human relationship is no longer the same. Adam and Eve then hear the sound of God 'walking in the garden in the cool of the day', as if taking an evening stroll. God the Almighty is looking for his human companion, whom he has just created. God calls out to Adam, 'Where are you?' (Genesis 3:9).[18] Despite his great power and might, God nonetheless longs for human company. This longing by God for human company only arises after the giving of the command, which suggests that the giving of the command has resulted in a kind of separation, or at least a feeling of separateness, between God and humankind. But Adam and Eve are in hiding. In the words of Adam, 'I was afraid ... and I hid' (Genesis 3:10). Fear, particularly the fear of authority, has entered the Garden: Adam and Eve are now conscious, indeed acutely conscious, of the power differential between them and God. They are now aware of their vulnerability in the face of this overwhelming power.[19]

When Adam's wrongdoing is discovered, he does what generations of men after him are fond of doing: blame it on the woman. In Genesis 3:12, the man says, 'The woman whom thou gavest to be with me, she gave me the fruit of the

---

[16] This is, actually, Robert Burt's speculation, which I have made my own; see Burt, *In the Whirlwind: God and Humanity in Conflict*, ch 1–3.
[17] Dershowitz, *The Genesis of Justice*, 33.
[18] I take this question to be a genuine question. At this stage in the narrative, all that God knows is that he has given humans a command. God has not yet found out about the breach of the command. One could rebut this reading of the text by positing that God is omniscient, but that would be reading (or forcing) omniscience into the text. There is no indication in the text that God is omniscient.
[19] Magonet, 'The Themes of Genesis 2–3', 39, 44.

tree, and I ate'. More than blaming the woman, who is Adam actually blaming? God! And who does Eve blame? In Genesis 3:13, 'the woman says, "The serpent beguiled me, and I ate."' After witnessing the world's first blame game, God curses Adam and Eve, and expels them from the Garden of Eden.[20] A story that begins with blessings in abundance ends with curses aplenty. The story moves swiftly from rapture to rupture. It shows the two faces of human nature: prelapsarian and fallen. Humans start off as noble savages, but end up as nasty brutes. Rousseau and Hobbes are each half right.

Prelapsarian Human: The Noble Savage

In examining the foundations of society, Hobbes took the journey back to the state of nature, but, as Rousseau points out, Hobbes did not go back far enough.[21] If Hobbes had gone back far enough, he would have found the prelapsarian human: a noble savage. Instead, as Hobbes stopped halfway, what he actually found was merely the fallen human, the human whose life is nasty, brutish and short (a nasty brute, for short). I will say more in Section 2 about the fallen human, or Hobbes's nasty brute. In this section, let's go back all the way and examine more closely the original human: the prelapsarian human, or Rousseau's noble savage. Neither Rousseau nor Hobbes used the phrase 'noble savage' or 'nasty brute', but I am using them here as convenient shorthand for the kinds of human beings that Rousseau and Hobbes describe in their respective portrayals of the state of nature.

Notwithstanding the tragic end to the Edenic story, in our literary imagination, we still think of the Garden of Eden as paradise on earth, as a place of perfect harmony between God, humankind and nature, as a place of abundance and everlasting life. Prior to the Fall, in the Garden of Eden, man and woman are in paradise. There is neither scarcity nor competition in Eden – instead, it is a site of boundless, self-renewing fecundity that satisfies and nurtures all forms of life.[22] Not only is there no scarcity and competition, prior to the giving of the prohibitive command, there is also no notion of obedience to authority. It is only with the giving of the command that obedience, or disobedience, to God's authority becomes a distinct and

---

[20] The story not only contains 'the first breach of the law', but also 'the first criminal prosecution' and 'the first sentencing decision'. Fox, 'Sentencing in the Garden of Eden', 4. See also Lytton, 'Due Process and Legal Authority in the Garden of Eden: Jurisprudence in Aggadic Midrash'.
[21] 'The philosophers who have examined the foundations of society have all sensed the necessity of going right back to the state of nature, but none of them has arrived there'. Rousseau, *Discourse on Inequality*, [5].
[22] Burt, *In the Whirlwind*, 13.

comprehensible possibility.[23] Prior to that, there is nothing to obey or disobey – indeed, the very concept of obedience to an external authority would have been unintelligible in the absence of any assertion of authority.

Like Eden, Rousseau's state of nature is also a site of boundless, self-renewing fecundity that satisfies and nurtures all forms of life: 'the earth, left to its natural fertility and covered with immense forests never mutilated by an axe, offers at every step storehouses and shelters for animals of all species'.[24] 'The productions of the earth provided him all the necessary help' and 'instinct prompted him to make use of them'.[25] Like the prelapsarian dwellers of Eden, Rousseau's noble savages 'live in the most profound security and without the slightest inconvenience'.[26] Neither the prelapsarian couple nor the noble savages have any notion of obedience to authority: so complete is the absence of any notion of obedience to authority among the noble savages that 'people would have great difficulty even explaining what servitude and domination are' to them.[27] Rousseau's noble savages 'could not have been either good or bad' – for they have 'not the slightest idea of goodness' and they are perfectly 'ignorant of vice' – like Adam and Eve prior to the eating of the fruit from the tree of the knowledge of good and evil.[28]

In the first creation account, man and woman live in a state of union and oneness with each other and with God: they are created together, and together they are in the image and likeness of God. In the second creation account, God creates man in an intensely physical, even erotic, manner when God molds man from clay and breathes into man's nostrils the breath of life. Woman, in turn, is created out of the ribs of man: man and woman are of 'one flesh' (Genesis 2:24), and they carry within them the breath of God. In their primordial state in Eden, Adam and Eve are one with each other and with God. More than merely being in the presence of God, they are in the image and likeness of God. Their every desire is satisfied in the universe that they find themselves in, like a fetus in the mother's womb. The idea of 'the Garden as a womb' is linked to a psychoanalytic – in particular, a Jungian – reading of the story, in which the initial state of the Garden represents 'the ego's original oneness with nature and deity'.[29] God, Adam and Eve are complete in themselves, until the giving of the prohibitive command.

---

[23] Burt, *In the Whirlwind*, 28.
[24] Rousseau, *Discourse on Inequality*, Pt 1, [3].
[25] Rousseau, *Discourse on Inequality*, Pt 2, [2].
[26] Rousseau, *Discourse on Inequality*, Pt 1, [8].
[27] Rousseau, *Discourse on Inequality*, Pt 1, [60].
[28] Rousseau, *Discourse on Inequality*, Pt 1, [43]–[44].
[29] Cunningham, 'Type and Archetype in the Eden Story', 292.

The turning point of the story comes in the giving of the command, not in the breach of it. It is the command that changes everything. Borrowing Rousseau's terminology, the giving of the command marks the momentous transition from the natural order to the social order (or more accurately, the social *dis*order). The subsequent breach of the command is merely the playing out of the logic of law initiated by the prior giving of the command. The relationship between God, Adam and Eve will never be the same again once the command is issued. They lose their original organic union, not at the point of transgression, but at the prior point of prohibition, when God issues the prohibitive command. The command fractures the hitherto undifferentiated state of union between God and humanity. It creates a power hierarchy in their relationship. It differentiates between the ruler and the ruled. It gives rise to a relationship of power between God and humanity, eventually leading to a power struggle between them. The serpent tempts humanity to eat the forbidden fruit by holding forth the promise that, by eating the forbidden fruit, humans will become like God: 'For God knows that when you eat of it your eyes will be opened, and you will be like God' (Genesis 3:5). The temptation is not just about the fruit; more than the fruit, the temptation is about the desire of the ruled to be the ruler. When the prohibition is issued, the transgression is doomed to follow. From that point in the narrative, we, the readers, are merely waiting for the inevitable – the transgression – to happen. Throughout the Hebrew Bible, we see a continuous proliferation of the dialectic of law and its transgression.

Prior to the command, there may have been a difference between the creator and the created, but it is a difference that binds, not one that divides. The creature is bound to the creator in the act of creation. However, as soon as the command is issued, Adam becomes a distinct legal subject – subject to the sovereignty of God. When God chooses to adopt the logic of law, the result is that there is a changed relationship between creator and creature.[30] Their relationship becomes one of sovereign and subject. For the first time, a battle of wills – between the human will and the divine will – becomes a distinct possibility. There could now be a clash between sovereign and subject, between authority and autonomy. The hierarchy between God and Adam is later replicated in the hierarchy between Adam and Eve. After the eating of the fruit, God says to the woman that, henceforth, the man 'shall rule over' her (Genesis 3:16). The hierarchy is also replicated in the relationship between human and nature. After the eating of the fruit, God says to the serpent that, henceforth, 'he shall bruise your head, and you shall bruise his heel'

---

[30] Magonet, 'The Themes of Genesis 2–3', 42.

(Genesis 3:15). Again, to adopt Rousseau's terminology, 'man is born free', but after the Fall, 'everywhere he is in chains'.[31] God chooses to adopt the logic of law in his dealing with humanity by issuing the prohibition at a specific point in the narrative, thereby transforming forever the nature of the divine–human relationship. Why does God do that? Only God knows.

Although only God knows, we could speculate. In order for God to be God, he needs another independent being to recognize him as such. God needs humans to be independent beings in order for humans to be in a relationship of mutual recognition with him. On this view, God needs humans, just as humans need God, for mutual recognition. The obvious counterargument here is that God is entirely self-sufficient, that he has no need for anything or anyone. This counterargument is obvious, but not obviously correct. The importation of the idea of divine self-sufficiency into the Genesis narrative, which is not mentioned at all in the text, requires as much justification as the idea of divine longing for human recognition. Without this mutual recognition, God will revert to the state of divine solipsism that he was in before the creation of the world.[32] The Baltimore Catechism of 1885 for schoolchildren states as much in the following couplet: 'Why did God make you? God made me to know him'.[33] One could give the answer a more explicit Hegelian twist by saying that God made me to *recognize* him. God and humans become fully aware of their existence as self-conscious beings when they mutually recognize each other's self-consciousness. As Hegel says, 'self-consciousness exists in and for itself when, and by the fact that, it exists for another; that is, it exists only in being acknowledged'.[34] Or as Jung says, 'Loudly as his power resounds through the universe, the basis of its existence is correspondingly slender, for it needs conscious reflection in order to exist in reality – existence is only real [in psychoanalytic terms] when it is conscious to somebody – that is why the Creator needs conscious man'.[35]

In order for humans to recognize God as a self-conscious being, humans themselves have to be self-conscious beings. For this process of mutual recognition to begin, humans have to grow in self-consciousness. A subject starts on the path toward self-consciousness through the experience of desire, for desire makes the subject aware of the faculty of the will, especially self-will. Nothing stimulates desire as much as a prohibition. 'Once there is a contrast

---

[31] Rousseau, *The Social Contract*, Bk I, ch 1.
[32] I am leaving aside angels, whose existence is not corroborated in the Genesis creation story.
[33] *A Catechism of Christian Doctrine, Prepared and Enjoined by Order of the Third Council of Baltimore* (1885), Pt 1, Question 6.
[34] Hegel, *Phenomenology of Spirit*, §178.
[35] Jung, *Answer to Job*, 11.

1 Cosmological Beginning: The Story of Eden

between the world of which I am aware and the world as I want it to be, and once I act on the world in order to make it conform to my desires, I may acquire some minimal consciousness of myself as something distinct from the rest of my world'.[36] God desires and wills that humans not eat the forbidden fruit, but humans desire and will the direct opposite: to eat the forbidden fruit. Humans are unlike the vegetables that God created earlier. Humans have a will that is different from God's. They can resist the will of God. Humans can talk back to God in the way that vegetables cannot. God cannot bend humans to suit his will in the way that he can with vegetables.

In order for God to attain full self-consciousness, he needs to be recognized by another self-conscious subject with an independent will. God needs a human subject, not another object. The possibility of mutual recognition between God and humans arises when these two strong willed and self-conscious beings confront each other. The possibility hovers between 'the radical denial of the other and the promise of mutual recognition'.[37] Throughout the Hebrew Bible and into the Christian Bible, God will threaten to deny his human subjects repeatedly, only to return later to reengage with them. On numerous occasions, God will threaten to end the relationship there and then, once and for all, but he is never quite able to. Humans, too, will walk away from God repeatedly, only to come back to God later to reengage with him. The story of the divine–human relationship is the story of them falling out and coming back together, only to fall out again and come back together again. They need each other to create this intersubjective space, within which they can both attain full self-consciousness in mutual recognition. However, the price that must be paid for the attainment of this mutual recognition is the end of the prelapsarian state.

The giving of the command signals the beginning of the end of the prelapsarian state. The giving of the command introduces the logic of law into the world, even if it is not yet a full-blown legal regime. I will provide detailed accounts of law, love and freedom in Chapter 2, but, for the time being, even without any detailed accounts at hand, one could venture, tentatively, to make certain impressionistic and intuitive observations about law, love and freedom in the story. The prelapsarian human knows no law. In that prelaw state, there is no individual me, but only a collective we. Can we speak of love in the absence of individuality? Yes, but only in the sense of love as union and oneness. In the first creation account, God calls things into being simply by an act of performative utterance. He simply says, 'Let it be so', and it

---

[36] Norman, *Hegel's Phenomenology*, 46.
[37] Bird-Pollan, 'Hegel's Grounding of Intersubjectivity in the Master-Slave Dialectic', 244.

is so. God's 'creative fiat induces a spasm of realization of new forms' in nature.[38] God's word, his logos, is so all encompassing that it would be impossible 'to conceive of rebellion, or even of dialogue'.[39]

Law fractures the state of love as undifferentiated union. Law introduces differentiation, and consequently, individuation. After the eating of the forbidden fruit, the first thing that Adam and Eve do is to cover their bodies. The love that is manifested in the intimacy of nudity is gone. The bare body is now the object of shame. Before the Fall, 'they are not aware of being distinct beings, neither distinct from each other or from God'.[40] After the Fall, they become aware, not only of their nakedness, but also of their separateness: the man and the woman begin to see that they are 'separate and different' from each other and from God. 'The final realization of separation and difference comes when God enters the Garden, and Adam and Eve hide because they do not know how to respond to God as a totally separate being'.[41] However, when one door closes, a window opens: the loss of love as union closes a particular experience of love, but it opens up the possibility of a new experience of love. The newfound sense of individuality makes possible a new plethora of experiences that require some kind of distinctness and distance between persons. One such experience is the experience of longing. A new way of loving becomes possible: love in the sense of paying attention to the other as the other, that is, as a separate and distinct being.

Just as we can distinguish between prelapsarian love and fallen love, so we can distinguish between prelapsarian freedom and fallen freedom. For the prelapsarian human, freedom consists in complete identification with the other beings in the close-knit world: man and woman are created in the image of God, woman is created out of the ribs of man, and both carry within them the breath of God. Their identity bleeds and blends into one another. Humans share in the creativity of God, in their nature (which is to be fruitful and multiply) and in their actions (as when Adam goes around naming animals). What they lack, however, is independence. They get their first feel of independence when God gives them the command not to eat the forbidden fruit. It is at this point that humans become independent agents in the world. Humans can now exercise their will. They can choose to obey or disobey: they can choose to eat or refrain from eating the forbidden fruit. They can choose to live within or without the norm. Henceforth, they will have a will that is

---

[38] Zornberg, *Genesis: The Beginning of Desire*, 18.
[39] Zornberg, *Genesis: The Beginning of Desire*, 18.
[40] Fletcher, 'Thinking about Eden', 18.
[41] Fletcher, 'Thinking about Eden', 20.

different from God's. One could say that the final gift that God gives to humankind in Eden is the gift of independence. Rousseau puts tremendous emphasis on this quality of freedom as the independence of the will: 'For physics explains in some manner the mechanical working of the senses and the formation of ideas, but in the power to will or rather to choose and in the feeling of this power one finds only purely spiritual acts, about which nothing is explained by the laws of mechanics'.[42] The first person to assert this freedom as independence is Eve when she takes the first bite of the fruit. Adam will soon follow suit. Eve chooses to act independently, to do her own thing. God's final question to Eve affirms obliquely her independence: 'What is this that you have done?' (Genesis 3:13).

Law creates an authority structure that the prelapsarian human knows nothing of. In so doing, it also creates the possibility of transgression as a mode of resistance and an assertion of individuality. In psychoanalytic terms, one could read the Edenic story, not only as a creation myth, but also as a maturation myth: 'the expulsion from Paradise is just as necessary, and just as painful, as a child's maturation and subsequent socialization through the Oedipal stage'.[43] Adam and Eve have to leave the garden and grow up. Separation is painful, for the transition from attachment to independence is never easy. Nonetheless, the child must eventually separate from the parent, and the parent must allow the child to discover his or her own reality: 'where there was one, there must be two'.[44] The transition is marked by transgression. Having made the transition, they now have to find their *own* way in the world: 'the enchantment of childlike existence in the garden is past'.[45] Like a child growing up, Adam and Eve must find a 'space of separateness' in order to be their own man and woman.[46] Having been expelled from Eden, the outside world is full of unexplored possibilities. God created them with his hands, but now, they are free from his iron grip. They can now go out and create a world for themselves. In a roundabout way, this craving to create a world for themselves was what they wanted all along when they ate the forbidden fruit: to be like God, the creator of the world. The prelapsarian human has finally fallen – and grown up. In the poignant words of Milton:

> Some natural tears they dropped, but wiped them soon;
> The world was all before them, where to choose

---

[42] Rousseau, *Discourse on Inequality*, Pt 1, [17].
[43] Parker, 'Mirror, Mirror on the Wall, Must We Leave Eden, Once and for All?', 20.
[44] Zornberg, *Genesis: The Beginning of Desire*, 20.
[45] Carr, *Erotic Word*, 46.
[46] Zornberg, *Genesis: The Beginning of Desire*, 21.

> Their place of rest, and Providence their guide.
> They, hand in hand, with wandering steps and slow,
> Through Eden took their solitary way.[47]

Fallen Human: The Nasty Brute

Earlier, I noted that, in examining the foundations of society, Hobbes took the journey back to the state of nature, but, as Rousseau points out, Hobbes did not go back far enough. Had he gone back far enough, he would have found, not the fallen human, but the prelapsarian human. Hobbes stops at the nasty brute, when he should have found the noble savage. Hobbes begins his narrative by asking us to imagine a state of nature in which there are three principal causes of quarrel arising out of 'the nature of man': competition, diffidence and glory – 'the first maketh men invade for gain; the second, for safety; and the third, for reputation'.[48] The desire for glory quickly turns into vainglory. Humans 'do not merely wish to survive; we wish to survive *better* than anyone else', which 'introduces a kind of scarcity that nothing can cure and a kind of competition to which there can be no end'.[49] The state of nature is a state of war, 'where every man is enemy to every man'.[50] 'To this war of every man against every man ... nothing can be unjust': 'where there is no common power, there is no law; where no law, no injustice'. There are only force and fraud.

To attain peace, we need to get out of the Hobbesian state of nature – but how? Hobbes's solution is that we enter into a social contract among ourselves to set up a common, coercive, compelling power – in short, the Leviathan – to instill fear in us and keep us in awe. As Hobbes says, 'the passion to be reckoned upon is fear'.[51] There needs to be a sense of 'terror' among the subjects, for 'covenants, without the sword, are but words'.[52] Those who refuse to enter the state of civil society would be 'left in the condition of war he was in before; wherein he might without injustice be destroyed by any man whatsoever'.[53] Hobbes applies the same logic to the divine–human relationship: 'To those

---

[47] John Milton, *Paradise Lost*, 12.645–9.
[48] Hobbes, *Leviathan*, ch 13.
[49] Ryan, *The Making of Modern Liberalism*, 226.
[50] Hobbes, *Leviathan*, ch 13.
[51] Hobbes, *Leviathan*, ch 14.
[52] Hobbes, *Leviathan*, ch 17.
[53] Hobbes, *Leviathan*, ch 18. This is like Cain, who exclaims after being exiled for murdering Abel: 'I shall be a fugitive and a wanderer on the earth, and whoever finds me will slay me' (Genesis 4:14).

1 Cosmological Beginning: The Story of Eden

therefore whose power is irresistible, the dominion of all men adhereth naturally by their excellence of power; and consequently it is from that power that the kingdom over men, and the right of afflicting men at his pleasure, belongeth naturally to God Almighty; not as Creator and gracious, but as omnipotent'.[54] In Hobbes's theory, 'we don't find an obligation to God based on either God's creation or our gratitude, but simply on God's irresistible power'.[55] The choice of the Leviathan as the imagery for the state is particularly telling. The Leviathan is the magnificent sea monster in the Book of Job. In the Book of Job, God asks Job rhetorically, 'Can you draw out Leviathan with a fishhook?'[56] Of course, Job can't and God can. Job finally submits to God when God asserts not so much his right as his might. Job realizes that might makes right. As Job submits, so must we – both to God and the State.

Unlike Adam and Eve in Eden, and unlike 'bees and ants',[57] no natural unity is to be found among the nasty brutes in the Hobbesian state of nature. The only form of unity that can be achieved among a multitude of nasty brutes is artificial unity through the artificial person of the sovereign: 'A multitude of men are made one person when they are by one man, or one person, represented ... for it is the unity of the representer, not the unity of the represented, that maketh the person one'.[58] A group of persons become 'a people' through the artificial unity of the sovereign. Hobbes has a legalistic view of sovereignty: 'a sovereign is by definition one who governs through law', and who is able to have its commands 'recognised as law'.[59] Within this political order, 'the relationship between sovereign and subject is mediated by law'.[60] The law of the sovereign has to be obeyed by the subject, for it was disobedience that got us into trouble in the first place; consequently, obedience to the law of the sovereign is the remedy that is necessary to save troubled humanity in its fallen condition. While Hobbes recognizes that there are two sets of laws – natural unwritten laws and civil enacted laws – he qualifies it by saying that natural laws are really just dictates of reason: 'they [natural laws] are but conclusions or theorems concerning what conduceth to the conservation and defence of themselves; whereas law, properly, is the word of him that by right hath command over others'.[61] Hence, natural laws 'achieve effective force only

---

[54] Hobbes, *Leviathan*, ch 31.
[55] Rawls, *Lectures on the History of Political Philosophy*, 44.
[56] Book of Job 41:1.
[57] Hobbes, *Leviathan*, ch 17.
[58] Hobbes, *Leviathan*, ch 16.
[59] Dyzenhaus, 'Hobbes and the Legitimacy of Law', 464, 483.
[60] Dyzenhaus, 'Hobbes's Constitutional Theory', 453.
[61] Hobbes, *Leviathan*, ch 15.

when they are enforced by the sovereign through incorporation into the civil law'.[62]

If the state of civil society is a state of legal order, then conversely, the state of nature is a state of lawlessness. In contrast to Eden where the state of pre-lapsarian lawlessness is portrayed as an oasis of peace and harmony, in the Hobbesian account, the state of lawlessness is persistently portrayed as the site of chaos and violence. While lawlessness merely denotes, in a literal sense, a state of being without law, in the context of the Hobbesian narrative, it connotes tumult and turmoil. The more negative the lawlessness in the state of nature is, the more positive the legal order in the state of civil society will look. The horror of the state of nature is designed to alert us to 'the dangers facing humans who doubt the need to defer to a single authority'.[63] Hobbes tries to convince us that 'an effective sovereign is over all, over everything else, a desirable thing to have'.[64] He does that by showing that 'however bad some sovereigns may be, the state of war [in the state of nature] is still worse'; therefore, 'so far as people are rational, then, they will want to avoid having things collapse back into a state of nature'.[65] While we dream of returning to Eden, the Hobbesian state of nature is so deplorable that no one would seek to return to it. Anything is an improvement on the Hobbesian natural condition. Where there is no security or order at all in the state of nature, any law is better than none. Without law, we would be left in the state of nature, where no humane relationships could ever survive, let alone relationships of love. In the Hobbesian state of nature, we have, not maximal freedom, but no freedom at all.

If the Edenic state of nature is paradise on earth, the Hobbesian state of nature is the direct opposite – it is hell on earth. Having been expelled from Eden, Adam and Eve may have fallen into something like the Hobbesian state of nature, where life is indeed nasty, brutish and short. One could line up the Edenic state and the Hobbesian state of nature chronologically: the Fall is a fall from the Edenic state into the Hobbesian state of nature. The prelapsarian human becomes the fallen human. The noble savage becomes the nasty brute. Hobbes's state of nature is a description of the condition after the Fall, but before the establishment of a full-fledged legal system.[66] Out of Eden, one son, Cain, kills another, Abel; and humankind is pitted against God and nature in the Great Flood. Hobbes specifically

---

[62] May, *Limiting Leviathan*, 38.
[63] Williams, 'Normatively Demanding Creatures', 305.
[64] Rawls, *History of Political Philosophy*, 48.
[65] Rawls, *History of Political Philosophy*, 51, 73.
[66] Thornton, *State of Nature or Eden?*, 166.

associates his state of nature with Cain's killing of Abel after the Fall: 'But someone may say: there has never been a war of all against all. What! Did not Cain out of envy kill his brother Abel?'[67] After Cain kills Abel, God has to intervene as a judge to make a ruling against homicide. After the Great Flood, God again has to intervene, but this time, it is to make a constitutional ruling to bind himself from ever destroying the world by flood again – God's covenant with Noah is then sealed through the sign of the rainbow. In Eden, law fractures the divine–human relationship. Out of Eden, law patches up the divine–human relationship. In Eden, or in Rousseau's state of nature, law is the problem. Out of Eden, or in Hobbes's state of nature, law becomes the solution. To phrase the paradox more sharply, out of Eden, law becomes the solution to the problem that law creates in Eden. Law is simultaneously a tragedy and a triumph, a blessing and a bane.

In this fallen world, we are caught between the nightmare and the noble dream.[68] Our image of the state of nature and the natural state of humankind is beset by two extremes: the Hobbesian nightmare and the Edenic dream. Beset by these extremes, the prelapsarian vision confronts the fallen reality. The utopian meets the dystopian. Looking within ourselves, we find both a noble savage and a nasty brute. Sensing the nasty brute within, we are fearful that, without law, we will be back in the Hobbesian nightmare, where neither love nor freedom is possible. As Hobbes tells us, in that state, there are only force and fraud. Social and political order needs to be established before any meaningful relationships could be formed. Love is impossible without law. In a state of war, where 'every man is enemy to every man' and 'nothing can be unjust',[69] there is, not unlimited freedom, but no freedom at all. Security has to be imposed before freedom could be enjoyed. It takes law to constitute our freedom.

Hobbes's solution for the creation of a legal order is the Leviathan. The Leviathan, however, leaves a bad taste in the mouth. The Leviathan imposes its will by instilling fear. To keep us in awe of it, there needs to be terror. The Leviathan has to be terrible. As Locke remarks, to think that people would accept the Leviathan would be 'to think that men are so foolish, that they take care to avoid what mischiefs may be done them by pole-cats, or foxes; but are content, nay, think it safety, to be devoured by lions'.[70] Locke could see no conceivable reason why people in the state of nature would submit

---

[67] Hobbes, *Leviathan with Selected Variants from the Latin Edition of 1668*, 1–2.
[68] This excellent turn of phrase is borrowed from H. L. A. Hart, 'American Jurisprudence through English Eyes: The Nightmare and the Noble Dream', 989.
[69] Hobbes, *Leviathan*, ch 13.
[70] Locke, *Second Treatise of Civil Government*, ch 7, §93.

voluntarily to a terrible and terrifying, lion-like, Leviathan. But what if the people were to identify with the Leviathan, in the way that Rousseau exhorts the people to identify with the General Will? While Hobbes places the figure of the Leviathan at the center of his account, Rousseau places the abstract object of the General Will at the center of his.[71] The General Will arises in the moment when the community is founded and a people constituted; once the General Will has arisen, it maintains a hovering spiritual presence over the community.[72] If one identifies with the Leviathan in the way one identifies with the General Will, then the normative scene changes. If we learn to be patriotic – that is, if we learn to love the law – then the *love* of the *law* will set us *free*.

Neither Hobbes nor Rousseau was the first person who thought about this puzzle of law, love and freedom. The first thinker in the Judeo–Christian tradition who perceived, most acutely and astutely, this puzzle was the person who stood at the very heart of the Judeo–Christian tradition: Paul. Paul was not a treatise writer, but a letter writer. Paul did not write systematic treatises. Instead, he wrote disparate letters to his scattered communities who were struggling with this precise question of how to lead a life of law, love and freedom. Paul sought to answer this question and recreate Eden in these nascent Christian communities, thus reclaiming the paradise that was lost, if not immediately, then eventually at *eschaton*. Paul presents Christ as the new Adam, who is supposed to fulfill our Edenic dream and bring us back to paradise. However, the paradise to which we will return will be an improved version of the old: it will be Paradise 2.0, for 'life in the *new* Garden of Eden would encounter no such problems as had befallen the first paradise'.[73] To get a glimpse of the new Eden, we will have to turn to Paul. The Book of Genesis and the Letters of Paul provide, respectively, an account of the cosmological beginning and a vision of the eschatological end.

II ESCHATOLOGICAL END: TURN TO PAUL

Paul lived at the turn of the Common Era. Before he became Paul the Apostle, he was Saul of Tarsus. Saul became Paul on the road to Damascus, when he converted from being the persecutor of Christians to being a Christian himself. Prior to his conversion, Saul of Tarsus was not simply a Jew, but a Pharisaic Jew. He was not simply a Pharisee, but a Shammaite Pharisee,

---

[71] Gans, *The Scenic Imagination*, 63.
[72] Gans, *The Scenic Imagination*, 62.
[73] Sawyer, 'The New Adam in the Theology of Saint Paul', 114.

which was as strict as it got in those days.[74] If Saul was zealous as a Jew, Paul was equally zealous as a Christian. As Saul, he opposed the Christians who compromised his Jewish vision; as Paul, he opposed the Judaizers who compromised his Christian vision. Paul's letters are 'wild, ecstatic and confused': they show someone who has a 'brilliantly tormented view of human nature', and who is 'racked by self-contradiction, whose life is pulled in two conflicting directions'.[75] Paul moves from singing praises to screaming condemnation about the law, sometimes in the same breath.

Paul sees Christ as a continuation of the Genesis creation story. If Jesus is the Messiah, as Paul thinks he is, then it means that the messianic age is upon us. The messianic age has cosmological implications: 'once more God was directly involved in the world, as had been the case when the heavens and the earth were being brought into existence; therefore this messianic age is once again the age of creation, parallel and transcendent to the former age of Adam'.[76] The world will be renewed, with Jesus as the new Adam. Paradise was lost with the first Adam, but it has been regained with the new Adam, 'for as in Adam all die, so also in Christ shall all be made alive'.[77] The prophecy of Isaiah is being fulfilled in Christ: 'For behold, I create a new heaven and a new earth'.[78] Paul exhorts his Christian communities to 'walk in the newness of life',[79] and to 'put on the new nature, which is being renewed in knowledge after the image of its creator'.[80] The idea of the messianic age contains within it 'the idea of a return to paradise' and the restoration of 'the world and humankind to their former glory'.[81] Crucially, the messianic age heralds a return to the perfect paradise, a paradise where there will be no need for law.

I am not alone in advocating a turn to Paul. A number of contemporary philosophers have embarked on various projects to reclaim Paul for a secular audience. For example, Agamben wants to 'restore Paul's letters to the status of the fundamental messianic text for the Western tradition',[82] and Badiou presents Paul as the foundation of universalism in the West.[83] They want to make Paul 'an interlocutor of our time'.[84] Like them, I too hope to present

---

[74] Wright, *What Saint Paul Really Said*, 26.
[75] Wilson, *Paul: The Mind of the Apostle*, 57, 122, 239.
[76] Sawyer, 'The New Adam in the Theology of Saint Paul', 105.
[77] 1 Corinthians 15:22.
[78] Book of Isaiah 65:17.
[79] Letter to the Romans 6:4.
[80] Letter to the Colossians 3:10.
[81] Sawyer, 'The New Adam in the Theology of Saint Paul', 105, 115.
[82] Agamben, *The Time that Remains*, 1.
[83] Badiou, *Saint Paul: The Foundation of Universalism*.
[84] Miller, 'Time of the Antichrist: Paul's Subversion of Empire', 565.

a reading of Paul that extracts from his letters certain enduring philosophical insights. As far as legal philosophy is concerned, in reading Paul, one needs to move back and forth between particular jurisprudence and general jurisprudence. Particular jurisprudence is the philosophical study of particular legal traditions, such as the common law, Jewish law or Roman law. General jurisprudence, on the other hand, attempts 'to show, not what is law here or there, but what is law' as such, wherever and whenever it is found.[85] On one level, Paul's jurisprudence is particular jurisprudence – it presents a critique of the Torah as a religious legal system. But, on a higher level, it may have something to say that is of interest to legal theory generally, that is, to general jurisprudence. Although in the first instance the term 'law' in Paul's letters refers specifically to the Torah, 'what interests Paul is the "lawness of law", whatever the particular law or obligation might be'.[86] Paul may have something to tell us about the quality of life under law as such. If Paul's particular jurisprudence could be generalized, then 'Paul's comments may add something to our repertoire of ways of viewing systems of law'.[87]

Critique of Law

In his Letter to the Romans, Paul proclaims that Christ is the end of law.[88] In his Letter to the Galatians, Paul says that Christ has set his people free.[89] The new Christian community promises to be a free people, sustained not by law, but by love. Law imprisons, but love liberates.[90] The law is the source of our bondage – the law is 'that which held us captive'[91] – for all who rely on the law are 'under a curse'.[92] Law does not constitute, but constricts, our freedom. These are histrionic pronouncements. Paul has grand ambitions, and he is not one who is prone to understatement. In ascribing messianic status to Jesus, Paul treats Jesus qua Christ 'as a catalyst, negatively, for radical criticism of the existing order; positively, of dreams at long last come true'.[93] In order to appreciate the grandiosity of Paul's critique of law, we have to begin with the concept of law in the Hebrew Bible.

---

[85] Austin, *Lectures on Jurisprudence or the Philosophy of Positive Law*, 32.
[86] Keck, *Paul and His Letters*, 86.
[87] Waldron, 'Dead to the Law', 305.
[88] Letter to the Romans 10:4.
[89] Letter to the Galatians 5:1.
[90] See Neoh, 'Law Imprisons, Love Liberates'.
[91] Letter to the Romans 7:6.
[92] Letter to the Galatians 3:10.
[93] Davies, 'From Schweitzer to Scholem', 344.

After the expulsion of Adam and Eve from Eden, God set about developing an elaborate legal regime to structure his relationship with his human subjects. The process that begins in Eden, with the giving of the one commandment not to eat the forbidden fruit, culminates in the Book of Exodus, with the giving of the Ten Commandments on Mount Sinai. The commandments would later multiply and increase exponentially in the Book of Leviticus, which contains an elaborate set of rules and regulations governing all matters big and small. Law becomes part of Israel's juridical–theological covenant with God. The covenant with God is an 'alliance between God and his people [and the] observance of the law is what cements it'.[94] Righteousness requires the maintenance of status within the covenantal community through obedience to the law of God, as revealed to Israel, the people of God.[95] The law of God exists as positive law, as law that is posited by God to the Israelites at specific points in the narrative: 'It presents itself canonically in written form, as a book or a code'.[96] Admittedly, biblical law includes more than rules and commandments. In addition to rules and commandments, it consists of wisdom and prophecy. But it is nonetheless true that the Bible, whether the Hebrew Bible or the Christian Bible, contains a lot of rules and commandments.

It is against this backdrop that we have to understand Paul's critique of the law. Paul mounts a critique of the law on three fronts: logical, psychological and political. According to Paul, 'where there is no law there is no transgression'.[97] There is a fairly simple logical point here, which is that 'transgression logically presupposes law'.[98] Hence, the logic of law is also the logic of transgression. 'Law is presented to its addressees as a set of ... non-negotiable requirements, prescribing or proscribing the named action'.[99] This feature is sometimes called the deontic character of law. Laws are not 'set out simply as rules of thumb or rather good ideas'.[100] Law does not just commend; it commands. Law governs conduct by requiring that certain acts be done and by prohibiting other acts from being done. Law demands obedience. It 'tracks our observances and transgressions', and makes them 'available as occasions for punishment'.[101]

---

[94] McNulty, 'The Event of the Letter', 2209.
[95] Sanders, *Paul and Palestinian Judaism*, 544.
[96] Waldron, 'Dead to the Law', 307.
[97] Letter to the Romans 4:15.
[98] Waldron, 'Dead to the Law', 311.
[99] Waldron, 'Dead to the Law', 315.
[100] Waldron, 'Dead to the Law', 316.
[101] Waldron, 'Dead to the Law', 317, 325.

In addition to the relatively straightforward logical point, there is also a more complicated *psycho*logical critique, when Paul states that 'through the law comes knowledge of sin'.[102] Just as sin requires knowledge of the law, such that those who know the law cannot say that they sinned unwittingly, so reciprocally, law brings with it the knowledge of sin. Later, Paul adds that 'our sinful passions [are] aroused by the law'.[103] One is here reminded of the forbidden fruit in the Garden of Eden. As the saying goes, the forbidden fruit is the sweetest. Prohibition increases desire and stimulates transgression. Law 'makes all the more desirable the very thing it prohibits'.[104] 'By naming and individuating particular transgressions, the law actually puts them before our minds in a way that heightens their appeal to us'.[105] The knowledge of the law is causally related, in a psychological way, to its transgression. Consider, for example, the exhibitionism of Diogenes of Sinope, who deliberately masturbated in the marketplace of Athens. He knew that 'the Athenians objected to his mode of life in general and to this form of behavior in particular'.[106] In fact, he did what he did for that very reason. Diogenes' contumacy was 'largely based on creating incongruity, such as his deliberate disregard for propriety and for social space boundaries'.[107] The existence of conventions controlling what one could not do stimulated Diogenes to do just that. The existence of prohibitions provokes the desire to do exactly that which is prohibited. As it is sometimes said, rules are meant to be broken. The presence of prohibitions feeds and fuels exhibitionist tendencies, then as now.

The psychological origins of desire are manifold. Rene Girard, for example, locates the origin of desire in mimesis: we desire what others desire and we want to have what others have.[108] Both Hobbes and Rousseau place a great deal of emphasis on mimesis: in Rousseau's state of nature, there is the 'positive mimetic moment' that triggers the feeling of pity; while in Hobbes's state of nature, there is the 'negative mimetic moment' that triggers the universal war of all against all.[109] However, we also want to have what we may not have: we also desire that which is forbidden. The forbidden fruit is desirable precisely because it is forbidden. Given the fecundity in the Garden

---

[102] Letter to the Romans 3:20.
[103] Letter to the Romans 7:5.
[104] Hill, 'Romans', 1096.
[105] Waldron, 'Dead to the Law', 313.
[106] Geuss, *Public Goods, Private Goods*, 12.
[107] Bosman, 'Selling Cynicism', 103.
[108] See Girard, *Deceit, Desire, and the Novel*.
[109] Gans, *The Scenic Imagination*, 53.

II Eschatological End: Turn to Paul

of Eden, Adam and Eve would have been spoilt for choice in terms of fruits to eat. They would not have paid any attention to the forbidden fruit had the fruit not been forbidden. The prohibition transforms the fruit into an object of desire: 'the law chains us to an object precisely by forbidding it'.[110] Law binds our conduct. In binding our conduct, it subordinates our will to its extraneous will. In subordinating our will to its will, it stimulates within its subjects a desire for transgression – it stimulates the desire for autonomy in response to the heteronomy of law. Law becomes the site of resistance and transgression, and the concomitant assertion of the independence of the individual will. Law is a prerequisite, if not the stimulant, for the self-assertion of the individual will. If individual independence lies in the transgression of boundaries, then law has to impose those initial boundaries in the first place. Law sets the stage for the transgression that is to follow.

The two logical and psychological arguments hint at a deeper political critique of law. In the Garden of Eden, when the prohibition against eating the forbidden fruit is issued, the nature of the relationship between God and humankind changes from an immediate relationship to a relationship that is mediated by law. Hence, when Adam and Eve eat the forbidden fruit, the transgression carries with it enormous political significance. Beneath the logic of transgression, there is a political psychology that is at work. The transgression signifies human disobedience and rebellion against the rule of God. As the Book of Genesis says, humans want to be like God.[111] The ruled wants to be the ruler. Underlying this transgression, there is a political struggle – that is, a struggle for power between the ruled and the ruler. Between God and humankind, one is to be dominant and the other subordinate. The forbidden fruit looks particularly tempting, not only because it is juicy and tasty, but also because the eating of it represents the human desire to be free from the constraints of God's law: 'Only with the coming of the Law does man's sin take on the character of open rebellion'.[112] Law exposes 'the deliberateness of human disobedience'.[113] It becomes the 'primary source of human alienation' from God.[114]

In the prelapsarian state of divine–human harmony prior to the promulgation of the prohibition, there is an immediacy in the divine–human relationship. However, that immediacy is lost as soon as the prohibition is issued. That prohibition now stands between God and humanity. The prohibition is a prelude to the Fall: when the law is issued, its transgression is bound to

[110] Caputo, 'Postcards from Paul', 5.
[111] Book of Genesis 3:5.
[112] Davies, 'Paul and the Law', 1480.
[113] Hill, 'Romans', 1094.
[114] Hill, 'Romans', 1086.

follow as a matter of course. 'With the law, the [human] subject has definitively exited from unity, and from innocence'.[115] Law's prohibition awakens human pride. Instead of saving Adam and Eve from death, God's prohibition in the Garden lures them to their death.[116] In the words of Paul, 'I was once alive apart from the law, but when the commandment came, sin revived and I died'.[117] 'The law is no longer just an inadequate solution to the problem of sin; the law itself is the problem'.[118] All this leads to the climax of the Letter to the Romans, when Paul proudly proclaims that 'Christ is the end of law'.[119] Christ, as the new Adam in the renewed Eden, restores the immediacy in the divine–human relationship. 'Therefore, if anyone is in Christ, he is a new creation; the old has passed away, behold the new has come', for as Paul says, 'in Christ, God was reconciling the world to himself'.[120] 'The eschatological end is a return to the cosmological beginning'.[121]

End of Law: Love and Freedom

The land beyond law promises to be a land of milk and honey, that is, of love and freedom. This land beyond law is the new Promised Land. Paul exhorts his community to embark on the new Exodus to the new Promised Land, where 'the creation itself will be set free from its bondage to decay and obtain the glorious liberty of the children of God'.[122] In the first Exodus, God sets his chosen people, the Israelites, free from the dominion of the Egyptians. Journeying from Egypt to the Promised Land, God sets his people apart by giving them his law on Mount Sinai. Having left the dominion of the Egyptians, the Israelites enter the dominion of the law of God. In the second Exodus, God will set his new chosen people, Christians of both Jewish and Gentile origin, free from the dominion of the law itself.[123] The freedom of the second Exodus is accomplished in Christ: 'For freedom Christ has set us free'.[124] In the messianic age that Christ inaugurates, the law becomes a paper tiger. The prescriptions of the law become adiaphorous, at best. Christians are free to observe them or disregard them. It does not matter either way. 'For in Christ Jesus, neither

---

[115] Badiou, *Saint Paul: The Foundation of Universalism*, 82.
[116] Hill, 'Romans', 1097.
[117] Letter to the Romans 7:9.
[118] Hill, 'Romans', 1096.
[119] Letter to the Romans 10:4.
[120] 2 Corinthians 5:17–19.
[121] Wolfson, *Venturing Beyond: Law and Morality in Kabbalistic Mysticism*, 263.
[122] Letter to the Romans 8:21.
[123] See Letter to the Romans ch 6–8.
[124] Letter to the Galatians 5:1.

II   Eschatological End: Turn to Paul   33

circumcision nor uncircumcision has any value. All that matters is faith, expressed through love'.[125] Having been freed from the law, Paul exhorts Christians to be enslaved again, but this time, by love. Christians should not be enslaved by law, but by love: 'For you were called to freedom ... but through love be servants of one another'.[126]

For Paul, Christ is love personified. The new Christian community promises to be a community sustained not by law, but by love. Paul has been called the apostle of love. His praise of love in his Letter to the Corinthians, for example, is a staple lectionary reading for marriage liturgies.[127] His zeal for love reinforces his proclamation of Christ as the end of law. In contrast to Moses who establishes the rule of law on Mount Sinai, Paul proclaims the power of love over law. According to Paul, 'He who loves his neighbor has fulfilled the law. The commandments, "You shall not commit adultery, You shall not kill, You shall not steal, You shall not covet," and any other commandment, are summed up in this sentence, "You shall love your neighbor as yourself." Love does no wrong to a neighbor; therefore, love is the fulfilling of the law'.[128] Love breaks the 'cycle of transgression and prohibition' by introducing a new way of being.[129] A few verses later, Paul says that 'the 'kingdom of God is not food and drink' [that is, dietary laws], but 'walking in love'.[130]

Paul reduces 'the multiplicity of legal prescriptions' into a single, affirmative maxim; 'this single imperative envelops no prohibition – it is pure affirmation'.[131] Paul contracts and recapitulates the entire corpus of Mosaic law 'in the figure of love'.[132] As Paul says, 'love is genuine'.[133] Love is that 'which alone effectuates the unity of thought and action in the world'.[134] For Paul, love is both a verb and a noun. As a verb, it denotes a particular way of

---

[125] Letter to the Galatians 5:6.
[126] Letter to the Galatians 5:13.
[127] 1 Corinthians 13:1–8: 'If I speak in the tongues of men and of angels, but have not love, I am a noisy gong or a clanging cymbal. And if I have prophetic powers, and understand all mysteries and all knowledge, and if I have all faith, so as to remove mountains, but have not love, I am nothing. If I give away all I have, and if I deliver my body to be burned, but have not love, I gain nothing. Love is patient and kind; love is not jealous or boastful; it is not arrogant or rude. Love does not insist on its own way; it is not irritable or resentful; it does not rejoice at wrong, but rejoices in the right. Love bears all things, believes all things, hopes all things, endures all things. Love never ends'.
[128] Letter to the Romans 13:8–10.
[129] Caputo, 'Postcards from Paul', 5.
[130] Letter to the Romans 14:15, 17.
[131] Badiou, *Saint Paul: The Foundation of Universalism*, 89.
[132] Agamben, *The Time that Remains*, 108.
[133] Letter to the Romans 12:9, according to Hill's translation: Hill, 'Romans', 1104.
[134] Badiou, *Saint Paul: The Foundation of Universalism*, 91.

acting in the world. But, more importantly, as a noun, it denotes a particular way of being in the world. Hence, it makes sense to say that God *is* love. Love as a noun precedes love as a verb: the state of being in love leads to the performance of certain acts and endows those acts with a certain quality, such that we can call them acts of love.

We sometimes say that love is blind. Love is radically contingent, even arbitrary – it appears as if from nowhere. One could express the same sentiment by saying that love is grace. Love as grace 'happens to everyone without an assignable reason'; 'grace is the opposite of law insofar as it is what comes *without being due*'.[135] Law operates within the logic of right and duty, 'granting to each part of the whole its due'. By contrast, grace is 'superabundant' with respect to 'the fixed distributions of the law'.[136] Grace is a gift, an unmerited favor, in contrast to a right or an entitlement.[137] Law makes an act referable to a norm. By contrast, grace is divorced from any norm; it is a 'lawless eruption ... a pure act'.[138] In Paul's terms, 'law came in', but 'grace abounded all the more'.[139] Love as grace has the 'capacity to erase the stain of guilt completely since it exceeds the dichotomy of right and wrong'.[140] Nietzsche recognizes this feature of love when he remarks that 'whatever is done from love occurs beyond good and evil'.[141] Love returns us to the prelapsarian condition, before Adam and Eve ate the fruit of the tree of the knowledge of good and evil.

Love is an act of grace that is rooted in faith. It is rooted in an abiding sense of fidelity to the subjective being of the other. Unlike the twelve apostles, Paul does not know Jesus in the flesh; he does not know the historical Jesus of Nazareth. He only knows Jesus as Christ.[142] His knowledge of Jesus Christ is purely a matter of faith. Love is 'tightly interwoven with faith'.[143] Like love and grace, faith too could be contrasted with law. The contrast that Paul draws between Abraham and Moses is precisely the contrast between faith and law – Abrahamic faith is contrasted with Mosaic law. And it is vitally important for Paul that Abrahamic faith precedes Mosaic law. In his words, 'the promise to Abraham and his descendants, that they should inherit the world, did not come through the law but through the righteousness of faith'.[144] Faith is not

---

[135] Badiou, *Saint Paul: The Foundation of Universalism*, 76–7.
[136] Badiou, *Saint Paul: The Foundation of Universalism*, 78.
[137] 'His grace as a gift': Letter to the Romans 3:24.
[138] Badiou, *Saint Paul: The Foundation of Universalism*, 84.
[139] Letter to the Romans 5:20.
[140] Wolfson, *Venturing Beyond*, 229.
[141] Nietzsche, *Beyond Good and Evil*, §153.
[142] Agamben, *The Time that Remains*, 126.
[143] Agamben, *The Time that Remains*, 129.
[144] Letter to the Romans 4:13.

a set of precepts, but a form of life.[145] Speaking to the new Christian community in Rome, Paul says, 'We are discharged from the law, dead to that which held us captive, so that we serve not under the old written code but in the new life of the Spirit'.[146] The word of faith cannot be reduced to a text – 'it cannot impose itself as a law'.[147]

Some have called this contraction and recapitulation of the law in terms of love 'the law of love'. In a similar vein, others have characterized this move from law to love as transcendence, fulfillment or completion: that law is transcended / fulfilled / completed in love. That is all fine, so long as one does not lose sight of the point that, when love breaks in, in the way that it does for Paul, the law can no longer remain the same. Paul has never claimed that Christ has not come to abolish the law: it was Matthew who put this statement into the mouth of Christ in his Gospel.[148] The Gospel of Matthew was written after Paul in a very different context for a different audience, so it is important that we do not conflate the two. I have analyzed the jurisprudential import of that Matthean claim elsewhere,[149] but here, we need to deal with the Pauline, not the Matthean, view. For Paul, the pressing problem was what to do with particular legal prescriptions under this new dispensation of love, or the law of love, if one prefers that formulation. The problem was presented in its most acute form in the circumcision debate. Circumcision was the most basic legal prescription in the law. It was the sign of the covenant and the entry point into the covenantal community. Just as citizenship makes one a member of the constitutional community, so circumcision made one a member of the covenantal community. It is very telling that Paul came down on the 'no circumcision' side of the debate. His negative position on this most central question about the law speaks volumes about his general view of the law.

Paul's Paradox

While Paul harbors antinomian tendencies, he never crossed the Rubicon into antinomianism. Paul is not antinomian. He could not be. For 'a messianic community that wants to present itself as an institution faces a paradoxical task'.[150] A messianic community looks toward *eschaton*, when the Messiah will

---

[145] Agamben, *The Time that Remains*, 122.
[146] Letter to the Romans 7:6.
[147] Agamben, *The Time that Remains*, 137.
[148] Gospel of Matthew 5:17.
[149] See Neoh, 'The Rhetoric of Precedent and Fulfillment in the Sermon on the Mount and the Common Law'.
[150] Agamben, *The Time that Remains*, 1.

return at the end of time, also known as the Second Coming, to make things whole again. At *eschaton*, the world will finally be restored to perfection. In that perfect world, which is projected into the indefinite future, there may well be no need for law. However, Paul's messianic community is not there yet. There is an eschatological tension, or a temporal gap, between the 'now' and the 'not yet'. In Paul's view, the Age to Come, the time of the end, has already begun – for it has been inaugurated by Christ – although the Present Age, the time of sin, is still proceeding apace.[151] Christians are living in the overlapping epoch of the Present Age and the Age to Come. In the time that remains from now till 'the end of the world', Paul needs law as much as he may detest it. After driving a wedge between law and love, Paul still has to 'offer guidance for behavior'.[152] 'In practice, what Paul expects of his converts is a fairly typical Jewish morality'.[153] Hence, Paul has to 'reinstitute Jewish laws with Christian warrants' by 'legislating rules of behaviour ad hoc'.[154] Paul did not create 'a law-free religion': Christianity, like Judaism, has always had laws.[155] After all his condemnation of the law, it turns out that there is a Christian list of acceptable behavior, 'a Christian "law"'.[156]

At key points in his letters, Paul recoils from his condemnatory tone and adopts a conciliatory tone toward the law in a series of rhetorical questions. 'Do we then overthrow the law by this faith? By no means! On the contrary, we uphold the law'.[157] 'What then shall we say? That the law is sin? By no means! ... The law is holy, and the commandment is holy and just and good'.[158] Like the prodigal son, Paul never ventures out of the law for too long. He soon returns to the law. Paul's thinking is still very much conditioned by the legal imagination. For example, Paul conceptualizes Christianity as a covenant, albeit a new covenant. To speak in covenantal terms is already to speak in the language of law. The ancient theological covenant reminds us of the modern legal constitution. The Last Judgment, when justice would be done, is another classic example of legal language, couched in the form of judicial eschatology: 'the final judgment will legitimate believers by punishing unbelievers' – 'justice then becomes a dividing up' of one's due, which is the quintessential role of the law.'[159] Even the term 'justification' is a Jewish law

---

[151] Wright, *What Saint Paul Really Said*, 37.
[152] Sanders, *Paul, the Law and the Jewish People*, 152.
[153] Hill, 'Romans', 1087.
[154] Hill, 'Romans', 1087.
[155] Hill, 'Romans', 1087.
[156] Davies, 'Paul and the Law', 1478.
[157] Letter to the Romans 3:31.
[158] Letter to the Romans 7:7–12.
[159] Badiou, *Saint Paul: The Foundation of Universalism*, 93–4.

court term, in which the unrepentant sinner will be condemned and the truly righteous will be vindicated.[160]

Given the strongly negative statements that Paul has made about the law, there is a sense of 'embarrassment about giving full weight to the positive statements which Paul makes about the law'.[161] If one were to read Paul in the Lutheran tradition, the negative statements make a lot of sense, but one would have to fudge the positive statements; conversely, if one were to read Paul in the Calvinist tradition, the positive statements make a lot of sense, but one would have to fudge the negative statements.[162] He makes very little effort to reconcile the two sets of statements, 'prolaw' and 'antilaw'; instead, he places them side by side.[163] Paul is caught between 'his native conviction that the law was given by God and is good' and 'his new conviction that life comes only through Christ and that therefore the law cannot save'; but he does not resolve the tension between the two convictions – 'he states them both as facts'.[164] Consequently, Paul switches back and forth between prose and poetry: Paul endorses the law for the prosaic aspects of life, but switches to lawlessness in his poetic moments.[165] By cherry-picking, one could accuse Paul of antinomianism as much as one could accuse him of legalism. Paul's letters are an attempt to 'grapple with the perennial and often insoluble dilemma' between the two extremes of legalism and antinomianism.[166]

The scholarly movement called the New Perspective on Paul attempts to reconcile the prolaw and antilaw statements in his letters using different hermeneutic techniques. The three musketeers of the New Perspective are E. P. Sanders, James Dunn and N. T. Wright. Sanders makes the hermeneutic distinction between 'getting in' and 'staying in'. According to Sanders, Paul uses the term 'law' in two distinct contexts: one in discussing how one gets into the community of the elect, and the other in discussing how one who is already in the community of the elect stays in.[167] One does not get in by keeping the law. Getting in is a matter of love, faith and grace. All the antilaw statements deal with this point about getting in. However, one who is already in stays in by keeping the law. Staying in is a matter of obedience to the law. All the prolaw statements deal with this point about staying in. Paul's polemic

---

[160] Wright, *What Saint Paul Really Said*, 33.
[161] Sanders, *Paul, the Law and the Jewish People*, 159.
[162] Wright, 'New Perspectives on Paul', [5].
[163] Gager, *Reinventing Paul*, 9.
[164] Sanders, *Paul, the Law and the Jewish People*, 138.
[165] The prose–poetry distinction is borrowed from Leibowitz, 'Religious Praxis: The Meaning of Halakhah', 13.
[166] Raisanen, 'Paul's Conversion and the Development of His View of the Law', 416.
[167] Sanders, *Paul, the Law and the Jewish People*, 10.

against the law is directed primarily against those who make obedience to the law an entrance requirement. However, once you are in, you are expected to behave in certain prescribed ways. For example, one should not engage in 'reveling and drunkenness', 'debauchery and licentiousness', and 'quarrelling and jealousy'.[168] It is inevitable that 'when he dealt with human behaviour [within the community of the elect] he had recourse to the law', using the language of 'punishment for transgression and reward for obedience'.[169]

If one accepts Sanders's interpretation of Paul, then the only question that remains to be solved is the simple one of distinguishing between the operative parts and the inoperative parts of the law of the Torah for those who are in the new Christian community of the elect. It is simply a matter of sorting out which part of the Torah is retained and which is rejected. In this respect, Dunn follows in Sanders's trail. According to Dunn, what is rejected is the content of the law of the Torah that functions as ethnic boundary markers, especially the 'rituals and practices which distinguished Israel from the nations'.[170] Paul is conscious of and concerned about the Gentile mission. He wants to enable Gentiles to become Christians without becoming Jews. He needs to find a way for Gentiles to relate to Jews on an equal footing in the community of Christ. Much of Paul's writings on law cluster around the two crises of law: one at Jerusalem on the question of circumcision, and the other at Antioch on the question of dietary laws. These legal requirements on circumcision and diet 'were widely regarded as characteristically and distinctively Jewish'.[171] They function as ethnic identity markers of Jewishness. They have become a sign of nationalism, and 'a badge not of Abraham's faith but of Israel's boast'.[172] For that reason, Paul rejects them both. Other than such types of laws, Paul is happy to keep the rest. For example, Paul is happy to keep laws that regulate moral conduct, for in this domain, 'the law serves as a measure of sin, defines sin, makes sinners conscious of their sin, and provides a yardstick by which sin will be judged'.[173] This pick-and-choose approach explains how Paul could condemn and endorse the law in the same breath.

Wright, the third of the trio, places Paul's approach within the story of God's relationship with humanity from Adam to Abraham, culminating in Christ. Adam is the patriarch of humanity, while Abraham is the patriarch of the Jewish people. God starts by dealing with humanity as a whole. When that

---

[168] Letter to the Romans 13:13.
[169] Sanders, *Paul, the Law and the Jewish People*, 153, 159.
[170] Dunn, 'The New Perspective on Paul: Whence, What, Whither?', 8.
[171] Dunn, 'The New Perspective on Paul (1983)', 98.
[172] Dunn, 'The New Perspective on Paul (1983)', 109.
[173] Dunn, 'The New Perspective on Paul: Whence, What, Whither?', 49.

II Eschatological End: Turn to Paul

ends in disaster in the Garden of Eden, God's alternative strategy is to deal with one particular people on earth, instead of the entirety of humanity. God chooses Abraham, and through him, the Jewish people. God enters into a covenant with the Jewish people, and makes them his chosen race, a people set apart. However, the plan has always been to use the Jewish people to restore the entirety of humanity to its prelapsarian condition. After the Fall, God makes the covenant with the Jewish people in order to use law as a means of salvation for the world. The salvation history begins with the Jewish people, but it is destined to end beyond the Jewish people. The initial covenant is made with the Jewish people, but the covenant is to be extended to include all the peoples of the earth. In Christ, the covenant is not broken, but broadened to include all who believe. Paul is in grips of this vision of the covenant. God has bound himself to the covenant: 'through this covenant he has promised not only to save Israel but also, thereby, to renew creation itself'.[174] The God of Israel, who is also the God of the whole world, will 'finally put the world to rights', which is the world that is meant to be before the Fall.'[175] According to Wright, this covenantal thinking explains the various law court imageries in Paul's letters. Hence, Paul could state that 'the doers of the law will be justified'.[176] Justification is about covenantal justice, 'about God putting the world to rights, with his chosen and called people as the advance guard of that new creation' in the renewed Eden.[177]

These interpretations by Sanders, Dunn and Wright, which jointly constitute the New Perspective on Paul, are all intelligible and intelligent solutions to Paul's paradox. I have no quarrel with them. What I want to add is merely the following. All are agreed that Paul wants to move away from law in some respects. All are also agreed that Paul does not go all the way and jettison law altogether. Paul settles for a middle position. The New Perspective on Paul tries to flesh out the middle position. Its proponents attempt to construct a scheme of harmonization that will unify the structure and elaborate the requirements of the middle position. That interpretive exercise is commendable, indeed necessary for certain purposes. Nonetheless, there remains the question of what is stopping Paul from going all the way. What is holding him back from jettisoning law altogether? What is the philosophical source of his theological scruples about going all the way? There is no way for anyone to get

---

[174] Wright, 'New Perspectives on Paul', [18].
[175] Wright, 'New Perspectives on Paul', [29].
[176] Letter to the Romans 2:13.
[177] Wright, 'New Perspectives on Paul', [54].

inside Paul's mind, so any guesses are necessarily speculative. Here is my speculation.

Paul is torn between the prelapsarian and the fallen view of human nature. Had Paul lived today, we could say that Paul is torn between the Rousseauan and the Hobbesian view of the natural condition of humankind. In Rousseau's prelapsarian state of nature, law destroys love and freedom. Hence, 'man is born free, but everywhere he is in chains'.[178] In Hobbes's fallen state of nature, law is necessary for love and freedom. Without law, life would be 'nasty, brutish and short'.[179] Paul is in a bind. From this bind, law emerges as a compromise solution. Paul's thoughts reflect the division between the prelapsarian vision and the fallen reality: between the eschatological desire to escape from law and the earthly gravitational pull back to law. A community, even one as otherworldly as the early Christian community, needs law to govern behavior and mediate interpersonal conduct. Despite their best efforts to escape this world, the early Christians were still living in this world. Living in this world means living under governments and under laws, whether civil or ecclesiastical. Standing at the cusp of the Judeo–Christian tradition, Paul struggled to articulate the relationship between law, love and freedom for the new community that he was trying to build.

Paul has a vision, in which love would make law superfluous, and in which freedom would be secured by love, not law. However, that vision clashes with the stark reality of our fallen state. In our fallen state, lawlessness may not be a return to the prelapsarian Edenic paradise, but a descent into the Hobbesian state of nature, where there is nothing but war, and life is nasty, brutish and short. Lawlessness has to be distinguished from unlawfulness: the unlawful is not the lawless. Crime, for example, is unlawful in that it contravenes the law. But crime, though unlawful, is part and parcel of the order and logic of law. In contrast, lawlessness is to step outside the order and logic of law entirely. Paul is simultaneously drawn to and repelled by lawlessness. Paul feels that law is inadequate; therefore, Paul dreams of love and freedom beyond law. However, there is the fear that, if one abandons law, one may end up, not in the dreamland of love, but in the nightmare of war, for 'all's fair in love and war'.[180] When one abandons law, the fear is that, instead of recovering Eden, one may end up in the Hobbesian state of nature: like Golding's boys, we may find ourselves killing each other and worshipping the Lord of the Flies.[181]

[178] Rousseau, *The Social Contract*, Bk I, ch 1.
[179] Hobbes, *Leviathan*, ch 13.
[180] This proverb, in its current form, is often attributed to Smedley, *Frank Fairleigh*.
[181] Golding, *Lord of the Flies*; see also Hobbes, *Leviathan*, ch 14, in which he describes the state of nature as 'a condition of war of every one against every one'.

II Eschatological End: Turn to Paul

A move beyond law could either be an ascent into love or a descent into hate. Giving up law, one could either rise up to heaven or fall into hell. Lawlessness could be either utopian or dystopian.

Paul approaches the rule of law and its role in relation to love and freedom with deep ambivalence. Even as he acknowledges the role and rule of law, he simultaneously imagines a world beyond law: he wants to be 'both under law and beyond it'.[182] In that vein, Grant Gilmore writes that 'in Heaven there will be no law, and the lion will lie down with the lamb, [while] in Hell there will be nothing but law, and due process will be meticulously observed'.[183] Paul, in his Letter to the Romans, proclaims that law is of the flesh, but we are truly of the spirit. The truth seems harder still: we are inevitably both flesh and spirit.[184] As we are both flesh and spirit, and as we are neither in heaven nor in hell, we individually and as a community, whether religious or political, have to continue to grapple with the question of law, love and freedom. Law, love and freedom exist in tension in the liminal space between our fear of descending into the Hobbesian state of nature and our dream of returning to the Edenic paradise on earth.

Paul leaves unresolved the question of how one could lead a life of law, love and freedom in this world. Subsequent generations will have to pick up the tab. Much of this book will be about how subsequent generations have tried to pick up the tab and resolve the puzzle. For the sake of conceptual clarity, the next chapter will provide fairly detailed accounts of law, love and freedom. The subsequent chapters will chart the story of how subsequent generations, from the ancient through the medieval to the modern, have struggled with this Pauline dilemma. The modern political state carries with it this ancient theological dilemma. Paul introduces 'a polemic that is as much in play today as it was in his own time'.[185] Some parts of the book will be theology-heavy, but that is as it should be if Schmitt is right that 'all significant concepts of the modern theory of the state are secularized theological concepts'.[186]

---

[182] Kahn, *Law and Love*, xi–xii.
[183] Gilmore, *The Ages of American Law*, 111.
[184] Kahn, *Law and Love*, 173.
[185] McNulty, 'The Event of the Letter', 2238.
[186] Schmitt, *Political Theology*, 37. See also Neoh, 'Political Theology and Legal Theory'.

2

Conceptual Bipolarities

The previous chapter introduces the ideas of law, love and freedom by recounting a story of their emergence in the Garden of Eden and their eventual consummation in the vision of Paul. We have encountered tensions and contradictions in the story of their emergence and in the vision of their consummation. The traditional way of reconciling these contradictions would be to employ the hermeneutic method, which was originally invented and specifically intended for interpreting biblical texts. Traditional biblical hermeneutics posits a fourfold sense of scripture: literal, allegorical, moral and anagogic.[1] There are different formulations of this fourfold sense. According to Dante, the literal operates at the level of sight and sound ('hearing the word and seeing the text'); the allegorical operates at the level of contemplation; the moral operates at the level of faith; and the anagogic operates at the level of 'the beatific vision that fulfils faith'.[2] In another formulation, it is said that 'the literal meaning teaches you what happened; the allegorical what you ought to believe; the moral what you should be doing about it; the anagogical what you may hope for'.[3] Aquinas uses the example of the verse in Genesis, 'Let there be light',[4] to illustrate the fourfold sense of Scripture: the 'light' refers literally to physical light, allegorically to the light of Christ, morally to spiritual illumination, and anagogically to the final glory of the Kingdom of God.[5] Under the traditional method of biblical hermeneutics, the literal meaning of law, love and freedom will have a spiritual extension (at the allegorical level), an ethical application (at the moral level) and an eschatological implication (at the

---

[1] Gregory the Great is regarded as the principal initiator of this fourfold division: see Cousins, 'The Fourfold Sense of Scripture in Christian Mysticism', 123.
[2] Frye, *The Great Code: The Bible and Literature*, 223.
[3] Atkinson, *Martin Luther and the Birth of Protestantism*, 91.
[4] Book of Genesis 1:3.
[5] Aquinas, *Commentary on Saint Paul's Epistle to the Galatians*, ch 4, §7.

anagogical level). What cannot be reconciled at the literal level might be reconciled at the allegorical, moral and anagogical level. The end result is to arrive at a unified and harmonious view of the world, especially of the spiritual world.

Biblical hermeneutics connects divine revelation with human understanding: the assumption is that the text is cryptic, so the exegetical discipline of hermeneutics is required to decipher the divine message, and to make patent to the human intellect the spiritual insight that is latent in the text. As effective as the biblical hermeneutic method might be for spiritual edification, this book will not be pursuing this method, for the primary task of the book is not exegetical, but philosophical. The philosophical task is neither to reconcile contradictions in the text nor to discern the mind of God through the text. This book is not in search of a divine message. Rather, the central task of the book is to pursue a philosophical reflection on the nature and structure of values. Insofar as it is interpretive, it is primarily interpretive, not of the biblical text as such, but of the moral imagination that lies behind the text and the moral practices that flow from the text. There is no reason to assume that the moral imagination or the moral practices are unified or coherent. The philosophical task is to discern both the convergent and the divergent moral values that are embedded in the moral imagination and expressed through moral practices. It is an exercise in conceptual analysis, specifically of moral concepts. This chapter will dissect the concepts of law, love and freedom analytically. It will demonstrate that law, love and freedom are concepts that are beset with bipolarities. It will begin by explaining what is meant by bipolarities, before proceeding to reveal the bipolarities in these three concepts. The purpose of this analytical exercise is to disentangle the multiple and contradictory senses that are intertwined in these value–laden concepts. It seeks to untie the Gordian knots in the three concepts of law, love and freedom.

Concepts do not come to us in neat packages. Their contents are messy and their contours blurry. Theorists who are interested in giving concepts a certain shape and form often have to devise strategies to clean up the mess. A popular strategy is to select a central case and construct a focal meaning for the concept, or to construct an archetype for it. For example, according to Finnis, the philosophy of law should start with the central case and focal meaning of the concept of law. He is, however, quick to point out that the focal is not univocal. There can be a focal meaning ('X *simpliciter*') and multiple secondary meanings ('X *secundum quid*').[6] Although social arrangements can be more or less legal, law is fully instantiated only when its focal meaning is

---

[6] Finnis, *Natural Law and Natural Rights*, 366.

fully instantiated.[7] Finnis devotes his magnum opus toward setting out the focal meaning of law. The focal meaning is fully instantiated in the central case of law. Where Finnis uses the notions of focal meaning and central case, Simmonds deploys the notion of an archetype to structure the concept of law. An archetype is an ideal of infinite depth, and there is no full instantiation of the archetype in the world. There are only approximations. According to Simmonds, the concept of law is best understood 'in terms of an intellectual archetype to which actual instances of law merely approximate to various degrees'; in this way, 'the idea of law might provide both the general criterion whereby instances of law count as such, and a guiding ideal by reference to which all such instances ought morally to be judged'.[8] Simmonds then draws on Fuller's eight desiderata to construct the archetype of law and he links the archetype to the moral value of liberty.[9]

These strategies, whether focal or archetypal, erect a pole and plant a lodestar for our concepts. The conceptual lodestar promises to restore order to the conceptual universe. But that might not do the trick for certain concepts. For some concepts are not guided by one lodestar, but two. They do not have one pole, but two: north and south.[10] For these bipolar concepts, there is a recurrent bipolar conceptual disorder. This chapter will argue that law, love and freedom are bipolar concepts. They are imbued with moral significance, but with competing moral significations. These concepts are guided by two opposing ideals that exist concurrently in tension. The opposing ideals exist as alternative ideals; hence, it is not possible to eliminate any one of them as a secondary, non-focal or lesser form of the other. One cannot be reduced or collapsed into the other. They both compete for our allegiance.

Morris Cohen calls this conceptual structure 'the principle of polarity'. Although the principle of polarity has some overlap with deconstructionism in its emphasis on binary oppositions, it does not carry as much continental connotation as full-blown deconstructionism. Deconstruction is made to do a lot of moral work in continental philosophy. According to Derrida, 'deconstruction is justice'.[11] Deconstructionism seeks to uncover, not just binary oppositions, but *hierarchical* binary oppositions, in which 'one of the terms

---

[7] Finnis, *Natural Law and Natural Rights*, 277, 279.
[8] Simmonds, *Law as a Moral Idea*, 52.
[9] Fuller's eight desiderata of law are set out in Fuller, *The Morality of Law*, 33.
[10] Or to use an astronomical image: 'Astronomers once said planets must have circular orbits. When they finally accepted the reality of elliptical orbits, which have two focal points, their theories became simpler, more elegant and more powerful': Schmidtz, *Elements of Justice*, 4.
[11] Derrida, 'Force of Law', 945.

dominates the other (axiologically, logically, etc.), and occupies the commanding position'.[12] Hence, the project of deconstructionism is not only about uncovering the logic of binary opposition, but it is also about effectuating a modal reversal of its hierarchy. The cutting edge of deconstructionism is the ethical edge. Through a 'double gesture' of uncovering the binary opposition and reversing its hierarchy, 'deconstruction will provide the means of intervening in the field of opposition it criticizes'.[13] In contrast to deconstructionism,[14] the 'principle of polarity' does not go that far. More pertinently, it does not subscribe to the ethical project that is entailed by deconstructionism. The principle of polarity is something more homely and more at home in the analytic tradition. The principle of polarity is an analytic method of inquiry that functions as 'a maxim of intellectual search'.[15] As a maxim of intellectual search, it says that, whenever you find a contradiction, look for a distinction.[16] The principle tells us that, heuristically, 'the way to get at the nature of things is to reason from opposing considerations'.[17] The methodological version of the principle is derived from the metaphysical version, which posits that, ontologically, there exist conceptual complexes in which 'contrary tendencies are conjoined', with the result that, for these concepts, 'opposite predicates are equally true'.[18] The binary oppositions uncovered by the principle of polarity might be hierarchical, but they need not be. Even if they were hierarchical, no reversal might be required. The binary oppositions uncovered in this book through the principle of polarity are *not* hierarchical, and *no* reversal is required after the oppositions are uncovered.

Borrowing from Cohen, Fuller illustrates the principle of polarity through his contrast of reason and fiat in the development of case law.[19] On the one hand, there are those who try to 'eliminate the branch of fiat by maintaining that the whole of law is, or at least can be, the expression of reason'; on the other hand, there are others who try to 'convert the whole of law into fiat' by insisting that a rule can never be a rule of law 'until it has been stamped as such by the judge, or the state, or the sovereign, or the Rechtsmacht, or the basic norm, or whatever standard of authoritativeness the particular faction of the

[12] Derrida, *Positions*, 41.
[13] Derrida, 'Signature, Event, Context', 195.
[14] Deconstructionism is multifaceted. The concept of deconstructionism itself could be deconstructed. It can mean different things to different people. The passage above merely distinguishes the principle of polarity from *a particular version* of deconstructionism.
[15] Larsen, 'Morris Cohen's Principle of Polarity', 587.
[16] Bronstein, 'The Principle of Polarity in Cohen's Philosophy', 45.
[17] Cohen, *A Dreamer's Journey*, 171.
[18] Cohen, 'Concepts and Twilight Zones', 677–8.
[19] Fuller, 'Reason and Fiat in Case Law', 376.

school happens to sponsor'.[20] The intellectual obsession to reduce the development of case law into either reason or fiat is due to the fact that philosophers 'have never been very ready to acknowledge that their thinking contains anything like an unresolved state of tension'.[21] Fuller argues that 'this antinomy is in fact inescapable', and that it is better for theorists to face it with 'its full force and depth'.[22] The antinomy reflects simultaneously the objective plurality, or at least the duality, of values, and the subjective desire for their unification; hence, the state of tension.

It requires a certain capaciousness of mind to 'retain at once two opposing tendencies in their full force'.[23] The two parts of the antinomy 'fight and reinforce each other at the same time'.[24] One could try to effect a reconciliation by appealing to notions like 'both' or 'between', that is, by arguing that any given phenomenon will encompass 'both' sides of the antinomy or that any given phenomenon will be situated 'between' the two extremes of the antinomy. Such reconciliation is possible. However, any such reconciliation is going to be tentative and temporary, for a living concept, like any living person, is always an evolving 'bundle of tensions and contradictions'.[25] Even if the contradictions are soluble or dissolvable, the point still stands that there are contradictions to begin with. At times, there may be good reasons to solve or dissolve the contradictions; at other times, there may be good reasons to hold up the contradictions and stare at them unflinchingly. Sometimes, unresolved contradictions may be more instructive than resolved ones. They remind us that our values, like ourselves, are complex.

The following sections will show that law, love and freedom are subject to this principle of polarity. They are bipolar concepts. The cause of the bipolarity does not lie in the duality of linguistic meanings, but the duality of ideal values. Each of these concepts has two opposing ideals embedded within it, which reflect profoundly divergent conceptions of the good life. From the perspective of one ideal, the other will often appear as wrong and misguided. Law, love and freedom are normative concepts, whose contour and content are essentially contested. One could view the bipolarity as a form of contestation over the definitions of law, love and freedom, but with one crucial caveat: 'definitions cannot settle fundamental questions'; they can only serve as 'proxy for the deeper issues at stake'.[26] Definitions

---

[20] Fuller, 'Reason and Fiat in Case Law', 382.
[21] Fuller, 'Reason and Fiat in Case Law', 381.
[22] Fuller, 'Reason and Fiat in Case Law', 377.
[23] White, *When Words Lose Their Meaning*, 152.
[24] Fuller, 'Two Principles of Human Association', 73.
[25] Fuller, *The Problems of Jurisprudence*, 717.
[26] Winston, 'The Ideal Element in a Definition of Law', 89.

are helpful insofar as they create 'a particular point of view' that enables one to 'grasp more clearly certain fundamental ideas'.[27] With this understanding of definition in mind, I am happy to present the following sections as providing definitions of law, love and freedom. However, the following sections present, not one, but two definitions for each term. Each term has two alternate and competing definitions.

Before plunging in, let me state one more caveat. The following analysis of the conceptual structure of law, love and freedom cannot avoid taking sides in contested philosophical debates. Each step of the way is open to various and well-known objections, which in turn have received equally various and well-known replies. I will indicate some of them in the following sections, but I will not be able to explore them with the depth that they deserve. One can talk about these issues till the cows come home, but at some point, I will have to bracket these controversies and move the argument along. Otherwise, we will get mired in them and get nowhere. In order to get going, the book will have to leave some of these controversies behind.

I LAW

The controversy that confronts us from the get-go is whether the practice of law embodies any moral value. The threshold question that confronts us here is whether the concept of law is a moral concept. To get at this question, let's start with the content of law, and work our way to the concept of law. The content of law is normative. It deals with what one ought to do. It is not what one ought to do all things considered, but it is what one ought to do from a particular perspective. Explaining the normativity of the content of law has been a central preoccupation of jurisprudence. However, it is not only the content of law that is normative; the concept of law is normative too. On this view, the normativity of the content of law is traceable to the normativity of the concept of law. One ought to follow *this* law because one ought to follow *the* law. The former refers to the content of law, while the latter appeals to the concept of law. Both content and concept are normative. The appeal from the content to the concept of law implicates the moral value that underpins law. Legal normativity is, at bottom, a species of moral normativity. Legal subjects use the concept of law, not only 'to grasp particular obligations that they might have', but also 'to grasp the desirability of being governed in certain ways'.[28] The concept of law is used to pick out certain salient features that distinguish

---
[27] Winston, 'The Ideal Element in a Definition of Law', 95.
[28] Waldron, 'Normative (or Ethical) Positivism', 427.

law from other forms of governance; it is used to 'grasp what is at stake when a distinction is drawn between legal rules and other sorts of rules'.[29] Therefore, what a theorist says about 'what law is' will inevitably have a connection to 'why law is seen as an importantly distinct mode or aspect of governance'.[30] Even when jurisprudence appears to be engaged in conceptual analysis, it is always geared toward giving an account of legal institutions that renders them as 'intelligible social enterprises with a certain, perhaps very complex, meaning or point'.[31]

A general theory of law is not a neutral description of legal practice, but 'an interpretation of it that aims not just to describe but to justify it – to show why the practice is valuable'.[32] It aims to show, as precisely as possible, the distinct value of the practice. We understand our practices better 'by designing conceptions of our values that show what, on reflection, we find most valuable in them'.[33] As a result, different values generate different theories of law. These theories differ because they emphasize different values in their accounts of law. If you like, you can call the practice 'law' and its value 'legality', but as far as the argument of this section is concerned, nothing much hangs on this terminological distinction. The same point still holds: realizing the value of legality requires the practice of law in a particular way. Practiced in the right way, law promises to realize the value of legality. The critical connection here is the relationship between the practice of law and the promise of legality. In the following section, I will argue that there are two opposing values that one could find in law, and they exist concurrently in tension in the practice of law. These two opposing values make up the bipolarity of the concept of law.

Law as Authority v Law as Resistance

Law as Authority

Let's return to Finnis's focal meaning here. According to Finnis, the central case of law is the law 'of a complete community, purporting to have authority to provide comprehensive and supreme direction for human behaviour in that community'.[34] Law's authority is central to the focal meaning of law. Finnis provides an account of how law's authority is justified with reference to the

---

[29] Waldron, 'Normative (or Ethical) Positivism', 425.
[30] Waldron, 'Normative (or Ethical) Positivism', 420.
[31] Postema, *Bentham and the Common Law Tradition*, 334.
[32] Dworkin, 'Hart's Postscript', 2.
[33] Dworkin, 'Hart's Postscript', 32.
[34] Finnis, *Natural Law and Natural Rights*, 260.

common good. The empirical fact that so-and-so can settle coordination problems by its say-so has normative significance, with the relevant normative principle being that authority is good because it is 'required for the realization of the common good'.[35] Authority is necessary to realize the common good in a common life.

The political philosopher who did most to foreground the need for authority as the justification for law is Hobbes. His portrayal of the state of nature presents starkly the awful fate that awaits humanity in the absence of law. Law provides authoritative solutions to problems in the state of nature. The previous chapter has examined the Hobbesian state of nature in some detail, but it may nonetheless be helpful to recapitulate briefly the key points from that examination. The Hobbesian state of nature is a fallen world. The humans in that world are quarrelsome. There are three principal causes of quarrel arising out of 'the nature of man': competition, diffidence and glory.[36] The state of nature is a state of war, 'where every man is enemy to every man'.[37] 'To this war of every man against every man ... nothing can be unjust': 'where there is no common power, there is no law; where no law, no injustice'. There are only force and fraud. To attain peace, we need to get out of this deplorable condition. The way out is to create a common, coercive, compelling power that could rule with authority. The authoritative ruler is known idiomatically as the Leviathan, but is technically called the sovereign. Crucially, the Hobbesian sovereign is one who exerts its authority through the medium of law. Hobbes has a legalist view of sovereignty: 'a sovereign is by definition one who governs through law', and who is able to have its commands 'recognised as law'.[38] Within this political order, 'the relationship between sovereign and subject is mediated by law'.[39]

The linkage of law, Leviathan and sovereignty relies on a particular reading of Hobbes's narrative of the state of nature, specifically Dyzenhaus's reading. On this reading, law is central to Hobbes's solution for getting out of the state of nature. Law is an integral part of the social contract, which creates the Leviathan. The Leviathan is a sovereign within a constitutional order. Law creates the locus of authority in the sovereign. Sovereignty is a legal concept and the sovereign is one who normally governs through law. This definition of the sovereign still stands even if one agrees with Schmitt that the 'sovereign is he who decides on the exception'.[40] Normally, the sovereign governs through

[35] Finnis, *Natural Law and Natural Rights*, 246.
[36] Hobbes, *Leviathan*, ch 13.
[37] Hobbes, *Leviathan*, ch 13.
[38] Dyzenhaus, 'Hobbes and the Legitimacy of Law', 464, 483.
[39] Dyzenhaus, 'Hobbes's Constitutional Theory', 453.
[40] Schmitt, *Political Theology*, 5.

law; exceptionally, the sovereign may step outside it. This reading of Hobbes posits a tight connection between law and Leviathan, sovereignty and authority – they all arise simultaneously. Another reading of Hobbes is possible, which shows them as arising consecutively – this alternative reading locates the value of law, not in authority, but in resistance. This alternative reading will be explored in the next section, which deals with the second half of law's bipolarity. For now, let's press ahead with the value of law as authority.

The humans in the Hobbesian state of nature do not need to be selfish in order to generate this need for the authority of law. It is sufficient that they are self-interested, that is, they are interested in their own projects and causes. Their projects may be thoroughly altruistic and their causes truly benevolent. They may be full of goodwill. Yet, their projects may clash. Then, there will be the need for the authority of law. To motivate this thought, Finnis imagines a 'world of saints'[41] and Raz conjures up a 'society of angels',[42] and asks whether law would be needed in that alternate universe. Finnis is a natural lawyer, while Raz is a legal positivist. Both theorists, a natural lawyer and a hard legal positivist, arrive at the same answer: absolutely yes. Even a world of saints or a society of angels would have the need for law, for even they would have the need for coordination. With all the goodwill in the world, they would have an abundance of 'intelligence, dedication, skill and commitment' that would 'multiply the problems of coordination'.[43] The authority of law 'shapes, supports, and furthers patterns of coordination' by bringing 'definition, specificity, clarity, and thus predictability' into their interactions, without which neither angels nor saints could live together.[44] Law is needed, regardless of whether the angels and saints converge on the same set of universal moral norms. If they do not converge, then law is needed to manage their disagreements.[45] If they converge, law is still nonetheless needed to render these universal moral norms more determinate, through the process of *determinatio*.

The concurrence of a natural lawyer and a legal positivist on this point is unsurprising, especially if Dworkin's interpretation of positivism is correct. Dworkin thinks that, notwithstanding what they say, positivists too are seeking to understand law by 'understanding what is distinctly important and valuable in it'.[46] What they perceive to be the most valuable quality in law is its

[41] Finnis, *Natural Law and Natural Rights*, 269.
[42] Raz, *Practical Reason and Norms*, 159.
[43] Finnis, *Natural Law and Natural Rights*, 232.
[44] Finnis, *Natural Law and Natural Rights*, 267–8.
[45] See Waldron, *Law and Disagreement*.
[46] Dworkin, 'Hart's Postscript', 31.

authority, that is, its ability to 'provide authority in circumstances when authority is needed', inter alia, to solve coordination problems.[47] In Hart's famous just-so story, law, in the form of secondary rules, is needed in response to the inefficiency, uncertainty and stasis of primary rules in the prelaw state. This high valuation of 'law's role in substituting crisp direction for the uncertainties of customary or moral imprecation'[48] is carried over from Hart to Raz, who, being harder than Hart in his positivism, places authority front and center in his account of law.[49]

On this view, legal positivism, too, is a normative thesis about law, just as natural law is. This view of legal positivism is definitely true of the early positivists, like Hobbes and Bentham, who champion legal positivism for its ability to set 'the conditions necessary for coordination, for conflict resolution, and for the general stability of expectations in people's dealings with one another'.[50] Law cannot create these moral conditions unless it is set up positivistically, that is, 'unless it is set up in a way that enables people, by and large, to determine what the law is on a given subject without having to exercise moral judgment'.[51] Law cures the defect of the prelaw state through the creation of authority: 'the nerve of legality is authority, and that authority is damaged or undermined unless its directives can be identified without recourse to the kinds of reasons for action that citizens have before authority has spoken'.[52] If moral tests are included as part of the criteria of legal validity, so the normative positivist argument goes, they will 'allow citizens and officials who disagree, often strenuously, about what morality requires to substitute their own judgment about what standards have been established: the consequent disorganization will produce not utility but chaos'.[53] Therefore, for moral reasons, moral tests should not be included as part of the criteria of legal validity.

If we accept that legal positivism too is a normative thesis, the jurisprudential landscape could be remapped, not in terms of the positivist–antipositivist divide, but in terms of the ideals that the respective theorists value in the law. On this remapped landscape, Hart, Raz and Finnis may find themselves on the same side of the border. The difference between Hart and Finnis is that Hart values the authority of law for human survival, while Finnis values the authority of law

[47] Dworkin, 'Hart's Postscript', 31.
[48] Dworkin, 'Hart's Postscript', 28.
[49] Raz, *The Authority of Law*, 30.
[50] Waldron, 'Normative (or Ethical) Positivism', 413.
[51] Waldron, 'Normative (or Ethical) Positivism', 430.
[52] Dworkin, 'Hart's Postscript', 28.
[53] Dworkin, 'Hart's Postscript', 28.

for human flourishing. Using the Aristotelian distinction, one could say that Hart is concerned with the role of law in life, while Finnis is concerned with the role of law in the good life.[54] For Hart, secondary rules, the emergence of which marks the emergence of law itself, are needed to cure the defects of a system of primary rules; whereas for Finnis, law is needed for the pursuit of the common good, within which individuals can participate in the basic goods that constitute the good life. Both Hart and Finnis value law as a mode of authority, albeit for different reasons. On this remapped landscape, the boundary between legal positivism and natural law theory is no longer as black and white as it was thought to be. Natural law theory is not opposed to positive law; instead, what it does is 'offer a normative account of the functions of positive law'.[55] Natural law theory yields an account of positive law, which finds its proper place within natural law.[56] They supplement, not supplant, each other.

Kant's theory of law, too, proceeds along similar lines. Kant is a strong proponent of natural law, in the sense of the existence of a set of universal moral norms. Nonetheless, he recognizes the immense advantage that positive law brings when one moves from the state of nature, where each person decides what is right for themselves and simply does what seems right to them, to the state of civil society, where the law is posited as authoritative for all.[57] The benefits of positive law are derived from its ability to provide authoritative directives. 'Disagreement about justice (even honest disagreement among people of good will) constitutes a problem – a problem to which positive law (that is, law accepted as authoritative without regard to the justice of its content) is the solution'.[58] Notwithstanding his belief in a set of universal moral law, Kant recognizes that 'when one thinks about justice, one must recognize that others [too] are thinking about justice and that one's confidence in the objective quality of one's own conclusions is matched by others' confidence in the objective quality of theirs';[59] hence, the need for positive law as a political solution to the fact of moral disagreement. What Kant has given us is a normative account of positive law that is centered on the value of authority in the face of moral disagreement. If on this side of the border are those who value law as a mode of authority, on the other side of the border are those who value law as a mode of resistance.

---

[54] Aristotle, *Politics*, 1252a29, 1280a30.
[55] Waldron, 'Normative (or Ethical) Positivism', 415.
[56] Finnis, 'What Is the Philosophy of Law?', 138.
[57] Waldron, 'Kant's Legal Positivism', 1537.
[58] Waldron, 'Kant's Legal Positivism', 1536.
[59] Waldron, 'Kant's Legal Positivism', 1566.

Law as Resistance

At the polar opposite of the ideal of law as authority is the ideal of law as resistance. On this opposing view, the value of law does not lie in the provision of authority, but in resistance. Submitting to authority means subjecting oneself to a certain degree of restraint. Those who resent the restraint have one option: resist. Law allows its subjects to resist authority. There is an alternative reading of Hobbes that locates the value of law in resistance. On this reading, the creation of the Leviathan gives birth to an entity with supreme might, which gives rise to the fear that the Leviathan may end up devouring the subjects. Therefore, law is instituted to bind the Leviathan, to rein in its reign. On this account, what gets us out of the state of nature is the creation of an entity with supreme might. However, once that is in place, there arises the worry about the concentration of power in the one entity. Law comes later to control the concentration of power. This account is part of what Shklar calls the 'liberalism of fear', which comes from the fear of having created a monster.[60] Law is a device to restrict the Leviathan. Law allows the subject to resist the sovereign.

Moving on from Hobbes's Leviathan, one could make a similar observation about Fuller's Rex. The creation of law is always an act of sovereign self-binding, as Rex in Fuller's parable learns the hard way. Fuller tells the story, or what he calls an allegory, of the 'unhappy reign of a monarch', who 'came to the throne with the zeal of a reformer', but 'died, old before his time and deeply disillusioned'.[61] With the zeal of a reformer, Rex set out to create a legal system. The creation of law requires that Rex restrict his own actions to conform to the 'inner morality of law', which is the 'morality that makes law possible'.[62] Rex's failure to conform to the inner morality of law meant that, 'not only did he not succeed in introducing the needed reforms, but he never even succeeded in creating any law at all, good or bad'.[63] If Rex refuses to tie his own hands, then the only option that he has left is to give up the legal enterprise altogether, which is exactly what Rex's successor, Rex II, did. 'The first act of his successor, Rex II, was to announce that he was taking the powers of government away from the lawyers and placing them in the hands of psychiatrists and experts in public relations'.[64] He could still govern, not through law, but through managerial direction. A sovereign who governs

[60] Shklar, 'The Liberalism of Fear', 21.
[61] Fuller, *Morality of Law*, 33.
[62] Fuller, *Morality of Law*, 33.
[63] Fuller, *Morality of Law*, 34.
[64] Fuller, *Morality of Law*, 38.

through law necessarily has to tie its own hands, and thereby leave room for the subject to resist its authority. The inner morality of law is, on one reading of it, the morality of resistance. It is the morality of the sovereign holding back in order for the subject to step forward. Hence, the decision to create a legal system and to rule through law always evinces a moral commitment on some level, which is Fuller's main anti-positivist point.

Resistance is all the rage for critical legal theorists of all shapes and sizes. For the critical race theorists, law is the site of resistance against white supremacy; for the feminist legal theorists, law is the site of resistance against male patriarchy; for the postcolonial legal theorists, law is the site of resistance against colonialism; for the queer legal theorists, law is the site of resistance against heteronormativity. In their resistance, sometimes they win, sometimes they lose. When they win, it is of great importance that their victory is a legal victory, for they fight the law through the law. The critical race theorists will celebrate the civil rights cases; the feminist legal theorists will celebrate the abortion cases; the postcolonial legal theorists will celebrate the native title cases; and the queer legal theorists will celebrate the same-sex marriage cases.

Critical legal theory has, not a pejorative conception of law, but an ambivalent conception of law: 'a pejorative conception views law fundamentally as an ideological practice for mystifying and legitimating injustice ... in the ambivalent conception, law is both ideology and promise; it can be one resource among others in a project of political redemption'.[65] It may well be the case that law is a tool for the strong to oppress the weak, for the rich to oppress the poor, for whites to oppress blacks, and for men to oppress women. However, 'even if law is a supple tool of power, law also serves as a discourse of ideas and ideals that can limit, channel and transform the interests of the powerful, sometimes in unexpected ways that the powerful cannot fully control'.[66] It provides the terms for the powerless to talk back to power: 'recourse to law forces the powerful to talk in terms in which the powerless can also participate and can also make claims'.[67] Recall the bumper sticker slogan of critical legal theory that 'all law is politics'. Properly understood, the slogan is not at all pejorative toward law. What it does is to draw attention to the political nature of law and the 'the political values that legal culture and rights discourse might serve': 'legal culture and institutions are valuable to critical theories of law because they are a way of doing politics, in the sense of shaping, restraining and challenging power'.[68]

---

[65] Balkin, 'Critical Legal Theory Today', 65.
[66] Balkin, 'Critical Legal Theory Today', 67.
[67] Balkin, 'Critical Legal Theory Today', 67.
[68] Balkin, 'Critical Legal Theory Today', 71.

A cynic could bracket and set aside these critical legal theories as being merely concerned with the contingent content of law, for they say little about the necessary features of the form of law. So, let me say something about the necessary features of the form of law, and show how, on that score too, law's value may be understood to lie in resistance. Let's return to Simmonds's archetype here. According to Simmonds, the moral value of the archetype of law consists in the value of liberty, understood as independence from the will of others, including that of the state. The form of law, understood in terms of Fuller's eight desiderata, promotes and protects individual independence.[69] Insofar as law obtains, there will necessarily be a range of legally permissible options, within which an individual could exercise his or her own will. The range may be widely or narrowly circumscribed, but within that sacrosanct zone, the exercise of one's will is protected by law. Within that zone, 'I can act as I choose, without regard to the fact that others may intensely object to what I am doing, relying solely upon the fact that my actions are legally permissible and will receive the protection of the law'.[70] Even saints might disagree, in perfect good faith, with one another. Their disagreement could range over matters of fact and norm. Law enables persons, whether saintly or not, to act in the face of objection and disagreement. On this view, law is needed even in a world of saints, not for saints to coordinate, but to enable saints to have a modicum of liberty, without which they would not be individual saints. Saints, too, have to be selves.

The value of law is put to the test, not when all is well, but when the chips are down. Law has interstices, which, when push comes to shove, are transformed into interstices of resistance. For example, an evil regime may pass a law requiring a particular style of salute. However, for the law to be intelligible and obeyable, 'it must define what is to count as a salute, what are the appropriate circumstances for giving a salute, and so forth': 'such definitions will almost certainly create the possibility of performing ironic or mocking forms of salute that would nevertheless count as complying with the legal requirement', such as 'a salute with the arm raised rather limply, or a quiet smile accompanying the stiffly raised arm'.[71] Law can regulate anything, but it can't regulate everything. No matter how precisely the style of the salute is specified, there will inevitably be *some* interstices of underspecification, and hence, of resistance. Those subject to law can always rely

---

[69] Fuller's eight desiderata are generality, publicity, prospectivity, clarity, comprehensibility, obeyability, constancy and congruence: see Fuller, *The Morality of Law*, 33.
[70] Simmonds, *Law as a Moral Idea*, 142.
[71] Simmonds, *Law as a Moral Idea*, 87.

on it strategically. Faced with the ever-present possibility of resistance under law, the evil regime may finally decide to throw in the towel and throw law out the window, and give the proverbial Joe a beating. When that happens, law has ceased to obtain, which only goes to show that, insofar as law obtains, there is always the possibility of resistance in and through the law.

Like Simmonds, Rundle too draws on Fuller's eight desiderata of law, but she associates them with a different value: the value of individual agency. According to Rundle, 'for Fuller, there can be no meaningful concept of law that does not include a meaningful limitation of the lawgiver's power in favour of the agency of the legal subject'.[72] An agent, in this thick Fullerian sense, is 'a person capable of purposive action, in possession of her capacities, and who is to be regarded as an end in herself . . . with a life to live of her own'.[73] The inner morality of law is the morality of agency: 'law is intrinsically moral for how, if it is to function, it must maintain and communicate respect for that status of agency'.[74] Notice how different this conception of the value of law is from the view of law as authority. Here, the focus is not on the lawgiver, but on the legal subject; not on authority, but on agency. The legal subject is an autonomous agent, who is capable of having an individual plan of life. On the one hand, the law provides a collective plan for communal life;[75] on the other hand, the legal subject has an individual plan for his or her own life. As an autonomous agent, the legal subject is capable of interacting with the law to further his or her individual plan. If the law supports one's individual plan, one could use it. If the law obstructs one's individual plan, the nature of law is such that one will have the option of resisting it.

Resistance is an ever-present possibility within the law, be it state law or God's law. The law could always be deployed against the lawgiver, even if the lawgiver is God. Just as state law could be deployed against the state, so God's law could be deployed against God. The possibility of resistance inheres in the discourse of law. Law, once given, has an independent existence from the lawgiver. By existing apart from the lawgiver, the law puts a brake on the arbitrary will of the lawgiver. The Talmudic tale of the Oven of Akhnai highlights this particular feature of law brilliantly. In the tale, the rabbis are arguing about the ritual purity of a tiled oven based on the ritual laws that were given by God. Rabbi Eliezer argues that the oven is clean, but his fellow rabbis disagree. To prove his point, Rabbi Eliezer says, 'If the law is as I say, then this

[72] Rundle, *Forms Liberate*, 2.
[73] Rundle, *Forms Liberate*, 10.
[74] Rundle, *Forms Liberate*, 3.
[75] Shapiro, *Legality*, ch 5.

carob tree will prove it'. The carob tree jumps a hundred cubits. However, the other rabbis respond by saying, 'One does not prove anything from a tree'. Rabbi Eliezer then says, 'If the law is as I say, then this aqueduct will prove it'. The water in the aqueduct begins to flow upstream. However, the other rabbis again respond by saying, 'One does not prove anything from an aqueduct'. Rabbi Eliezer then says, 'If the law is as I say, then the wall of the academy will prove it'. The wall begins to fall. Rabbi Joshua reprimands the wall saying, 'If scholars argue a point of law, what business is it of yours?' Finally, Rabbi Eliezer says, 'If the law is as I say, it shall be proven from heaven'. A voice of heaven cries out that 'the law is always as he says'. In response, Rabbi Joshua quotes Deuteronomy 30:12 saying, 'It is not in heaven'. Rabbi Jeremiah explains this verse to mean that, once God gave the law to Moses on Mount Sinai, heavenly voices no longer have any say in legal matters. The law confers on the rabbis the exclusive authority to decide legal questions and requires that internal disputes be resolved by majority vote. When Rabbi Eliezer refuses to back down, he is excommunicated.[76]

If the law, once given by God, is independent of God, as the Talmudic tale suggests, then it follows that the law of God could be used against God himself. Abraham comes close to doing just that in the Sodom and Gomorrah episode.[77] Sodom is known for sodomy. God wants to destroy Sodom and Gomorrah as punishment for the wrongdoing of its inhabitants. When God reveals his intention to Abraham, Abraham starts haggling with God. In haggling with God, Abraham deploys the basic legal concepts of guilt and innocence and of judging and justice. Abraham asks God:

> Will you really wipe out the innocent with the guilty? Perhaps there may be fifty innocents within the city. Will you really wipe out the place and not spare it for the sake of the fifty innocent within it? Far be it from You to do such a thing, to put to death the innocent with the guilty, making innocent and guilty the same. Far be it from you! Will not the Judge of all the earth do justice?[78]

Abraham's rhetorical questions hold God to account by God's own pronounced standards. These promulgated standards bind even God himself. God immediately concedes and says, 'If I find at Sodom fifty righteous in the city, I will spare the whole place for their sake'.[79] The haggling continues as

---

[76] Babylonian Talmud, Bava Melzia 59b, in Walzer, *The Jewish Political Tradition*, 263–4. The Talmudic tale is also recounted in Shapiro, 'Authority', 382–3.
[77] Book of Genesis 18:17–33.
[78] Book of Genesis 18:23–25.
[79] Book of Genesis 18:26.

Abraham bargains the amount down to forty-five, to forty, to thirty, to twenty, and finally, to ten.

II LOVE

The initial threshold question for law is whether, in addition to being a practice, it is also a value. For love, there is less controversy that it is a value. What is more controversial is in identifying the kind of value love is. The initial threshold question for love is whether the value of love is part of aesthetics or ethics. Is the experience of love an ethical experience or an aesthetic experience? Is love directed to the good (in which case it is part of ethics) or is love directed to the beautiful (in which case it is part of aesthetics)? Is love concerned with a life well lived (in which case it is part of ethics) or is love concerned with beauty (in which case it is part of aesthetics)? My response to this dilemma is to deny it. This dichotomy is a false one.

As Wittgenstein points out, 'ethics and aesthetics are one'.[80] Or as Nietzsche aphorizes, we should turn our lives into works of art: 'To "give style" to one's character – a great and rare art! It is practiced by those who survey all the strengths and weaknesses of their nature and then fit them into an artistic plan until every one of them ... delights the eye'.[81] Ethics is concerned with a life well lived, while aesthetics is concerned with a beautiful life. However, if one holds the view that a life well lived is a beautiful life, then ethics and aesthetics converge. In aesthetics, 'the work of art is the object seen *sub specie aeternitatis* [from the perspective of the eternal]'; in ethics, 'the good life is the world seen *sub specie aeternitatis*'.[82] In aesthetic and ethical contemplation, 'the whole of consciousness is inhabited by the object contemplated',[83] be it the work of art or the good life. In living one's life well, one transforms one's biological life into a biographical work of art.

Love gives meaning and beauty to one's life. It makes one's life meaningful and beautiful. Love may be other-regarding, but it is also self-enriching. A life with love is both a life well lived and a beautiful life. Hence, insofar as love is concerned, Wittgenstein is right: 'ethics and aesthetics are one'.[84] However, the question still remains as to what the aesthetic and ethical value of love consists in. I will argue below that the value of love consists in two bipolar

---

[80] Wittgenstein, *Tractatus*, §6.42.
[81] Nietzsche, *The Gay Science*, §290.
[82] Wittgenstein, *Notebooks 1914–1916*, §7.10.16.
[83] Collinson, 'Ethics and Aesthetics Are One', 268.
[84] Wittgenstein, *Tractatus*, §6.42.

ideals: love as leading to a union of distinct persons versus love as enabling a sustained attention to the distinctness of persons.

Love as Union v Love as Attention

Love as Union

The idea of love as union is traceable to antiquity: the Aristophanes myth of love tells us that 'human nature was originally one and we were a whole, and the desire and pursuit of the whole is called love'.[85] On this mythical view, love is not 'the union of the strange, but the reunion of the estranged'.[86] Turning from the Greco-Roman world to the Judeo–Christian world, we find the same idea of love as union. In the Book of Genesis, we are told that the relationship of the primordial couple, who gives birth to the rest of humanity, is one of union, in which 'two become one'.[87] In the Trinity, 'three are one' because of the bond of love between the Father and the Son, with the bond of love being the Holy Spirit. Philosophers, both continental and analytic, continue to draw on this notion of love as union. Hegel posits love as 'the dissolution of the opposition between self and other, so a finding of oneself in the other'.[88] Rawls points out that those who love 'acquire strong attachments to persons',[89] attachments that enable them to overcome the 'separateness of persons and of the ends they pursue'.[90]

In the first creation account in Genesis, man and woman live in a state of union and oneness with each other and with God: they are created together, and together they are in the image and likeness of God. In the second creation account in Genesis, God creates man in an intensely physical, even erotic, manner when God molds man from clay and breathes into man's nostrils the breath of life. Woman, in turn, is created out of the ribs of man: man and woman are of 'one flesh',[91] and they carry within them the breath of God. In their primordial state in Eden, Adam and Eve are one with each other and with God. This prelapsarian form of love as union – the original oneness of creator and creature – was lost with the Fall. However, for Paul, that was not the end of the story. Christ continues the story of creation. In the sequel to the

---

[85] Aristophanes' speech in Plato, *Plato's Symposium*, 520.
[86] Tillich, *Love, Power and Justice*, 25.
[87] Book of Genesis 2:24.
[88] Bernstein, 'Love and Law: Hegel's Critique of Morality', 415.
[89] Rawls, *A Theory of Justice*, 573.
[90] Mendus, 'The Importance of Love in Rawls's Theory of Justice', 68.
[91] Book of Genesis 2:24.

creation story, the paradise that was lost in Adam is regained in Christ. In describing the effect of the new creation in Christ, Paul returns to the original idea of love as union. Having discovered the love of Christ, Paul has recovered the love of God. In the words of Paul, 'It is no longer I who live, but Christ who lives in me; and the life I now live in the flesh I live by faith in the Son of God, who loved me and gave himself for me'.[92]

We find the same idea at work in the phenomenology and psychology of love. Nozick argues that lovers are 'united to form and constitute a new entity in the world, what might be called a *we*'.[93] Lovers who constitute a *we* unite not only their well-being but also their autonomy: 'they limit or curtail their own decision-making power and rights; some decisions can no longer be made alone'.[94] The union of love alters the constitution of the self to include the other. It unites 'the most radically separated beings, namely individual persons'.[95] This ascription of the end of love as the formation of a *we* also explains two related features of love: infatuation and unrequited love. The function of infatuation is 'to pave and smooth the way to uniting in a *we*: it provides enthusiasm to [overcome] the hurdles of concern for one's own autonomy, and it provides an initiation into a *we*-thinking by constantly occupying the mind with thoughts of the other'.[96] When one's mind is occupied with thoughts of the other, these thoughts could be realistic or, as is more often the case, fantastic. Infatuation still works even if it is founded on fantasy. Love is, after all, blind. Defects in the beloved, which are obvious for all to see, are blind spots in the eyes of the lover. The claim here is not that infatuation is love; rather, the claim is that infatuation is a step along the way to love as union. The reality of the other matters less for the ideal of love as union, as compared to the ideal of love as attention that we will encounter later. In unrequited love, the desire to form a *we* is still there, but it is not reciprocated. Consequently, no *we* is actually formed, but the desire remains as long as the love endures, albeit unrequited.

In Arendt's study of Augustine's idea of love, Arendt shows that Augustine sees *appetitus* as lying at the root of love, whether *caritas* or *cupiditas*. Each of these italicized terms is loaded. *Appetitus* is a kind of craving that is 'tied to a definite object, and it takes this object to spark the craving itself, thus providing an aim for it'.[97] *Appetitus* is a motion toward a definite object.

[92] Letter to the Galatians 2:20.
[93] Nozick, 'Love's Bond', 418.
[94] Nozick, 'Love's Bond', 419.
[95] Tillich, *Love, Power and Justice*, 26.
[96] Nozick, 'Love's Bond', 424.
[97] Arendt, *Love and Saint Augustine*, 9.

Hence, love is both motion and emotion. *Appetitus* turns into *caritas* or *cupiditas* depending on its object; hence, 'the right love consists in the right object'.[98] *Caritas* is *appetitus* that is directed toward the eternal (the divine), while *cupiditas* is the love that is directed toward the temporal (the world). There is no doubt what Augustine's preferred option is: *caritas*, not *cupiditas*. 'However, both right and wrong love (*caritas* and *cupiditas*) has this in common – craving desire, that is, *appetitus*'.[99] From Augustine, we get the twin maxims on love: 'love, and as do as you please', and 'love, but be careful what you love'. Arendt's Augustine-inspired triangulation of *appetitus*, *cupiditas* and *caritas* in Latin mirrors Tillich's triangulation of *eros*, *philia* and *agape* in Greek. According to Tillich, *eros* is 'the drive towards the unity of the separated': 'in the moment in which one is in love the fulfilment of the desire for reunion is anticipated and the happiness of this reunion is experienced in imagination'.[100] All love is erotic. *Philia* is directed toward particular persons, with whom one has a degree of personal familiarity and, as Aristotle would add, with whom one stands in a position of equality. The paradigmatic example of *philia* is friendship. *Agape*, on the other hand, is directed toward all. It is the unconditional universal love of all beings. *Agape* is the highest form of love: it is 'the depth of love or love in relation to the ground of life'.[101]

Aquinas develops Augustine's definition of love by linking the will with the intellect in the act of love. On this expanded conception, love as union is tied to an intimate knowledge of the beloved. According to Aquinas, '[love] draws the lover into the interior of the beloved, with the result that nothing remains in the beloved that is not united to the lover; just as the form enters deeply into the one informed by it, so too the lover in a certain way enters the beloved'.[102] Love directs the intellect to seek deeper knowledge of the beloved, which in turn deepens one's love for the beloved. For Aquinas, the paradigm for this movement of love is *caritas*, the love of God, for 'the more perfectly we know God, the more perfectly we love him'.[103] The movement between love and knowledge is bidirectional: 'the contemplation of spiritual good enkindles [the love of God] within us, while the love of God moves us to contemplate him more deeply'.[104] Something or someone, whether God or human, can be

---

[98] Arendt, *Love and Saint Augustine*, 17.
[99] Arendt, *Love and Saint Augustine*, 17.
[100] Tillich, 'Being and Love', 43–4.
[101] Tillich, 'Being and Love', 48.
[102] Aquinas, *Commentary on the Sentences of Peter Lombard*, III.27.1.1 ad 4.
[103] Aquinas, *Summa Theologica*, I-II.67.6 ad 3.
[104] Sherwin, *By Knowledge and By Love*, 233.

loved only if known: 'no one can love what he does not know'.[105] Therefore, if one wants to love that which is worthy of love, one needs to be able to grasp the relevant properties that make an object worthy of love, and hence, loveable. The better one's grasp, the better one's love.

Humans overcome their existential isolation through love. Love annihilates the distance between subject and object 'by transforming the subject into a lover and the object into the beloved'.[106] Love binds the lover to the beloved. To overcome one's existential loneliness, the self desires to unite with something outside itself and become entirely absorbed by the object of love, whereby 'the lover forgets himself in the pursuit of the beloved'.[107] The feeling of love is, in the words of Freud, oceanic. Freud defines the oceanic feeling as 'a feeling of an indissoluble bond, of being one with the external world': 'at the height of being in love, the boundary between ego and object threatens to melt away'.[108] To experience love is 'to experience this sense of completion'.[109] According to Raz, 'aspiring to such fusion includes the desire to have one [that is, a fused] will, not only through gradual adaptation, but also by the more immediate transformation of the will through love'.[110]

Love has an inflated status in our moral imagination today. We hear that 'all you need is love',[111] and 'love makes the world go round'.[112] Without putting love down, it is nonetheless important to put love in its place. There are two important caveats about love. First, love need not be among equals. Love can be marked by inequality, even deep inequality, of power. In such cases, the idea of love as union will incorporate a derivative notion of love as a submission to the will of the beloved. Of the power differentials that can exist in the world, none could be greater than the power differential between human and God. Loving God involves absolute submission to his will. To love God is to 'cling to him',[113] even if it requires the killing of one's son, as demonstrated in Abraham's sacrifice of Isaac.[114] The love of God – the desire to be one with him – supplies the motivation for obedience. 'If you love me',

---

[105] Aquinas, *Summa Theologica*, ST I-II 27.2.
[106] Arendt, *Love and Saint Augustine*, 18.
[107] Arendt, *Love and Saint Augustine*, 28.
[108] Freud, *Civilisation and Its Discontent*, 12–3.
[109] Kahn, *Putting Liberalism in Its Place*, 214.
[110] Raz, *Morality of Freedom*, 33.
[111] The Beatles, 'All You Need is Love' (1967).
[112] There is, of course, a grain of truth in these sayings. 'Sayings like "love makes the world go round" don't become trite for nothing': Wolf, *The Variety of Values*, 182.
[113] Arendt, *Love and Saint Augustine*, 19.
[114] For a close reading of this episode in the Book of Genesis, see Neoh, 'Law and Love in Abraham's Binding of Isaac', 237.

says Jesus, 'you will keep my commandments'.[115] By doing what the Lord commands, the disciple becomes one in mind and heart with the Lord, which is an example of how love works among unequals. However, it is sometimes said that love is the great equalizer, that 'love levels all ranks',[116] which is true, to some extent. Love does not eliminate entirely the power difference, but it reduces it in one crucial respect. Although there is a clear power difference between God and humans, God's love for humans renders him vulnerable to humans, for humans could withhold their love from him. Humans could spurn his love, as Adam and Eve did in the Garden of Eden. Hence, the Fall is tragic, not only for humans, but also for God.

Second, love need not be directed at the right object. The person or thing that you love might not be worthy of your love. Recall Augustine's two injunctions: love and do as you please, but be careful what you love. The latter injunction is important because you might love that which is undeserving of love. According to Augustine, two different objects of love define the two cities: 'the earthly city by a love of self carried even to the point of contempt for God, the heavenly city by a love of God carried even to the point of contempt for self'.[117] To the two Augustinian injunctions, we can add a third observation: such is each as his or her love. As Augustine says, 'hold fast rather the love of God, that as God is forever and ever, so you also may remain forever and ever: because *such is each one as is his love*'.[118] Love and do as you please, but be careful what you love, for such is each as his or her love. In *cupiditas*, whose object is temporal, 'man has cast the die that makes him perishable', while in *caritas*, whose object is eternity, 'man transforms himself into an eternal, nonperishable being'.[119] Well-ordered love means loving each in the right measure. For Augustine, 'every man is to be loved as a man for God's sake; but God is to be loved for His own sake'.[120] Humans are united with their objects of love: love the mundane and you become mundane, but love the sublime and you become sublime.

Love as Attention

Recall that in the Edenic narrative, the primordial community of God, man and woman start off with the experience of love as union. The Fall brings that

---

[115] Gospel of John 14:15.
[116] Gilbert and Sullivan, *HMS Pinafore*.
[117] Augustine, *City of God*, Bk XIV, §28.
[118] Augustine, 'Homilies on the First Epistle of John', Bk II, §14.
[119] Arendt, *Love and Saint Augustine*, 18.
[120] Augustine, 'On Christian Doctrine', Bk I, §28.

experience of love to an end. The immediate result of the Fall is differentiation, and consequently, individuation. After the eating of the forbidden fruit, the first thing that Adam and Eve do is to cover their bodies. The love that is manifested in the intimacy of nudity is gone. The bare body is now the object of shame. Before the Fall, 'they are not aware of being distinct beings, neither distinct from each other or from God'.[121] After the Fall, they become aware, not only of their nakedness, but also of their separateness: the man and the woman begin to see that they are separate and different from each other and from God. 'The final realization of separation and difference comes when God enters the Garden, and Adam and Eve hide because they do not know how to respond to God as a totally separate being'.[122] However, when one door closes, a window opens: the loss of love as union closes a particular experience of love, but it opens up the possibility of a new experience of love. The newfound sense of individuality makes possible a new plethora of experiences that require some kind of distinctness and distance between persons. One such experience is the experience of longing. A new way of loving becomes possible: love in the sense of paying attention to the other as the other, that is, as a separate and distinct being.

At the polar opposite of the view of love as union is the countervailing view of love as attention. The countervailing idea here is that love requires an appreciation of the other as an independent agent in the world. While love as union strives for the overcoming of separateness, love as attention strives, not for the overcoming, but the grasping of separateness. Separateness is not to be eliminated, but appreciated. It is not just about noticing separateness, but it is also about being attentive to the needs of the other as a separate individual. The egoistic narcissist only pays attention to the self, and to objects or persons that they perceive to be an extension of the self or to be somehow related to the self, either because they pose a threat or provide a benefit to the self. Love as attention pulls the person out of the self. It perceives the other as utterly different from the self, and yet still pays attention to the other as the other. It consists in an appreciation of the other, not in relation to, but apart from the self. 'Love is the extremely difficult realization that something other than oneself is real'.[123] It is the realization that the other, too, has an inner life of infinite depth. It calls for an accurate perception of the other, and willing the good of the other for their own sake. All these are unachievable if you and the other are absorbed into each other to the point of indistinction, which the view

---

[121] Fletcher, 'Thinking about Eden', 18.
[122] Fletcher, 'Thinking about Eden', 20.
[123] Murdoch, 'The Sublime and the Good', as quoted in Jollimore, *Love's Vision*, 149.

of love as union idealizes. In contrast to love as union, love as attention requires the preservation of the distinctness of the other. The human person is the quintessential object of love as attention: 'a person, unlike other objects of love, possesses a profound and complex inner life and exists as a subject in the world'.[124] Love as attention, then, is the effort to come to know that inner life in its full individuality. This kind of love is ineluctably particular. While love as union can accommodate a high degree of abstraction – one can strive for union with abstract entities like the nation, humanity, nature and, at its most abstract level, the universe – love as attention is different in that it focuses 'the lover's attention on the beloved as a concrete, particular individual'.[125]

On this conception, the relevant faculty of love is not the will, but sight (in the mind's eye). A lover needs to look at, attend to, and focus on the beloved.[126] It requires, not the fusion of will with the beloved, but the singling out of the beloved. Love is a way of seeing. In seeing the beloved differently, the world thereby looks different to the lover. The lover sees the world in light of the beloved. The beloved has the lover's attention in a special way, as evidenced by how the lover's attention is immediately captured by the beloved the moment she steps into the room. The room no longer looks, or feels, the same. The experience is true even if it is a crowded room with many other people in it. The addition of the presence of the beloved changes one's field of vision entirely. The lover sees the world with the beloved at the center. 'Love causes the lover's world to be transformed', but 'what looks to the lover like a transfigured world is really the result of a transformed eye'.[127]

To love her is to have knowledge of her. The use of the word 'knowledge' as a euphemism for sexual intercourse is an interesting play on words. Carnal knowledge may or may not be a necessary condition for romantic love, but it is definitely not sufficient. To truly know her often requires a lifetime of effort at seeing her for who she is. It is an endless task – till death do us part. The same applies to the love of God: to love God is to have knowledge of him. As an expression of love, prayer is not petition, but contemplation: it consists in simply being attentive to God.[128] The task of attention is lifelong: it goes on continuously and, often imperceptibly, 'it builds up structures of value' around the beloved.[129] It directs the lover's attention outward, away from the self toward the object of love. The same process is at work in falling in love as

---

[124] Jollimore, *Love's Vision*, xii.
[125] Jollimore, *Love's Vision*, 151.
[126] Murdoch, *The Sovereignty of the Good*, 22.
[127] Jollimore, *Love's Vision*, 3.
[128] Murdoch, *The Sovereignty of the Good*, 55.
[129] Murdoch, *The Sovereignty of the Good*, 37.

much as in falling out of love. If one wants to stop loving a particular object of love, it is often futile to force oneself to stop loving. What is needed in such a case is another object to attend to, that is, another object of love. What is needed is a reorientation: 'deliberately falling out of love is not a jump of the will, it is the acquiring of new objects of attention and thus of new energies as a result of refocusing'.[130]

This view of love also entails selflessness, but not in the sense of a loss of self in a fusion of will. Love as attention is not the thrusting forward of oneself toward a fusion of will, but a stepping back. Instead of looking at others from the vantage point of the self, love is the effort to look at the other independently of the self. It is selfless in precisely this sense. It is 'to recognize in a most fundamental way [the] value and significance [of the beloved] as an individual'.[131] It assumes that one could look at and love something without thereby seizing it.[132] Hence, 'loving someone always involves caring about the person for his [or her] own sake', willing and wishing his or her good, independently of one's own.[133] Love is selfless for it draws the lover out of the self to focus his or her attention on the needs, interests, desires and well-being of the beloved.[134] Love, on this view, consists in a selfless – that is, a non-self-centered – concern for the good of the beloved. The lover sees the beloved as a separate individual and desires that the beloved flourishes. Love, in this form, has no place for 'lust, obsession, possessiveness and dependency'.[135]

Consider Bernard William's example of having 'one thought too many'. A man sees two persons drowning, and he can only save one. One of them is a stranger. The other is his wife (let's assume that his wife is his beloved). What should he do? More crucially, *how* should he decide? Should he be expected to figure out, first, what general moral principle would render it permissible for him to save his wife? 'But this construction provides the agent with one thought too many: it might have been hoped by some (for instance, by his wife) that his motivating thought, fully spelled out, would be [just] the thought that it was his wife, *not* that it was his wife and that in situations of this kind it is permissible to save one's wife'.[136] The additional thought – 'that in situations of this kind it is permissible to save one's wife' – is 'one thought too many'. Seeing and sensing the need of his beloved provides him with a sufficient reason for

---

[130] Murdoch, *The Sovereignty of the Good*, 55.
[131] Jollimore, *Love's Vision*, 153.
[132] Murdoch, *The Sovereignty of the Good*, 65.
[133] Wolf, *The Variety of Values*, 189.
[134] Jollimore, *Love's Vision*, 150.
[135] Frankfurt, *The Reasons of Love*, 43.
[136] Williams, *Moral Luck*, 18.

action, 'without requiring that he think of any additional considerations and without the interposition of any general rules'.[137] Love is the reason, for it makes 'the beloved valuable to the lover'.[138]

III FREEDOM

'To raise the question, "what is freedom?" seems to be a hopeless enterprise. It is as though age-old contradictions and antinomies were lying in wait'.[139] After raising this cautionary note, Arendt proceeds to raise the question anyway, in an essay entitled 'What Is Freedom?' There are many ways to carve up freedom. Like Berlin, I do not propose to discuss the more than two hundred senses of this protean word: 'I propose to examine no more than two of these senses – but those central ones, with a great deal of human history behind them, and, I dare say, still to come'.[140] Berlin proposes, as his two senses of freedom, positive and negative freedom. Before Berlin, Constant proposes, as his two senses of freedom, ancient and modern freedom.[141] Arendt, in the essay referred to above, distinguishes philosophical free will from political freedom. I shall propose, as my two senses of freedom, independence and identification.[142] I do not think that I am saying anything particularly new here, but I am merely repackaging the old. The binary itself is as old as the hills. What underlies Constant's modern freedom, Berlin's negative freedom and Arendt's philosophical free will is freedom as independence. What underlies Constant's ancient freedom, Berlin's positive freedom and Arendt's political freedom is freedom as identification. On the former view, the value of freedom lies in the value of independence: what is good about freedom is to be found in what is good about independence. On the latter view, the value of freedom lies in the value of identification: what is good about freedom is to be found in what is good about identification.

The initial threshold question for law is whether it is simply a practice or a value-laden practice. The initial question for love is whether it is part of ethics or aesthetics. The initial threshold question that confronts us for freedom is whether it is political or metaphysical. Or to phrase the question more precisely, is freedom on the political plane continuous or discontinuous with freedom on the metaphysical plane? If one thinks that they are discontinuous,

---

[137] Frankfurt, *The Reasons of Love*, 37.
[138] Frankfurt, *The Reasons of Love*, 40.
[139] Arendt, 'What Is Freedom?', 143.
[140] Berlin, 'Two Concepts of Liberty', 121.
[141] Constant, 'The Liberty of the Ancients Compared with that of the Moderns'.
[142] This division is inspired by my reading of Bergmann, *On Being Free*.

then one could hive off the political from the metaphysical, and concentrate on the 'political, not metaphysical', as the Rawlsian slogan calls for. On the other hand, if one thinks, like Berlin, that they are continuous, then that kind of hiving off no longer seems possible or plausible. Any claims about freedom on the political plane will carry with them certain metaphysical presuppositions, whether articulated or not. For example, Berlin thinks that positive freedom is grounded on the metaphysics of rationality, while negative freedom is grounded on the metaphysics of free will. This section will adopt the continuous view and the argument that follows is best understood in that seamless fashion. The argument will move back and forth between the political and the metaphysical. However, even if you were to adopt the discontinuous view, the argument that follows would still work, albeit in a more clunky fashion: you could confine my remarks about political freedom to the political plane and my remarks about metaphysical freedom to the metaphysical plane.

Freedom as Independence v Freedom as Identification

Freedom as Independence

In Constant's memorable phrase, 'individual independence is the first need of the moderns'.[143] Individual independence consists in being left alone to do one's own thing. It is concerned with what Berlin calls negative freedom, which is 'the area within which the subject – a person or group of persons – is or should be left to do or be what he is able to do or be, without interference by other persons'.[144] As Berlin says, 'the wider the area of non-interference, the wider my freedom'.[145] Berlin's reference to noninterference is the classical liberal formulation. Republican theorists of freedom would emphasize non-domination over noninterference. Someone dominates another when 'they have sway over the other, in the old phrase, and the sway is arbitrary'.[146] Both the liberal and the republican formulations paint a view of the self with the ability to decide and choose what it wants to do with its own life, including what Nozick describes as 'the ability to regulate and guide its life in accordance with some overall conception it chooses to accept'.[147] We want to be left alone to lead our lives by our own lights, without the interference of others.

---

[143] Constant, 'The Liberty of the Ancients Compared with that of the Moderns', 321.
[144] Berlin, 'Two Concepts of Liberty', 121–2.
[145] Berlin, 'Two Concepts of Liberty', 123.
[146] Pettit, *Republicanism*, 52. See also Neoh, 'Just Jurisprudence', 237.
[147] Nozick, *Anarchy, State and Utopia*, 49.

III Freedom

This desire for freedom as individual independence did not arise with modernity. Its origin goes much further back. It goes all the way back to the Book of Genesis. Adam and Eve have their first taste of freedom as independence when they eat the forbidden fruit and leave the garden. In Eden, there exists only one prohibition. They can choose to obey or disobey the single prohibition: they can choose to eat or refrain from eating the forbidden fruit. They can choose to live within or without the norm. By choosing to disobey, they have, in effect, asserted a will that is different from God's. They have chosen not to accept the norm. The first person to assert this freedom as independence is Eve when she takes the first bite of the fruit. Adam will soon follow suit. Eve chooses to act independently, to do her own thing. God's final question to Eve affirms obliquely her independence: 'What is this that you have done?'[148] Having broken the one and only prohibition, there is now no prohibition left. With Eden behind them, 'som[e] natural tears they drop'd, but [they] wip'd them soon', for 'the world was all before them'.[149] They are now free to make a life and create a whole world for themselves. Out of Eden, they are left alone to do their own thing, to do or be what they are able to do or be. With the knowledge of good and evil, they can thenceforth decide and choose what they want to do with their own lives, to lead their lives by their own lights.

On this view of freedom, to be free is to be independent. That much is clear, but the question still remains: to be independent *from what*? To begin with, I need to be independent from the will of others, that is, I am free 'to the degree to which no man or body of men interferes with my activity'.[150] However, this independence from external obstacles is merely the necessary but insufficient condition for personal freedom. Much more is needed. One needs independence from something whose tentacles reach much deeper within one's self. Rationalism, from Plato to Kant, holds that to be truly free is to be independent from the hold of one's instincts and desires, impulses and inclinations. To be free is to be free from one's passion. Most of us have had the experience of longing to be free of a particular feeling that has a grip on us, such as fear, spite or lust, that we find within ourselves. Sometimes, these feelings come surging in. Like swimming against the tide, we struggle not to let them overwhelm us or get the better of us. The struggle is even more nerve-racking when one has to deal with those unconscious psychic forces – what Freud calls drives – that lurk in the dark and operate covertly in the deeper recesses of one's mind.

---

[148] Book of Genesis 3:13.
[149] Milton, *Paradise Lost*, Bk 12, line 645–6.
[150] Berlin, 'Two Concepts of Liberty', 122–3.

In these situations, the obstacles to freedom as independence are not external, but internal. In these cases, 'we have to make discriminations among motivations, and accept that acting out of some motivations' is not freedom, but 'a negation of freedom'.[151] To be truly free, according to the rationalists, one should act according to reason. Our brute desires are aroused in us by purely natural processes. To be free, I need to 'break loose from what is merely given by nature, including the brute facts of my inclinations, and direct my life by principles which I generate myself', in line with reason.[152] It is only when our actions are rationally determined that we are living up to our true status, not as brutes, but as rational creatures.[153] As Kant says, a rational agent 'should partake of no other happiness or perfection than that which he himself, independently of instinct, has created by his own reason'.[154]

In an almost symmetrical reversal, the romantics posit the direct opposite. According to the romantics, what we need to be free from is not passion, but reason. To be free is to be independent of reason. Reason is artificial. It is inauthentic. Schiller argues that Kant has invested reason with tyrannical powers, and this form of tyranny is uniquely vicious for it splits a person into two and pits one half against the other, making one half tyrant and the other half slave.[155] The romantics launch a revolt against reason. Rousseau's conjecture of the noble savage, for example, is hopelessly romantic. The noble savage in the state of nature follows his or her natural instincts, which lead to nothing but absolute tranquillity and perfect harmony. Over time, this romantic theme develops into what Taylor calls the ethic of authenticity.[156] To be free is to be authentic, which requires a return to nature and a reconnection with one's instincts and desires, impulses and inclinations. Hence, one should act in accordance with one's passion, for that is the only sure source of authenticity.

The existentialists absorb both the lessons of rationalism and romanticism, and absorb them well. For the existentialist, to be free is to be free from reason *and* from passion. To be free is to be free from everything and anything. It is to be completely independent. Therefore, only the capricious and whimsical act is truly free. Freedom, like the first creation, has to be *ex nihilo*: out of nothing. 'The act must have no basis whatsoever. It must arise suddenly as if from nothing and from nowhere, a spark with neither purpose nor direction'.[157] Contrariety

---

[151] Taylor, 'What's Wrong with Negative Liberty', 221.
[152] Taylor, 'Kant's Theory of Freedom', 325.
[153] Taylor, 'Kant's Theory of Freedom', 324.
[154] Kant, 'Idea for a Universal History from a Cosmopolitan Point of View', 13.
[155] Bergmann, *On Being Free*, 29.
[156] Taylor, *A Secular Age*, ch 13.
[157] Bergmann, *On Being Free*, 35.

III Freedom

and caprice are the sole proof of the complete independence of the individual. This kind of existential freedom has a 'deep subjectivity, gloomy flamboyance and desperate extravagance'.[158] First, one casts aside the cloak of reason, then the cloak of passion, revealing finally that the emperor has no clothes.

The existentialist moves from *achtung* to *angst*: while Kant's *achtung* despairs at the sensual and rejoices in the rational, the existentialist *angst* has neither the sensual nor the rational to fall back on, hence there is nothing but angst.[159] This view of freedom as radical independence ultimately ends up with 'the purity of the solitary will'.[160] 'Shell after shell would be cast off as hindering encumbrances, till one would be diminished to a point in space'.[161] The self is heroic: it yields to nothing and no one. The self is free to flee from reason and fly in the face of passion. Without reason or passion, the self is both lonely and alone: 'what it pictures is indeed the fearful solitude of the individual', who could only escape from this brave new world 'by a wild leap of the will'.[162] The independent self wants to begin everything *de novo*: 'with an almost poetic fancy, he strives to live each day as if it were his first, and he believes that to form a habit is to fail'.[163] One's life has to be scrubbed clean at the end of each day, so that on the next day, the independent self could start afresh, *tabula rasa*, with 'the blank sheet of infinite possibility'.[164]

This radical existential freedom of the unworldly self – of being in the world, but not of the world – is made possible by what Arendt calls an inward philosophical turn, in which freedom is turned into free will. According to Arendt, this inward turn 'was originally the result of an estrangement from the world in which worldly experiences were transformed into experiences within one's own self', that is, 'into an inwardness to which no other has access'.[165] Within this inward space, the self can enjoy absolute freedom as complete independence. Within it, I can direct my will as I see fit. This kind of free will 'is not experienced in association with others but in intercourse with one's self in the form of an inner dialogue which, since Socrates, we call thinking'.[166] It is to be found 'in the inner dwelling of the soul and the dark chamber of the heart'.[167] In this inner sanctum, the self is sovereign.

---

[158] Bergmann, *On Being Free*, 22.
[159] Murdoch, *The Sovereignty of the Good*, 39.
[160] Murdoch, *The Sovereignty of the Good*, 30.
[161] Bergmann, *On Being Free*, 49.
[162] Murdoch, *The Sovereignty of the Good*, 27.
[163] Oakeshott, 'Rationalism in Politics', 7.
[164] Oakeshott, 'Rationalism in Politics', 9.
[165] Arendt, 'What Is Freedom?', 146.
[166] Arendt, 'What Is Freedom?', 157.
[167] Arendt, 'What Is Freedom?', 158.

Freedom as Identification

In contrast to the liberty of the moderns that consists in individual independence, the liberty of the ancients consists in 'an active and constant participation in collective power', the exercise of which is a 'vivid and repeated pleasure'.[168] The ancients 'admitted as compatible with this collective freedom the complete subjection of the individual to the authority of the community'.[169] Not much importance is accorded to individual independence: 'the individual was in some way lost in the nation, the citizen in the city'.[170] Among the ancients, the basic unit of analysis is not the individual, but the polis. The individual citizen is a constituent part of the polis, and the citizen's role is to take an active part in governing the polis.[171] What is required to attain this sort of freedom is an identification of the self with elements outside the individual self; in this case, the polis. It expands the boundary of the self. Through the process of identification, the boundary of the self is expanded to include the polis. The self is constituted in the polis. At the polar opposite of the view of freedom as independence is the view of freedom as identification.

On this view, what is doing the work of freedom is not independence from things, but identification with things. The true ideal of freedom lies in identification, not independence. To flesh out this idea, let's start with some common everyday observations of the hoi polloi. Social psychologists tell us that people want to fit in, and they will do anything to fit in. To fit in, they will happily conform to the demands of the group. They also want to have a collective identity, even if it means making an enemy of those who are different from them. There is a herd for every lone wolf: 'people need a sense of solidarity and of communion'.[172] 'Provided the answer to "Who shall govern me?" is somebody or something which I can represent as "my own", as something which belongs to me, or to whom I belong', I can, in a sense, describe it as freedom.'[173] Professional philosophers often treat these sentiments as vulgar, if not vicious. The existence of a herd for every lone wolf leads to nothing but a herd mentality. Berlin cautions us that the 'sovereignty of the people could easily destroy that of individuals'.[174] Worse, it could lead to the demonization of difference, particularly of the other. After all, this is the stuff that leads to

---

[168] Constant, 'The Liberty of the Ancients Compared with that of the Moderns', 316.
[169] Constant, 'The Liberty of the Ancients Compared with that of the Moderns', 311.
[170] Constant, 'The Liberty of the Ancients Compared with that of the Moderns', 312.
[171] Flikschuh, *Freedom: Contemporary Liberal Perspectives*, 17.
[172] Bergmann, *On Being Free*, 6.
[173] Berlin, 'Two Concepts of Liberty', 160.
[174] Berlin, 'Two Concepts of Liberty', 163.

occasional outburst of collective hysteria. At its height, it leads people to shout, in a fit of madness, 'Crucify him, crucify him'. The philosophers' disdain and distrust of the masses is to be expected, for it was the mentality of the mass and the mob that led to the death of their ancestor, Socrates. However, there may be a method in the madness of the masses: it may do philosophers some good not to dismiss them too easily out of hand.

One could begin by thinking of freedom as the ability to act in accordance with one's *own* standards, as opposed to the standards of others. The crucial word here is 'own'. Identification is the be all and end all: something is one's own if one identifies with it and it is not if one does not. Identification does not require independence. One can be dependent on that with which one identifies, for the identification brings the hitherto external object into the orbit of the self. If I identify with something, that thing becomes a part of who I am. That thing may even become the entirety of me. Hence, when Paul identifies with Christ, he could say, 'It is no longer I who live, but Christ who lives in me'.[175] There we have an identification of the most thoroughgoing kind. Just as the key question under the view of freedom as independence is independence from what, so the key question under the view of freedom as identification is identification with what. 'An act is free if the agent identifies with the elements from which it flows', for 'freedom is the acting out of that identity'.[176] Where there is identification, there is freedom.

If Arendt is right that, in the Western intellectual tradition, freedom as independence is linked to an inward philosophical turn, then one could say that freedom as identification is linked to an outward political turn. Philosophical free will is distinguished from political freedom in that the former is found in the intercourse with oneself, whereas the latter is found in the intercourse with others. The former refers to 'an attribute of thought or a quality of the will', while the latter refers to one's standing among one's peers, which enables a person 'to get away from home, to go out into the world and meet other people in deed and word'.[177] The Greek polis, according to Arendt, was set up precisely for that purpose: to provide citizens with something with which to identify and within which to act. The polis is the theater of freedom: it is the space for the performance of freedom.[178] Courage is needed in politics because 'courage liberates men from their worry about life for the freedom of the world', for 'in politics, not life but the world is at stake'.[179] In the public

---

[175] Letter to the Galatians 2:20.
[176] Bergmann, *On Being Free*, 37.
[177] Arendt, 'What Is Freedom?', 148.
[178] Arendt, 'What Is Freedom?', 154.
[179] Arendt, 'What Is Freedom?', 156.

realm, what matters is not the independence of the self, but the identification of the self with the world that is the polis.

Under this ideal of freedom as identification, freedom is attained, not by escaping from political authority, but by identifying with it and integrating oneself into it. It is attained by making the political world 'part of oneself, no longer alien [or] obstructive, no longer a frontier [or] a field of force which hems one in, but on the contrary, that which one's own free activity would have made it, if one had been the demiurge, the creator'.[180] Berlin famously calls this kind of freedom positive freedom. The liberty of the ancients is a variant of positive freedom: 'not freedom from, but freedom to' – the freedom to 'lead one prescribed form of life', to be self-directed, to be one's 'own master'.[181] However, in contrast to freedom as independence, under this ideal of freedom as identification, being self-directed does not require that I alone, and no one else, make the decision on the direction of my life. I could still be free even if someone else other than myself makes the decision on the direction of my life, so long as I identify with the decision-maker or the decision-making process, that is, so long as I identify with the person or process that stands behind the decision.

Freedom requires that I am able to express myself, not that I am independent from myself. My self-expression is the expression of my identity, that is, my identifications. My identifications could be complex and multifaceted. I identify with different parts of myself with varying strength and intensity. As Taylor describes it, 'we experience our desires and purposes as qualitatively discriminated, as higher or lower'.[182] The higher ones we identify with more, and the lower ones we identify with less. Freedom lies in acting in accordance with our higher desires and purposes, that is, with desires and purposes that we identify with more deeply. When we act out of desires and purposes that we consider lower, over and against the desires and purposes that we consider higher, we feel unfree. We feel that we are acting in spite of ourselves, as if to spite ourselves. We experience some desires as fetters 'because we experience them as not [really] ours'.[183] I can lose a lower desire without any serious loss to my identity, for 'I feel that I should be better off without it, that I do not lose anything in getting rid of it, that I remain quite complete without it'.[184] This more complex view of freedom 'involves my being able to recognize adequately my more important purposes', and separate them from the lesser

---

[180] Berlin, 'Two Concepts of Freedom: Romantic and Liberal', 184.
[181] Berlin, 'Two Concepts of Liberty', 131.
[182] Taylor, 'What's Wrong with Negative Liberty', 220.
[183] Taylor, 'What's Wrong with Negative Liberty', 225.
[184] Taylor, 'What's Wrong with Negative Liberty', 222, 224.

ones.[185] I want to act, not in accordance with my false consciousness, but in accordance with my true identification. Therein lies the root of the complaint by Berlin that this conception of freedom splits the human personality into two: the self at its best and the debased self.

In the previous section, I situated rationalism and romanticism within the ideal of freedom as independence. In this section, I will show that rationalism and romanticism could be reconceptualized and resituated within the ideal of freedom as identification too. Their prescriptions for freedom can be reread as prescriptions for the appropriate forms of identification. The rationalists want us to identify with reason, and the romantics with passion. Let's start with rationalism. Rationalism splits the human personality into two: one noumenal and rational, and the other phenomenal and contingent.[186] In metaphysically splitting the human personality into two, the rationalists identify the higher self, or the truest self, or the self at its best, with the rational self. In order to attain this kind of freedom, one has to experience rationality, 'not as an impersonal voice that imposes alien commands on me', but 'as that which speaks most truly and authentically for me'.[187] One should say of reason what Paul said of Christ: 'It is no longer I who live, but reason that lives in me'.[188] Hence, 'everything that is dissonant from reason, that inveighs against it, must be dissociated from me'.[189] Berlin calls this rationalist move a form of secularized Protestantism, 'in which the place of God is taken by the conception of the rational life, and the place of the individual soul which strains towards union with him is replaced by the conception of the individual, endowed with reason, straining to be governed by reason and reason alone'.[190] To be free is to identify with a certain kind of rational moral order, what Kant calls the kingdom of ends.[191]

The romantics turn the rationalist prescription on its head. The romantics exhort us to identify, not with reason, but with passion. According to the romantics, freedom is not to be found in the rational mind, but the passionate will. To have a free will is to follow one's passion, not the dictates of reason. For a person to be free, the person needs to identify with a will that is free, and that will could be an individual will or what Rousseau calls the General Will. One becomes free by identifying with the General Will. Insofar as one could

---

[185] Taylor, 'What's Wrong with Negative Liberty', 228.
[186] Gray, 'On Negative and Positive Liberty', 519.
[187] Bergmann, *On Being Free*, 29.
[188] Cf Letter to the Galatians 2:20.
[189] Bergmann, *On Being Free*, 29.
[190] Berlin, 'Two Concepts of Liberty', 138.
[191] Taylor, 'Kant's Theory of Freedom', 326.

be made to identify with the General Will, one could be 'forced to be free'.[192] The General Will is the 'common self', or *moi commun*, in which the self is 'inflated into some super-personal entity – a State, a class, a nation, or the march of history itself'.[193] In *The Social Contract*, Rousseau uses the notion of the General Will to construct a form of association, in which 'each, while uniting himself with all, may still obey himself alone'.[194] The trick lies in the identification of the individual self with the whole community. Each becomes an indivisible part of the whole. The result is the creation of a 'public person, so formed by the union of all other persons', who are collectively called the people and severally called citizens: the General Will is their will.[195] Rousseau's famous formulation that 'freedom is obedience to the General Will' makes perfect sense once one sees that the kind of freedom referred to here is freedom as identification: 'a citizen would of course be free if he obeyed the General Will simply because the General Will is, so to speak, his very own'.[196]

Consider, as a parting image, Berlin's musician: 'For the musician, after he has assimilated the pattern of the composer's score, and has made the composer's ends his own, the playing of the music is not obedience to external laws, a compulsion and a barrier to liberty, but a free, unimpeded exercise'.[197] The image is even more stirring in the case of a musician engaging in a concerted action, that is, of a musician in a concert. In a concert, the musician identifies, not only with the symphony, but also with the orchestra: 'the more undeviating the adherence to the rules for concerted playing, the more fully satisfied the players feel, the fewer obstacles at that moment do they find in the universe about them'.[198] By being absorbed in and by the performance, the musician becomes part of the whole, and there is music in the air.

IV WHERE DO WE GO FROM HERE?

It seems that, at this point, we are left with a conceptual maze. The previous chapter shows that the values of law, love and freedom feature in both the Genesis myth of cosmological beginning and the Pauline vision of eschatological end. However, this chapter shows how messy this whole enterprise is.

---

[192] Rousseau, *The Social Contract*, Bk 1, ch 7.
[193] Berlin, 'Two Concepts of Liberty', 134.
[194] Rousseau, *The Social Contract*, Bk 1, ch 6.
[195] Rousseau, *The Social Contract*, Bk 1, ch 6.
[196] Bergmann, *On Being Free*, 38.
[197] Berlin, 'Two Concepts of Liberty', 141.
[198] Berlin, 'Two Concepts of Freedom: Romantic and Liberal', 185.

IV Where Do We Go from Here?

There are not only conflicts between these values, but there are also conflicts within them. Law is polarized between authority and resistance. Love is polarized between union and attention. Freedom is polarized between identification and independence. The conflicts *within* the respective values of law, love and freedom mean that they cannot be combined willy-nilly without creating conflicts *between* those values. An aspect of law might be reconcilable with one particular aspect of love, but not another; and reconcilable with one particular aspect of freedom, but not another. They all have to hang together in a particular way in order for them to work in the context of one's life – hence, the need for reflection and choice. Recall that our overarching aim is to find a way to lead a life of law, love and freedom. Where do we go from here? The next chapter will try to point a way forward to get out of the maze. The task of this chapter has been analysis; the task of synthesis will follow in the subsequent chapters. This chapter shows the ways in which the values in the concepts of law, love and freedom pull in opposite directions. If this chapter has been pulling concepts apart, hopefully, the subsequent chapters will be able to put Humpty together again.

3

Methodological Turn to Historical Narrative

Chapters 1 and 2 attempt to elucidate the philosophical puzzle surrounding the relationship between law, love and freedom. Chapter 1 presents the puzzle in a literary style by examining the emergence of law, love and freedom in the Garden of Eden. It shows that the values of law, love and freedom feature in both the Genesis myth of cosmological beginning and the Pauline vision of eschatological end. Chapter 2 presents the puzzle in an analytic style by examining the bipolar structure of the concepts of law, love and freedom. Chapter 1 is a show-and-tell, while Chapter 2 is more cut and dried. Chapter 2 ends with the note that law, love and freedom are bipolar concepts. Law is polarized between authority and resistance. Love is polarized between union and attention. Freedom is polarized between identification and independence. Chapter 2 leaves us with a conceptual maze. Our overarching aim is to find a way to lead a life of law, love and freedom. This chapter will try to chart a way forward, to get us out of the maze. If the task of the previous chapter has been analysis, then the task of the subsequent chapters will be synthesis. This chapter is the turning point of the book: it will lay the methodological foundation for the chapters to come.

 This chapter will argue for a turn to historical narrative. The way to bring some order to the bipolar conceptual disorder of law, love and freedom is not through further abstract conceptual analysis, but through a historical narrative approach. This chapter will explain why in four parts. The first two parts will link two staple philosophical distinctions: the descriptive–evaluative distinction and the practice–value distinction. The latter two parts will propound two methodological approaches that will vindicate the linkage of description and evaluation, and of practice and value: the narrative approach and the historical approach. Jointly, the method is one of historical narrative. Historical narratives tell stories that are rooted in histories. The final part of this chapter will provide synopses of the two historical narratives of law, love and freedom that

I will tell in the subsequent chapters. This book advances a jurisprudential thesis, but it is 'jurisprudence as a moral and historical inquiry'.[1]

I DESCRIPTION AND EVALUATION

Let's begin with a thought experiment by Anscombe. Imagine someone coming up to you to ask for a 'saucer of mud'. You will, understandably, ask him in response: what for? By expressing a desire for something, the person has implicitly 'characterised the thing wanted as desirable'; hence, your question in response tries to 'find out in what aspect the object desired is desirable'.[2] If the person replies that 'he does not want it for anything, he just wants it', his reply would strike many, including Anscombe, as nonsensical.[3] In order for a desire for something to be comprehensible, one has to be able to provide an account of it that is both intelligible and intelligent. By intelligent, I mean that the account should display some higher orders of thought beyond 'I want it because I want it'. In describing the object of one's desire, one is also, at the same time, evaluating its significance for oneself and for other similarly situated agents. 'For a human agent, to pursue a desire is not just to be pulled by a physical force; rather, it is to make an intentional, at least potentially conscious judgment that the desire is worth satisfying, and thus that the desired object is worth having'.[4]

In explicitly desiring an object, in situations where the desire is conscious and considered, one is also implicitly making a claim that the object is desirable, that is, as worthy of desire not just by me but also by others like me. Such a normative claim necessarily invokes a reference to a community of others, specifically of others like me, who *would* assent to my judgment of value.[5] Note the hypothetical *would*. The assent that is invoked does not have to be an actual agreement. It could be an idealized agreement among a hypothetical community of similarly situated subjects. With that, we move from one individual to a group of individuals, whether actual or imaginary, and we move from the individual viewpoint to the general viewpoint. When assessing the individual viewpoint, the actual attitude of the individual matters. However, there is a significant change when we move from the individual viewpoint to the general viewpoint, for the general viewpoint cannot depend upon the diverse and variable attitudes of actual individuals. One gets to the

---

[1] Simmonds, 'Jurisprudence as a Moral and Historical Inquiry', 249.
[2] Anscombe, *Intention*, §37.
[3] Anscombe, *Intention*, §37.
[4] Krasnoff, *Hegel's Phenomenology of Spirit*, 99.
[5] Krasnoff, *Hegel's Phenomenology of Spirit*, 99.

general viewpoint through normative generalization. Normative generalization differs from empirical generalization: while the latter relies on statistical aggregation, the former relies on evaluative judgment.

The ability to engage in normative generalization is what transforms 'plain persons' into 'moral philosophers'. The plain person asks, 'what is my good'; whereas the moral philosopher asks, 'what is the good'. Any persistent attempt to answer the former will soon lead one to ask the latter, so the plain person is always at the cusp of becoming a moral philosopher.[6] In thinking about what I should do here and now, I reflect simultaneously on what my life should be as a whole. In thinking about what my life should be as a whole, I reflect simultaneously on what human lives should be universally. I will not know what I should do here and now if I do not understand how that action fits into what my life should be as a whole; and I will not know what my life should be as a whole if I do not understand how my life fits into what human lives should be universally. In this way, 'our immediate practical concerns thus open out onto philosophical reflection, and philosophical reflection in turns opens out onto a radical evaluation of our lives, our characters, our values'.[7]

Normative generalization proceeds by asking what would be considered important or significant in that field of human action. The answer to this question does not lie in statistical frequency, that is, in counting heads and collating individual viewpoints. Instead, it is to be found in thinking about what an idealized person of practical reason would find important or significant in those circumstances. The general viewpoint is the viewpoint of practical reason. This undertaking cannot proceed without a descriptive knowledge of the practices, but neither can it proceed without an evaluative judgment of them. According to Finnis, 'no theorist can give a theoretical description and analysis of social facts without also participating in the work of evaluation'.[8] Without some evaluative judgment, the descriptive data will appear like a dog's breakfast: it will be an unintelligible mess. Evaluative judgment puts some sense into the nonsense. Therefore, law, love and freedom 'can be fully understood only by understanding their point, that is to say, their objective, their value, their significance or importance', as conceived by a person of practical reason who lives a life of law, love and freedom.[9] For the account of law, love and freedom to make sense, there needs to be a movement, to and fro, between the evaluative assessment of what is good

---

[6] MacIntyre, 'Plain Persons and Moral Philosophy', 3.
[7] Lear, *Love and Its Place in Nature*, 205.
[8] Finnis, *Natural Law and Natural Rights*, 3.
[9] Finnis, *Natural Law and Natural Rights*, 3.

I Description and Evaluation

in life and the description of the human situation in which the good is variously realized.[10] An intelligible account of law, love and freedom is not just a matter of achieving a careful description of the practices of law, love and freedom, but it is also a matter of grasping the point of those practices, including the values toward which those practices must be understood as oriented.[11]

If one does not like Finnis's idea of 'practical reason', one could use Dworkin's idea of 'constructive interpretation' to arrive at a broadly similar conclusion. Conveying a similar point with different terminology, Dworkin argues that an interpretation of social practice has to fit the practice and show it in its best light.[12] Fit and best light constitute the two dimensions of interpretation. Fit is descriptive and best light is evaluative: both are integral for a successful interpretation. An interpretive exercise is neither straightforwardly descriptive nor purely evaluative. It is both, and irreducible to either. Interpretation strives to make the object of interpretation the best that it can be. On the one hand, it cannot make it into something that it is not: it has to fit. On the other hand, it should not make it any less that it could be: it has to show it in its best light. Hence, an interpretation needs to have the integrity of fit and best light. An account of law, love and freedom has to fit the facts: it has to fit the experience of what it means for someone to be lawful, loving and free. However, the best constructive interpretation of these values would not only fit, but it would also show them in their best light: it would show why it is good for someone to be lawful, loving and free. Hence, the best constructive interpretation is both descriptive and evaluative.

Law, love and freedom are thick concepts. Thick concepts express a union of fact and value: 'the way these notions are applied is determined by what the world is like (for instance, by how someone has behaved), and yet, at the same time, their application usually involves a certain valuation of the situation, of persons or actions'.[13] The application of these thick concepts is simultaneously 'world-guided and action-guiding'.[14] Therefore, in order for an account of law, love and freedom to be intelligible and intelligent, it has to offer a thick description of what is going on in the lives of the lawful, the loving and the free. We do not just want to know what law, love and freedom are. We also want to know to whom they matter and why. A thick description of this sort

---

[10] Finnis, *Natural Law and Natural Rights*, 17.
[11] Simmonds, 'Reflexivity and the Idea of Law', 18.
[12] For a full exposition of Dworkin's theory of interpretation, see Dworkin, *Law's Empire*. For a quick summary, see Dworkin, 'Law as Interpretation'.
[13] Williams, *Ethics and the Limits of Philosophy*, 144.
[14] Williams, *Ethics and the Limits of Philosophy*, 155.

must include an evaluative judgment. To be sure, this requirement of evaluative judgment does not preclude the lawless, the loveless and the unfree from offering a thick description of law, love and freedom. An observer can talk about law, love and freedom without sharing or partaking in those values. In these circumstances, the insightful but noncommittal observer may be inclined to couch his or her use of these terms with qualifying phrases like 'so called', 'so to speak' or 'as they say'. Nonetheless, 'in imaginatively anticipating the use of the concept, the observer also has to grasp imaginatively its evaluative point'.[15] There is no escaping the evaluative point. One cannot strip the evaluation from the description.

The content of these values will have been worked out over a long period of time in a particular society. A coherent account of law, love and freedom, thickly understood, has to reflect the complexity of the *human society* in which these values are shaped. Such an account will be 'universal because it is *human*', but also 'particular because it is a *society*', for 'societies are necessarily particular because they have members and memories, members with memories not only of their own but also of their common life'.[16] The content of these values will be 'idiomatic in its language, particularist in its cultural reference, and circumstantial in the two senses of that word: historically dependent and factually detailed'.[17] Consequently, an account of these values will be 'richly referential, culturally resonant, locked into a locally established symbolic system or network of meanings'.[18] Later in this chapter, I will argue that the methodology to produce such an account is the historical narrative approach. However, before explaining the historical narrative approach, I have to tackle another staple philosophical distinction: practice and value.

II PRACTICE AND VALUE

The previous section links description with evaluation. This section will link practice with value. MacIntyre defines a practice as a 'coherent and complex form of socially established cooperative human activity ... [with] standards of excellence which are appropriate to, and partially definitive of, that form of activity'.[19] Every practice has its own standards of excellence; hence, to participate in a practice is to 'accept the authority of those standards' and 'subject [one's] own attitudes, choices, preferences and tastes to the standards

---

[15] Williams, *Ethics and the Limits of Philosophy*, 157.
[16] Walzer, *Thick and Thin*, 8.
[17] Walzer, *Thick and Thin*, 21.
[18] Walzer, *Thick and Thin*, xi.
[19] MacIntyre, *After Virtue*, 218.

which currently and partially define the practice'.[20] Practices have a social and intergenerational dimension: 'to enter into a practice is to enter into a relationship not only with its contemporary practitioners, but also with those who have preceded us in the practice, particularly those whose achievements extended the reach of the practice to its present point'.[21]

A practice can be all-encompassing, so much so that a practitioner can be entirely absorbed, heart and soul, into the practice. One can dedicate one's life to its pursuit and perfection, alongside other practitioners. Given the social dimension of practice, some practices may come to constitute a social form of life. To participate in a social form, one needs to con-form. The social form endows our actions with significance: it transforms our actions into a project. The shape of our projects depends largely on the social forms of life that are available to us. Hence, 'a person's well-being depends to a large extent on success in socially defined and determined pursuits and activities'.[22] Take, for example, the practice of friendship or fraternal love. Friendship is a socially determined form of human interaction, and it is through participating in the social form of friendship that one discovers new ways of living one's life.[23] Sharing a meal or watching a movie or going on a trip with another person are no longer random actions that one does, but they become part and parcel of the pursuit of friendship. Friendship endows these actions with the significance that they have. At its height, the pursuit of friendship can become so all-encompassing that one can say: 'Greater love has no man than this, that a man lay down his life for his friends'.[24]

Like standards of excellence, moral values too are embodied in social forms. Moral values find their home within a social form, that is, within the lived experience of individuals engaging in a social practice. As Williams tells us, ethical understanding always has a social dimension: 'if we are going to understand how ethical concepts work ... we have to have some insight into the forms of social organization within which they work'.[25] To appreciate a moral value, we need to understand its social form. To understand a social form, we need to grasp its moral value. Disembodied from practice, values will appear like castles in the air. Castles in the air are not real. Devoid of value, practices will appear like sandcastles. Sandcastles, though real, are not the real deal: they are not the sturdy castles that they try to mimic. Hence, any analysis

---

[20] MacIntyre, *After Virtue*, 221.
[21] MacIntyre, *After Virtue*, 226.
[22] Raz, *Morality of Freedom*, 309.
[23] Raz, *Morality of Freedom*, 216.
[24] Gospel of John 15:13.
[25] Williams, *Ethics and the Limits of Philosophy*, 145.

of a practice needs to account for this dual character of form and value. Therein lies the link between the practice and value of law, love and freedom.

There are two ways of conceptualizing the link between social practice and moral value. The link could be conceptualized in terms of the emergence of values in practices, or in terms of the projection of values on practices. The latter view is part of a larger scientific worldview that sees the world as in itself valueless: 'value, on this scientific image, is projected onto the world by humans'.[26] Even if this latter view is true of the natural world of objects, it cannot be true of the human world of practices, for in this domain, practices are not inert but constantly constructed and reconstructed, fashioned and refashioned, to create webs of significance. Values emerge in and through these structures of signification. Humans are thus suspended in these webs of significance that they themselves have spun.[27] The values of the self develop through the internalization of the values that emerge through the practices. Hence, for me to develop into a good enough person, there must be enough good in the world of practices.[28] For me to develop to be lawful, loving and free, there must be enough law, love and freedom in the world.

In an analytic fashion, Raz presents the link between practice and value in two theses: the special social dependence thesis and the general social dependence thesis. The *special social dependence thesis* claims that some values exist only if there are (or were) social practices sustaining them. The *general social dependence thesis* claims that, with some exceptions, all values depend on social practices either by being subject to the special thesis or through their dependence on values which are subject to the special thesis.[29] In a continental fashion, Simmonds presents the link through the Hegelian notion of the 'concrete universal'. For Hegel, the universal is not separated from the particular. On the contrary, the universal inheres in the particular; hence, the 'concrete universal'. Taking the cue from Hegel, Simmonds uses the notion of a 'concrete universal' to refer to particular practices within a form of life whose values 'are inhabited before they are reflected upon'.[30] Universal values are not separated from particular practices. On the contrary, universal values inhere in particular practices. We absorb those values through their practices before we reflect upon them. Any philosophical theory of universal values is always drawn, in part, from what one has already learned through particular practices.[31]

---

[26] Lear, *Love and Its Place in Nature*, 210.
[27] Geertz, 'Thick Description', 5.
[28] Lear, *Love and Its Place in Nature*, 219.
[29] Raz, *The Practice of Value*, 19.
[30] Simmonds, 'Jurisprudence as a Moral and Historical Inquiry', 252.
[31] MacIntyre, 'Plain Persons and Moral Philosophy', 19.

While it is true that an unexamined life is not worth living, one must first live the life before one could examine it. Philosophical examination of our lives can sharpen our perception of our moral values, but it cannot conjure up values where none exists. It cannot conjure up values from thin air. What it can do is to sharpen our perception of the moral values that are already latent in our practices. Philosophical examination can make the implicit explicit. Values are in here, not out there: they are in the world of concrete practices, not out there in the ether. The human world of practices is already a moral world, and 'we would do better to study its internal rules, maxims, conventions, and ideals, rather than to detach ourselves from it in search of a universal and transcendent standpoint'.[32] Hence, philosophical examination should start with an 'historically informed reflection upon our practices and institutions'.[33] Examining our practices in this way – like looking at ourselves in the mirror – we may be both shocked and impressed by what we see. We find our values in our practices, and thereby find ourselves.

To be sure, nothing of the foregoing implies stasis and immutability. Social forms are always open to revision and their accompanying moral values are open to reinterpretation. But the foregoing does imply that the social forms and the moral values that they embody have a degree of objectivity. They have an objective existence in the same way that language has an objective existence. They have an independent existence in relation to the individual. I, acting on my own, cannot change them. I can commit an error: I can make a grammatical mistake, just as I can fail as a friend. Their standards are independent of a person, though not independent of a people. Just as the speakers of a language, acting collectively over a period of time, can change the grammar of a language, participants in a social form, likewise, can change the content of the social form. In Arendt's famous phrase, 'men, not Man, live on the earth and inhabit the world'.[34] Hence, it is 'men, not Man', who can change the content of social forms.

Let me also address, and put to rest, two related concerns about the linkage of practice and value: the possibility of moral disagreement and the problem of evil. The linkage of practice and value does not rule out the possibility of moral disagreement either about or within a social form. Values are underdetermined by practice: 'the practice comes first and its significance is grasped (never fully and always imperfectly) subsequently'.[35] We discover our moral

---

[32] Walzer, *The Company of Critics*, ix.
[33] Simmonds, 'Jurisprudence as a Moral and Historical Inquiry', 256.
[34] Arendt, *The Human Condition*, 7.
[35] Simmonds, 'The Bondwoman's Son and the Beautiful Soul', 118.

values through our practices, but we only 'see through a glass, darkly'.[36] Each participant in the social form may see the social form, or more specifically, the moral value of the social form, slightly differently. They see the same object, but they see it from their own perspective or vantage point. 'For morality is, as it were, both intensely personal (a matter of conscience) and irreducibly shared (a matter of inherited language, form of association, and dialogue with others)': it straddles between 'shared practice and individual critical judgment'.[37] Social forms do not possess a natural value 'independently of our beliefs, ideas and categories of thought'; rather, their value becomes 'clear to us in our speaking of it'.[38] When we speak, we may disagree, but that is to be expected in a world that is inhabited by 'men, not Man'.

Moral argument presupposes moral disagreement. If there is no disagreement, there will be nothing to argue about. What is noteworthy is not that we argue and disagree, but whom we argue with and what we disagree about. We typically argue with our neighbors, our friends, our colleagues – in short, our fellows – about our practices. These moral arguments and disagreements occur within a set of collective practices that constitute our moral life. Without a set of collective practices, there could be neither argument nor agreement about anything. As Wittgenstein says aphoristically, 'if a lion could talk, we could not understand him', because the lion and us have nothing in common.[39] Therefore, any intelligible moral argument and disagreement should be understood as occurring within, and not without, the set of collective practices that render the argument and disagreement intelligible. We start with our shared social life, and 'we become critics naturally, as it were, by elaborating on existing moralities and telling stories about a society more just than, though never entirely different from, our own'.[40] Moral disagreements are, at bottom, interpretive disagreements about our values and practices. Starting from our practices, one looks for values that best explain these practices. Starting from our values, one looks for practices that best express these values. At both of these steps, people can disagree. We strive to align our values with our practices, and our practices with our values. As much as we try, we may not always succeed. When we fail, we fall into hypocrisy.

In addition to the risk of hypocrisy, there is also the risk of wicked practices. Differentiating right from wrong, and good from evil, in our practices is a matter of practical reason. However, practical reason is itself a practice, so

[36] 1 Corinthians 13:12.
[37] Simmonds, 'The Bondwoman's Son and the Beautiful Soul', 127.
[38] Simmonds, 'Jurisprudence as a Moral and Historical Inquiry', 260.
[39] Wittgenstein, *Philosophical Investigations*, 223.
[40] Walzer, *Interpretation and Social Criticism*, 65.

in a sense, it is turtles all the way down. The practice of practical reason requires an intelligent grasp 'of human wants and passions and of the conditions of human life'.[41] In the practice of practical reason within the Western tradition, 'philosophical reflection has identified a considerable number of requirements of method in practical reasoning': 'someone who lives up to these requirements is thus Aristotle's *phronimos* and has Aquinas's *prudentia*'.[42] Among the requirements of practical reason are that one should not make arbitrary preferences among values or among persons. As Finnis explains, although 'any commitment to a coherent plan of life is going to involve some degree of concentration on one or some of the basic forms of good, at the expense, temporarily or permanently, of other forms of good', the commitment would be unreasonable if it is done 'on the basis of a devaluation of any of the basic forms of human excellence'.[43] Practical reason requires that one concentrates on the basic forms of the good to which one is committed, while respecting the rest. Practical reason also requires a degree of 'fundamental impartiality among the human subjects who are or may be partakers of those goods', for those goods are human goods, which 'can in principle be pursued, realized, and participated in by any human being'.[44] In addition to these two, Finnis lists seven other requirements: having a coherent plan of life, a degree of detachment from one's projects, a degree of commitment to one's projects, the pursuit of efficiency within reason, respect for every basic value in every act, favoring and fostering the common good, and following one's conscience. Following these requirements of practical reason thus helps the reasoner to distinguish wicked practices from good ones. Evil consists in, inter alia, a failure in the practice of practical reason.

III NARRATIVE APPROACH

The previous two sections link description with evaluation, and practice with value. The two linkages are preludes to the following two sections, which will argue that, in order to vindicate the nexus between description and evaluation and between practice and value, the philosophical examination in this book will proceed by way of a narrative approach and a historical approach. This section will explain the narrative approach and the next section will explain the historical approach. Jointly, the method is one of historical narrative.

---

[41] Finnis, *Natural Law and Natural Rights*, 101.
[42] Finnis, *Natural Law and Natural Rights*, 102.
[43] Finnis, *Natural Law and Natural Rights*, 105.
[44] Finnis, *Natural Law and Natural Rights*, 106–7.

There are many kinds of narratives. Narratives can be personal or political, tragic or epic, mythical or historical. History is a kind of narrative. A turn to history is, *ipso facto*, a turn to narrative. Narrativity is a corollary of historicity. The pursuit of moral philosophy through historical narrative is an attempt at the *study* of values through a *story* of how different people throughout history have sought to accommodate different values and render them coherent in their lives.

Let's begin with a thought experiment by MacIntyre. Imagine that you are standing at the bus stop, and the person next to you suddenly says to you: 'The name of the common wild duck is *Histrionicus histrionicus*'. You would be dumbfounded, wouldn't you? You understand the meaning of the words in the sentence perfectly, but what you are puzzled by is the point of it. To understand the point of it, you will need to situate it within a story about what he is up to and evaluate it within that frame. He might have mistaken you for someone who yesterday had approached him in the library and asked whether he knew the scientific name of the common wild duck. Or he might have just come from a session with his psychotherapist who had urged him to break down his shyness by talking to strangers. Or he might be a spy, uttering a code word. 'In each case, the act of utterance becomes intelligible by finding its place in a narrative'.[45] The attainment of cognitive intelligibility is a narrative accomplishment. We organize our experience by 'telling stories, about ourselves and about others, to ourselves and to others'.[46] This requirement of narratability applies even to the extreme existentialist who desires that his or her action be free in the radical sense of being without foundation or justification. Even there, the action only makes sense within a narrative context of existentialism.

We are storytellers. Narratives not only help us to make sense of individual action; they also help us make sense of individual identity. The persistence of individual identity through time is one of those big philosophical puzzles of all time. MacIntyre addresses that puzzle by relating identity to narrative. According to MacIntyre, the unity of an individual life consists in the unity of a narrative embodied in a single life: 'the unity of a human life is the unity of a narrative quest'.[47] When asked to give an account of what I did with my life and why, the only way to give that account is to recount how I got here and where I am heading. In short, the only way that I could give that account is to tell a story of my life. To be able to tell you a story about my life as it unfolds in

---

[45] MacIntyre, *After Virtue*, 244.
[46] Geertz, *Available Light*, 193.
[47] MacIntyre, *After Virtue*, 253.

time endows my life with a sense of identity that persists through time. We speak of a life story to describe the time span between birth and death: 'the plot serves to make one story out of the multiple incidents'.[48] Stories, especially life-stories, are always a mix of description and evaluation.

Consider what happens in psychoanalysis. The analysand brings to the analyst 'scattered fragments of lived stories, dreams, primal scenes, and conflictual episodes'.[49] The role of the analyst is to help the analysand piece together these scattered story-fragments, including those that are repressed, into a coherent narrative, which would make the life of the analysand more intelligible, thus more bearable. Psychoanalysis helps the analysand to tell a story out of story-fragments. In telling that story, the analysand becomes the narrator, if not entirely the author, of his or her own life story. An examined life is a recounted life, for 'life can be understood only through the stories that we tell about it'.[50] Self-knowledge occurs in the narrative mode, in 'both the figuration of the character and the configuration of the plot'.[51] 'Man is a storytelling animal' who can only ever answer a question, 'What am I to do?', insofar as he or she has an answer to the prior question, 'Of what stories do I find myself part?'.[52]

Stories explain, not only individual action and identity, but also collective action and identity. Take, for example, what Balkin calls constitutional stories. 'At the heart of constitutions are stories: stories about foundings, to be sure, but also stories about people: the people who create the constitution and the people who continue it, the people who fight for it and the people who fight over it, the people who live under it and the people to whom it belongs'.[53] Hence, constitutional disagreements are, at bottom, narrative disagreements: 'unpack a disagreement about the Constitution and you will find a disagreement about stories, about what was done to whom by whom, what it means, and whether and why it is worth remembering'.[54] One advances a constitutional argument by telling a story, and one rebuts it by telling an alternative story. A story helps you see the point in a vivid way, and seeing is believing. 'Telling stories is not a way of escaping argument: it is a way of arguing'.[55] The stories describe how we got here and where we are heading.

---

[48] Ricoeur, 'Life in Quest of Narrative', 21.
[49] Ricoeur, 'Life in Quest of Narrative', 30.
[50] Ricoeur, 'Life in Quest of Narrative', 31.
[51] Ricoeur, 'Narrative Identity', 196.
[52] Laidlaw, *The Subject of Virtue*, 62.
[53] Balkin, *Constitutional Redemption*, 2.
[54] Balkin, *Constitutional Redemption*, 3.
[55] Balkin, *Constitutional Redemption*, 17.

They present characters and events, together with lessons in which evaluations of the past provide prescriptions for the future. Stories give us 'roles to fill and obligations to fulfill'.[56] My individual story is always embedded narratively within the story of my community. A character never starts *ab initio*; rather, 'they plunge *in medias res*, the beginnings of their story already made for them by what and who has gone before'.[57]

The story of my life is always embedded narratively within the story of my community, which in turn is embedded narratively within a tradition that stretches back in time. It is a story within a story. If this narrative account is true, what then is the role of philosophy? Walzer gives two images of the philosopher, particularly the moral philosopher. The moral philosopher could either be the eagle at dawn or the owl at dusk. The eagle at dawn goes out in search of new land and new values, like an explorer. The owl at dusk reflects on the past and interprets what has happened, like a sage. There is a place and a time for the eagle at dawn and the owl at dusk, for the explorer and the sage. Nonetheless, Walzer prefers the owl to the eagle. The owl speaks to the people by 'elaborating on existing moralities and telling stories about a society more just than, though never entirely different from, [its] own'; for the owl, 'it is better to tell stories'.[58] Walzer presents the prophet as the quintessential owl. The prophet reminds the people of the values to which they are already committed. The prophet lifts the mirror up to the people. Prophecy becomes self-fulfilling prophecy when the people remember. In the Book of Exodus, the people are reminded that: 'You shall not wrong a stranger or oppress him, *for you were strangers in the land of Egypt*'.[59] The message draws heavily on the memory of the narrative when the Israelites were strangers in the land of Egypt before their Exodus. If oppression were to continue in Israel, the experience of Exodus would come to naught. It implicates the entire self-narrative of the people.

The narratives carry the moral force that they do because they encode what Taylor calls the social imaginary, that is, 'the ways in which people imagine their social existence, how they fit together with others, how things go on between them and their fellows, the expectations that are normally met, and the deeper normative notions and images that underlie these expectations'.[60] The social imaginary helps us make sense of our collective practices, by connecting practice with value. It incorporates a sense of the 'expectations

---

[56] Balkin, *Constitutional Redemption*, 26.
[57] MacIntyre, *After Virtue*, 249.
[58] Walzer, *Interpretation and Social Criticism*, 57.
[59] Book of Exodus 22:21.
[60] Taylor, 'Modern Social Imaginaries', 106.

that we have of one another, the kind of common understanding which enables us to carry out the collective practices that make up our social life'.[61] Out of Eden, we have to build a world for ourselves, both a physical world to protect us from the elements and a moral world to protect us from evil. We have to create our own practices and find our values within them. By participating in a social form of life, we partake in the social imaginary, whose combination of practice and value make the social form of life possible. We inhabit the social form of life and the associated social imaginary before we are even aware of it. The task of the owl at dusk is to come *ex post*, belatedly, to make sense of what is happening, by telling a story about it.

IV HISTORICAL APPROACH

Looking into the past, we will be surprised by how seemingly antagonistic values 'could be brought together into a single world view'.[62] We could only make sense of the presence of these seemingly antagonistic values within a single worldview by examining the 'social history of the moral imagination'.[63] 'One purpose in telling the story is to uncover the meanings of those [values] in a narrative context, that is, in their time dimension'.[64] The story that I will tell in the subsequent chapters is a story of contingency, not of necessity. Contingent events will goad and guide the story's progression.[65] It is not a story of how events *must* unfold. Rather, it is a story of how, given the particular line-up of circumstances, events *have* unfolded. Although contingent, these events are not arbitrary. Their occurrence is not without rhyme or reason. Part of the motivation for telling the story is to explain the whys and wherefores of these events. However, the whys and wherefores could only be told with the benefit of hindsight. Looking into the future, a storyteller may be a prophet, but he is most definitely not a fortune-teller.[66]

The same underlying purpose motivated Berlin's turn from analytic philosophy to the history of ideas: 'For Berlin, the history of ideas was not only a subject of intrinsic fascination, but also a means to self-understanding ... to make sense of the concepts that dominated the politics of his day'.[67] The task

---

[61] Taylor, 'Modern Social Imaginaries', 106.
[62] Berman, *Law and Revolution*, 3.
[63] Geertz, 'Found in Translation', 788.
[64] Berman, *Law and Revolution*, 1.
[65] Balkin, *Constitutional Redemption*, 29.
[66] Balkin, *Constitutional Redemption*, 30.
[67] Cherniss, 'Isaiah Berlin's Political Ideas', xxiii.

of the historian of ideas is neither to condemn the ideas of the past (as progressives are wont to do), nor to hanker after them (as conservatives are wont to do). Rather, the task is to understand them, especially how they have 'shaped human experience over time, and continue to underlie the outlook of the present'.[68] The strangeness of the past is not to be deplored, but embraced. The stranger the past, the sharper the contrast is between past and present. Understanding a strange past brings the peculiarity of the present into sharp relief. By familiarizing ourselves with the past, we defamiliarize the present. The taken-for-granted features of the present will no longer be taken for granted. We see the present with new eyes, and thereby, get a better grasp of the predicament of the present. At its best, the history of ideas does for a culture what psychoanalysis does for the individual: to lay bare the origins of 'the often implicit, deeply embedded, formative ideas, concepts and categories', by means of which we order and interpret our experience.[69] It tells us 'who and what we are, and by what stages and often tortuous paths we have become what we are'.[70] We may even find that the surface differences between them in the past and us in the present will give way to a recognition of a more profound and fundamental similarity between us and them.

Examining the history of ideas is both a historical as well as a philosophical enterprise. It starts with the past but presses toward an understanding of the present. It applies the past to the present. It examines the time-bound practices of law, love and freedom in order to understand the values of law, love and freedom. These values assume a vast diversity of forms of realization. They are reiterated differently in different times and places. The reason why a philosopher needs to turn to history is that these values cannot be understood in isolation from their time-bound practices, for 'moral ideals are a sediment: they have significance only so long as they are suspended in a religious or social tradition, so long as they belong to a religious or social life'.[71] Another reason why a philosopher needs to turn to history is the Nietzschean reason. Many moral concepts possess 'not one meaning but a whole synthesis of meanings: the previous history of [the concept] in general, the history of its employment for the most various purposes, finally crystallizes into a kind of unity that is hard to disentangle, hard to analyze and, as must be emphasized especially, totally indefinable'.[72] Only that which has no history can be

---

[68] Cherniss, 'Isaiah Berlin's Political Ideas', xxiv.
[69] Hausheer, 'Introduction', in Berlin, *Against the Current*, xxxvii.
[70] Hausheer, 'Introduction', in Berlin, *Against the Current*, xliv.
[71] Oakeshott, *Rationalism in Politics*, 41.
[72] Nietzsche, *On the Genealogy of Morals*, 80.

defined.[73] That which has a history can only be narrated. History is, ultimately, a story.

History is a particular kind of narrative. It is a retrospective narrative. History is the past organized into a narrative, in a way that tells us something meaningful about ourselves.[74] It is the result of a process of reflection on the past to make sense of the present. Humans understand themselves 'retrospectively by telling a historical story about how they came to be what they are'.[75] If our values are found in our practices, we cannot give a philosophical account of those values without giving a historical account of how their corresponding practices came to be part of our society. It is an account of how values are actualized in practices and how practices reflect values over time. This kind of vindication of our values and practices is 'only available in hindsight, in a reconstructive account of what has already unfolded in the world'.[76] Historicity is often associated with linearity, but it need not be. It is equally compatible with a circular view of time, a kind of eternal recurrence on a grand scale. A historical narrative need not be part of a progressive narrative. History can tell us how we got to be who we are, but 'admiring ourselves at the end of the story is another matter'.[77]

The practices and values from a past age 'can be appreciated by us and can be recognized as intimating truths to which we subscribe', even if we no longer engage in precisely the same type of practices.[78] The skill that is required to accomplish this task is imaginative empathy, that is, 'the power of sympathetic, reconstructive imagination akin to those of the creative artist – the capacity to enter into and understand from "inside" forms of life wholly different from his [or her] own'.[79] Historians of ideas need to be able to 're-enact within themselves the states of mind of men [or women] tormented by questions to which these [ideas] claim to be solutions'.[80] To use Collingwood's example, imagine you are reading the ancient edict of an emperor. Merely reading the words in the edict will not get you very far toward grasping the full significance of the edict. To grasp its significance, you must 'envisage it as the emperor envisaged it': you must go through the process that the emperor went through in deciding to issue this edict, thereby reenacting in your own mind the experience of the

---

[73] Nietzsche, *On the Genealogy of Morals*, 80.
[74] Krasnoff, *Hegel's Phenomenology of Spirit*, 111.
[75] Krasnoff, *Hegel's Phenomenology of Spirit*, 151.
[76] Krasnoff, *Hegel's Phenomenology of Spirit*, 74.
[77] Krasnoff, *Hegel's Phenomenology of Spirit*, 160.
[78] Houlgate, *An Introduction to Hegel*, 9.
[79] Hausheer, 'Introduction', in Berlin, *Against the Current*, xxxvi.
[80] Berlin, 'Does Political Theory Still Exist?', 87.

emperor.[81] You must step into the shoes of the emperor. The historian of ideas is interested, not only in ideas, but also in the people who held those ideas: 'what they felt, imagined, desired and expressed in utterances'.[82]

Bernard Williams calls this kind of imaginative empathy 'the ethnographic stance'. The ethnographic stance is the attitude of 'an observer who has an imaginative understanding of a society's ethical concepts and can understand its life from the inside'.[83] The observer 'understands from the inside a conceptual system in which ethical concepts are integrally related to modes of explanation and description'.[84] Williams adopts the ethnographic stance in his own philosophical thinking, and invites his readers to do the same. Williams peppers his philosophical work with detailed references to the lives and times of ancient Greeks. 'While Williams does not of course suggest that his readers should wish to be or try to think or act like ancient Greeks, they are invited to take Greek thought and practice seriously as pertaining to themselves; sufficiently so for them to reconsider their own thoughts in the light of it'.[85] His readers are invited to see in those ancient and alien practices and values an aspect of themselves. The ancient and alien thus expands our moral horizon and enlarges our moral imagination. It is not necessary to believe what they believed in order to be able to understand their practices and appreciate their values. Perceiving a value in the practice of others in a different time and place does not automatically mean that one has to adopt it as one's own here and now, not least because the form of life available then may no longer be available now.[86]

In the next chapter, this book will explore the monastic conception of freedom. The monks thought that they were free. To put the point more strongly, the monks thought that their lives were the paradigm of freedom. In response to the monastic form of life, we have two options. We could dismiss the monks as being systematically deluded. It is easy to claim that they are systematically deluded from our contemporary vantage point. To adopt this position is to take the high ground and make us in the present the be all and end all. Assigning such superiority to the present is sheer hubris. Alternatively, we could invest more intellectual effort to have greater imaginative empathy: to see the value in their lives on their terms, to get inside their form of life, and to recognize that they, too, have a mode of experiencing

---

[81] Collingwood, *The Idea of History*, 283.
[82] Mali, 'Berlin, Vico and the Principles of Humanity', 61.
[83] Williams, 'Reply to Simon Blackburn', 203.
[84] Williams, 'Reply to Simon Blackburn', 204.
[85] Laidlaw, *The Subject of Virtue*, 214.
[86] Laidlaw, *The Subject of Virtue*, 224.

freedom that may be different from ours. The past is a foreign land. Entering the past is like going into a foreign land. Finding the monks in the past is like finding a tribe deep in the forest of the Amazon. They have to be approached with the same imaginative empathy, and humility, as when an anthropologist encounters the tribe for the first time.

The subsequent chapters will recount stories about the ancient and the alien. Stories could be factual or fictional. Each has its pros and cons. Either could convey truth about the human condition. In claiming to offer a historical narrative, I am partly claiming that my account is a matter of fact. Fact could be stranger than fiction, and hence, it might better reflect the complexity of the human condition. The historical narrative that I will tell is, of course, my interpretation of the facts of history. To be more precise, it is my interpretation of the facts as reported to me by historians. In addition, I will, on many occasions, recount biblical stories. To be clear, I am not offering those biblical stories themselves as historical facts, at least not straightforwardly. History is complex and multilayered. In the case of biblical stories, the historical fact is that someone, somewhere in the past, believed in those stories and structured their lives around them. For example, when I say that Paul believed in the Resurrection, I am not making any historical claim about whether the Resurrection happened. Rather, my historical claim is that someone called Paul believed that the Resurrection happened and wrote a series of letters about it. What I am doing is offering a historical narrative of Paul's historical narrative: I am claiming that my historical narrative is true to historical facts, but I am not making any claim about the veracity of Paul's historical narrative. Similarly, when I refer to the creation myth in the Book of Genesis, I am not claiming that the world was created in the manner that the myth says it was. Rather, my claim is that groups of people – Jews, Christians, Jewish-Christians – embraced the myth and the myth gave meaning to their lives.

I tell these historical stories to make a point. In making the point, I try to be as true to the facts as I can. One can challenge me on the factual accuracy of my story, insofar as it claims to be true to historical facts. Yet, 'showing that a story is incomplete or false does not always undermine its persuasive appeal'.[87] It may still have persuasive power because it makes you see things in a new light. Even if the historical narrative turns out to be factually off the mark, it could still, nonetheless, be thought provoking. A gripping historical narrative does not settle disagreements, but inspires them. The persuasive appeal of a historical narrative does not lie solely in its historical facticity.

[87] Balkin, *Constitutional Redemption*, 27.

V HISTORICAL NARRATIVES OF LAW, LOVE AND FREEDOM

In order to provide a coherent account of the relationship of law, love and freedom that combines description and evaluation, and which shows the dependence of value on practice, I propose to adopt a historical narrative approach. In the next two chapters (Chapters 4 and 5), I will tell two historical narratives of law, love and freedom. In the final chapter (Chapter 6), I will make an analytic claim that follows from the two historical narratives that I have told. What drives the analytic claim are the two historical narratives. Just as one should not put the cart before the horse, so I should not put the analytic claim before the historical narratives. The analytic claim will be presented in the final chapter.

I will tell two stories. Each story has two levels to it. On one level, it is a sociopolitical story concerning the transformation of practice. On another level, it is a conceptual story concerning the transformation of the values of law, love and freedom. It is important to emphasize that these are two levels of a single story, for values are always embodied in practice. It will be a story of roots and routes, which traces the twists and turns that the values of law, love and freedom have undergone. The two stories, in gist, are as follows:

1. The first narrative is a story of how the instability in Paul's structure of thought about law, love and freedom gave rise to the monastic ideal as a way of stabilizing the structure and giving it some kind of foundational coherence. Fast forward several centuries, the Reformation brought the monastic ideal out of the monasteries into the world, and through a long and winding road, it came to shape the modern project of constitutionalism. This narrative is the prior narrative, prior in the sense of being the first story that I will tell and in the sense of being the primary narrative.
2. The second narrative is a story of how the instability in Paul's structure of thought about law, love and freedom also gave rise to the antinomian ideal as another way of stabilizing the structure and giving it a different kind of coherence. Fast forward several centuries, the Reformation, in bringing the monastic ideal out of the monasteries into the world, triggered a tit for tat transformation of the antinomian ideal into anarchism. This narrative is the counter narrative.

There is a neat parallel between the prior narrative and the counter narrative. The plot in gist is as follows:

Prior Narrative: Paul → Monastic Ideal → Reformation → Constitutionalism
Counter Narrative: Paul → Antinomian Ideal → Reformation → Anarchism

Paul is the starting point and the Reformation is the turning point for both narratives. The prior narrative tells a story of the construction of an ordered form of life: religious order in monasticism and political order in constitutionalism. The counter narrative tells a story of its antithesis: contra religious order in antinomianism and contra political order in anarchism. Both narratives belong to the Pauline tradition. Although part of the same tradition, the two narratives are conflicting, which should not come as a surprise, as a tradition is more often than not 'sustained and advanced by its own internal arguments and conflicts'.[88]

Earlier, I have mouthed the Schmittian dictum that all modern political concepts of the state are secularized theological concepts. This way of telling the two stories – the prior narrative and the counter narrative – is my way of putting my money where my mouth is, which is to show how theological ideas of order and disorder are transformed into political ideas. Eventually, if this investment pays off, I want to cash out both narratives in terms of law, love and freedom.

The monastic ideal subscribes to a particular configuration of the values of law, love and freedom. The antinomian ideal subscribes to a rival configuration.

THE MONASTIC IDEAL	v	THE ANTINOMIAN IDEAL
Law as Authority		Law as Resistance
Love as Union		Love as Attention
Freedom as Identification		Freedom as Independence

The two narratives will recount how these two configurations of values came to be. What we have here are not simply 'two theories, but the theoretical specifications of two different ways of life'.[89] They present two different visions of a moral life within which the values of law, love and freedom could be realized. To be sure, these are not the only two visions available, but these are the two visions that the two narratives will shed light on. Other visions will require other narratives for them to see the light of day.

---

[88] MacIntyre, *After Virtue*, 302.
[89] MacIntyre, *After Virtue*, 137.

4

Prior Narrative: From Monasticism to Constitutionalism

Chapter 2 presented a bipolar account of law, love and freedom. Law is polarized between authority and resistance. Love is polarized between union and attention. Freedom is polarized between independence and identification. Having pulled these concepts apart, the next two chapters will try to put Humpty together again. If one wants to lead a life of law, love and freedom, one has to find a way to make those values coherent. The coherence of values is to be found within a particular form of life. A form of life manifests itself in historical perspective. A form of life does not appear out of thin air; rather, it is constructed over time. Neither is it like the flies of summer, here today gone tomorrow; rather, it persists through time. Hence, one needs to turn to historical narrative to make sense of values and see how they 'could be brought together into a single world view'.[1]

Chapter 3 argued that, in order to understand a form of life, one has to tell a story of its emergence and transformation. The coherence of values is not to be found in abstract conceptual analysis, but in a historical narrative of how values are combined and lived. This chapter will tell the story of how a particular form of life – from monasticism to constitutionalism – combines the values of law as authority, love as union and freedom as identification. This story is the prior narrative. The next chapter will tell the story of how another form of life – from antinomianism to anarchism – combines the values of law as resistance, love as attention and freedom as independence. The next story is the counter narrative.

PRIOR NARRATIVE	COUNTER NARRATIVE
Law as Authority	Law as Resistance
Love as Union	Love as Attention
Freedom as Identification	Freedom as Independence

[1] Berman, *Law and Revolution*, 3.

Chapter 1 showed that the tensions in law, love and freedom arise, in part, from the divided nature of humankind. In the Edenic myth of origin, we encounter two views of human nature: prelapsarian and fallen. Within the single myth, we find Rousseau's noble savage as well as Hobbes's nasty brute. Chapter 1 argued that this mythic equivocation permeated Paul's writings and it troubled Paul throughout his entire missionary career. The bifurcated image of human nature in the cosmological beginning is transposed into Paul's vision of the eschatological end. While the human condition might have been perfect in the beginning, and although the human condition will be restored to its prelapsarian perfection at the end, humans are, here and now, fallen. Humans are out of the earthly paradise, but not yet in the apocalyptic heaven. In the interim – in the time that remains till Christ comes again – there is the urgent task of building a Christian community here and now. A messianic community looks toward *eschaton*, when the Messiah will return at the end of time to make things whole again. At *eschaton*, the world will finally be restored to perfection. The perfect world is projected into the indefinite future. In the time that remains between now and then, Paul needs law as much as he may detest it.

A community, even one as otherworldly as the early Christian community, needs law to govern behavior and mediate interpersonal conduct. Despite their best efforts to escape this world, the early Christians were still living in this world. Living in this world means living under governments and under laws, whether civil or ecclesiastical. Given this fact, Paul leaves unresolved the question of how one could lead a life of law, love and freedom in this world. Subsequent generations will have to pick up the tab. This chapter will take up the story and continue where Chapter 1 left off. It will chart the story of how subsequent generations, from the ancient through the medieval to the modern, have struggled with this Pauline dilemma. The modern political state carries with it this ancient theological dilemma.

PAUL AND THE PERFECT CHRISTIAN

Paul is often referred to as the second founder, if not *the* founder, of Christianity, and for good reason. His letters were written well before the gospels. His letters set the scene for the clash of ideas that would later ensue within Christianity, and beyond. One way to approach Paul is to place him in the context of the various disputes that he was engaging in. Paul had to negotiate and differentiate his new Christian community from the monotheistic Jews, on the one hand, and the polytheistic Romans, on the other. He had one eye toward Jerusalem and another eye toward Rome. Negotiating between 'the Jews' and 'the Romans' was like navigating between Scylla and Charybdis. Consider, for example, the trick question: who killed Jesus? Was it 'the Jews' or 'the Romans'? The blame game was recorded in the trial scene itself. Jesus was shoved from the Sanhedrin to Pilate, that is, from the Jewish to the Roman authorities. In the Gospels, we have the two iconic images of 'the Jews' shouting 'let his blood be upon us and on our children', and Pilate washing his hands clean saying 'I am innocent of the blood of this man' after pronouncing the final judgment for the crucifixion. This blame game reflected the political realities at the time: schismatic antagonism against 'the Jews' and the need to kowtow to Rome as the ruling power.

Before his road to Damascus, Paul was a Jew and a Roman citizen. After his fateful trip to Damascus, Paul remained a Jew and a Roman citizen, in addition to his newly acquired identity as a Christian. His letters reflected this mix of identities. Juggling all these competing identities was an extremely difficult balancing act. The identity crisis in the early church in its relations with Jerusalem and Rome existed in microcosm in the person of Paul. On the Roman front, Christianity started life as a minority religion in Rome. However, unlike Judaism, it was a proselytizing religion that sought to convert both Jews and Gentiles. This proselytizing mission was due, in no small part, to Paul's vision as the apostle of the gentiles. He transformed Christianity from being a sect of Judaism to a universal religion when he proclaimed that, in Christ, 'there is neither Jew nor Greek, neither slave nor free, neither male nor female'.[2] All could be admitted into the family of Christ.

Christianity's proselytism was a blessing and a bane in its relationship with Rome. First, it made Rome the persecutor of Christians, before making it the protector of Christians. The change of role from persecutor to protector was marked by the conversion of Constantine. The conversion of Constantine was a decisive moment in both Christian and Roman history. The Church became Roman. A lot had to change, both in Rome and in the Church. Christians suddenly found themselves to be in the dominant position. They were no longer persecuted. The Roman Emperor moved from being an enemy to a friend, and Christianity moved from the margins of the empire to the heart of the establishment. With the changing fortunes of Christianity, there followed a change in the image of the perfect Christian. Christianity is a call to perfection, as Jesus tells his disciples: 'Be ye perfect'.[3] But who is the perfect Christian? More specifically, how should the perfect Christian live the gospel

---

[2] Letter to the Galatians 3:28.
[3] Gospel of Matthew 5:48.

and lead a life of law, love and freedom? As the political equation changed, the answer to these questions changed.

The earliest model of the perfect Christian was, without doubt, the *martyr*. Christ died a gruesome death. Dying to make a point was a central feature of Christianity. The religion started as a persecuted faith, hated by 'the Jews' and hunted by 'the Romans'. The first martyr, Stephan, was, ironically, persecuted by none other than Paul himself, prior to his conversion on the road to Damascus. Paul was zealous, whether as the persecutor or the persecuted. Paul was the persecutor who became the persecuted. Tradition has it that Paul was eventually martyred – beheaded, to be precise – in Rome during the reign of Emperor Nero. The decades of Roman persecution gave rise to a multitude of martyrs. Some sought out martyrdom, while others had martyrdom thrust upon them. The martyr opposed the state and bore the full force of the state willingly, often gladly. A martyr would not run away. He or she would not seek an escape. Instead, they would take pride in bearing the punishment meted out to them. The state's terrifying power over life and death – what the Romans call *vitae et necis potestatem* – means nothing to them. What can you do to control someone who does not fear death? You can do nothing. Hence, martyrs, then and now, are a constant threat to the polity. The fear of death no longer holds them captive. Think of the awesome image of the martyr: a lone individual standing upright, surrounded by hungry lions.

It takes two to tango. For there to be martyrs, there needed to be persecutors. With the conversion of Constantine, Rome made peace with Christianity and the age of the martyr came to a close. With no persecutors at hand, there was no opportunity for martyrdom. A new model of heroism had to be found. There needed to be a new image of the perfect disciple to replace the martyr. The new figure had to be more quietist to suit the new sociopolitical environment where Christianity had pride of place in the political establishment. The new figure had to be more peaceable.

The *hermit* fitted the bill. The hermit was heroic in a quiet and peaceful way. The hermit retreated into the desert to fight the devil in the soul through severe ascetic practices. Unlike martyrs, hermits minded their own business and did not create trouble for the state. The image of the perfect disciple thus shifted from the martyr fighting the Romans in the City to the hermit fighting the Devil in the Desert. The hermit replaced the martyr as the new soldier of Christ. The battle was projected inward. The political trial of the martyr in public was replaced by the spiritual struggle of the hermit in private. The courage of the martyr under persecution was replaced by the fortitude of the hermit under temptation. The fire of Christian zeal was no longer kindled in the City, but in the Desert. A new form of religious life came into being with the hermit. Hermits led solitary lives away from society. Their eremitic life was one of withdrawal. They sought to reduce the self to a point with no attachments in the world whatsoever. They were not quite Rousseau's noble savages, but they came close.

While they adopted ascetic practices, these practices were entirely voluntary: the practices were neither codified nor subject to any form of supervisory oversight. Hermits could come and go as they pleased, as and when they wanted. They could become a hermit one day, and cease to be one the next. They did not need to seek approval from anyone to be a hermit. All that the male aspirant needed to do was to remove himself to the outskirts of town and build himself a hermitage. No ordination, no training, no test. Several hermits might group themselves into a commune, but their lives remained individualistic. They might join forces and pull their resources to build a chapel nearby for Sunday Eucharist, but their lives otherwise remained solitary, so solitary that a hermit's death was often only discovered when he failed to turn up for Sunday Eucharist for several weeks in a row. Unlike the martyr, the hermit's attitude to the state was not hostile, but indifferent. They simply could not care less. The state did not matter to them, so long as they were left alone, literally alone, to do their own thing. The state was more than happy to leave them alone and let sleeping dogs lie. People would flock to the countryside to see these hermits, partly out of curiosity and partly to ask for miracles. Hermits were harmless; thus, unlike martyrs, they did not pose a threat to the state. Their asceticism consisted of withdrawing from the state and denying the self. Hermits dumbed the mind and numbed the senses in an effort to direct their entire attention to the single object of their love: God.

THE MONK AND THE MONASTIC IDEAL

Hermitry soon became the career of choice for those wishing to pursue a religious vocation, so much so that the countryside was filled with hermits of all sorts. Hermits were, by and large, a law unto themselves. While the state was happy to let them be, the Church began to feel uneasy about them. Note the capitalization in the Church. By this time, the Church became more structured and juridified as it became more powerful. The Church wanted to have greater and tighter control over the growth and direction of the religious life of its flock. There was an increased effort at codification and coordination. The hermit could no longer be given the free rein that they needed for their existence. A new model of the perfect Christian, again, had to be found.

The practice had developed of hermits banding together and pooling their resources. The Church seized on this practice, gave it a value and made it a norm. The Church rounded up the hermits and cloistered them. With that, the cenobitic monk came into existence, replacing the eremitic hermit. The cloisters became monasteries under the leadership of an abbot, who often ruled with an iron fist, albeit in a velvet glove. Monastic life would be marked by constant surveillance by other monks and ultimately by the abbot. Life would be anything but solitary. Alongside this development in practice, polemical attacks against the life of the hermit began to circulate. The solitary life was rebranded as being selfish, while the common life of monks became exalted as the model of a perfect community. This inversion – the transvaluation of values – could be seen in the course of John Cassian's *Conferences of the Desert Fathers*, written sometime in the fifth century. Cassian started his *Conferences* by praising the eremitic life, but this praise of the eremitic life gradually thinned and eventually disappeared as the *Conferences* progressed. By the end of the *Conferences*, Cassian left his audience in no doubt that 'the only practicable form of monasticism that he could recommend' was the cenobitic form.[4] The *Rule of the Four Fathers* was even more unequivocal in its prescription that 'the desolation of the desert and the terror of various monsters do not permit the brothers to live singly [as hermits]'.[5] Hence, the brothers ought to live in community, as monks. With this shift, the charisma of the exemplary 'holy man' passed to the 'holy community'.[6]

Rules governing monastic life began to be codified, one of the earliest of which was the *Rule of Saint Augustine*. Augustine established his first monastery in Thagaste in 388 and his second monastery in Hippo in 391, and wrote the Rule in 397. In Thagaste and later in Hippo, Augustine created an alternative society of men who rejected sex, wealth and power in favor of chastity, poverty and obedience. Obedience was central in creating well-regulated monasteries: the monks should obey their 'superior as a father, always with the respect worthy of his position, so as not to offend God in him'.[7] In his treatise on the *Work of Monks*, Augustine criticized the 'hypocrites in the garb of monks, who went through the provinces, sent by no authority, never stationary, stable, or settled'.[8] He contrasted the itinerant monks with the stable and stationary monks who lived under a superior and a Rule. In these salutary and stationary monastic communities, the Rule would be policed by the mutual surveillance of the monks themselves: 'mutually safeguard your purity ... by your mutual vigilance'.[9] 'Whoever

---

[4] Markus, *The End of Ancient Christianity*, 185.
[5] As quoted in Dunn, *The Emergence of Monasticism*, 85.
[6] Markus, *The End of Ancient Christianity*, 193.
[7] Augustine, 'Praeceptum', §7.1.
[8] Augustine, 'The Work of Monks', 384.
[9] Augustine, 'Praeceptum', §4.6.

happened to discover [an infraction of the rule] must report the offender', who upon conviction, 'must submit to the salutary punishment determined by the judgement of the superior', which included corporal punishment.[10] Even if, perchance, his actions were to escape the notice of his fellow monks, he still could not escape the constant surveillance of 'the One who keeps watch on high, from whom nothing can be hidden', for 'God sees everything'.[11] Although the Rule would be enforced rigorously, the obedience had to be done out of love and not fear, for the *mores* of the monastery should be founded on the *amores* of the monks.[12] The chief goal of the rule was to enable the multitude of monks 'to live harmoniously in the house and to have *one heart and one soul* seeking God'.[13] To that end, 'let no one work for himself alone, but all your work shall be for the *common* purpose'.[14] Ultimate freedom was to be found in complete obedience to the common rule.

The *Rule of Saint Augustine* was followed by the *Rule of the Four Fathers*, the *Second Rule of the Fathers*, the *Rule of Macarius*, the *Third Rule of the Fathers*, the *Oriental Rule* and the *Rule of the Master*, culminating in the *Rule of Saint Benedict* in the sixth century. As the rules developed, they became more elaborate, and the office of the abbot became more powerful. The Council of Chalcedon in 451 made clear that, although a monastery was subject to the territorial jurisdiction of the local diocesan bishop, the bishop could not exercise his episcopal powers within the monastery, and the monks, unless they were clerics, were subject to the authority of the abbot alone. When speaking of the different kinds of monks in the opening chapter, the *Rule of Saint Benedict* singles out 'those who live in monasteries and serve under a rule and an abbot' as 'the strongest kind of monks'.[15] The *Rule of Saint Benedict* asserts its own supremacy, when it prescribes that 'everybody should follow the Rule as a master in all things and nobody should rashly deviate from it', including the abbot, who 'should do everything in fear of God and in observance of the Rule'.[16]

Unlike hermits who founded their lives on total individual solitude, the monks founded their lives on the direct opposite: total communitarianism. They possessed nothing individually, not even their lives. They led a well and truly common life. The vow of poverty dispossessed them of their external

---

[10] Augustine, 'Praeceptum', §4.8–9.
[11] Augustine, 'Praeceptum', §4.5.
[12] Lawless, *Augustine of Hippo and His Monastic Rule*, 22.
[13] Augustine, 'Praeceptum', §1.2.
[14] Augustine, 'Praeceptum', §5.2.
[15] *Rule of Saint Benedict*, ch 1.
[16] *Rule of Saint Benedict*, ch 3.

goods, and the vow of obedience dispossessed them of their internal will. Thenceforth, whatever they owned, they owned in common, and whatever they willed, they willed in common. They saw themselves as creating the ideal Christian community here on earth. They created a separate world within the walls of the monastery. They provided those in the City of Man with a glimpse of the City of God. In humanity's fallen condition, the monastery was 'the nearest that men could get to a society in which the bonds between its members were restored to their original [prelapsarian] integrity'.[17] Monks became the new model of the perfect Christian.

To examine more closely the monastic form of life, let's consider the word *habit*. In common usage, habit denotes a regular way of doing things. On a larger scale, it can denote a way of being and acting, or even an entire way of life. In the monastic context, habit also refers to the robe that monks wear. Monks don the habit. The donning of the habit operates on two levels: it is the wearing of a physical item of clothing as well as the taking on of a particular way of life. These two levels of meaning merge through a process of allegorization, whereby each item of clothing is made to symbolize an aspect of the monastic way of life, for example, the hood is a symbol of simplicity, the mantle is a symbol of humility, the belt is a symbol of readiness to fight for Christ and so on.[18] Consider the other closely related word *inhabit*. Monks inhabit the monastery, and thereby, commit themselves to a form of communal habitation. They inhabit, not only a place, but also a style of dress and a form of life.

What is novel with the monks, as opposed to the hermit or the martyr, is that their form of life is created by law. Monks create their own legal structure in the monastery. Their rules are codified and read to them daily during mealtimes. They eat in silence as the lector reads them the rules. Their entire existence is regulated by the monastic code. Monastic codes contain an 'imposing mass of punctilious precepts and ascetic techniques, of cloisters and horologia, of solitary temptations and choral liturgies, of fraternal exhortations and ferocious punishments'.[19] They dictate, sometimes in fine detail, what to wear and what to eat, when to speak and when to keep silent, what prayers to say and what thoughts to think. In so doing, the code constructs a form-of-life: 'a life that is linked so closely to its form that it proves to be inseparable from it'.[20] The form-of-life is created through the mechanism of

---

[17] Markus, *The End of Ancient Christianity*, 80.
[18] Agamben, *The Highest Poverty*, 13–6.
[19] Agamben, *The Highest Poverty*, xi.
[20] Agamben, *The Highest Poverty*, xi.

rules. Obedience to authority, entrenched in the impersonal code and embodied in the person of the abbot, is total. Every hour of existence is regulated, such that a monk's entire existence is given up to what the Church calls the Liturgy of the Hours. The prescribed prayers throughout the day and night constitute the Divine Office, which transports the monks to a higher time than the secular time of the world. Unlike the rest of the world that lives in secular time (the *saeculum*), the monks live in sacred time, for every moment of the monk's life is sacralized by its submission to – or more accurately, its subsumption under – the monastic law. The monastic law is totalitarian, insofar as it claims to regulate, not only single acts and events, but the entire existence of an individual.[21] The monks live their lives under the constant gaze, not only of God, but also of the other monks. Theirs is a separate and parallel community to that of the family and the state, only better, for theirs is a more perfect communion. The authority of law makes all that possible for them.

The goal of this austere ascetic form of communal life is grand: love as union. Through this form of life, the monks seek to be of 'one mind and one heart', horizontally with each other and vertically with God. Augustine places tremendous emphasis on the quality of single-mindedness in the monastery: 'you [monks] have not only renounced carnal wedlock, but have also chosen to dwell with one accord in fellowship together under the same roof, to have "one soul and one heart" unto God'.[22] This union is achieved through the authority of law, for it is law that creates the common life for the monks which makes union possible. The other word for monasticism, *cenoby*, expresses this goal perfectly. *Cenoby* originates from the term *koinos bios*, which literally means the common life. The perfection that the monks seek is not individual perfection, but the formation of a perfect community. Monasticism provides us with a model of what a 'total communitarian life' would look like.[23] It offers us a glimpse of another world, with a different form of social organization.[24] The monastic community has always been anomalous amid the wider community, but 'in that anomaly resided its special function': its existence as an alternative mode of social ordering 'proclaims a challenge to all other forms of social existence' amid the society of the fallen.[25] Thus, when MacIntyre ends his book *After Virtue* by calling for 'the construction of new forms of community within which the moral life could be sustained so that both morality and civility might survive the coming ages of barbarism and darkness', he points to

[21] Agamben, *The Highest Poverty*, 26.
[22] Augustine, *Select Letters*, Ep CCXI, 377.
[23] Agamben, *The Highest Poverty*, 9.
[24] Siedentop, *Inventing the Individual*, 93, 99.
[25] Markus, *The End of Ancient Christianity*, 81, 159.

Saint Benedict.[26] When Saint Benedict wrote his Rule in 529, after the sack of Rome in 410, it must have looked like the end of civilization. The empire was in decay, and the future looked bleak. As the world descended into the dark ages, the monks made a strategic retreat from the world. The monks left the world to the barbarians and cloistered themselves behind the walls of the monastery. Within the monastery, they dedicated themselves to God and made a commitment to one another to set up a new form of moral order, as the dark ages descended upon Europe. The utopianism of monasticism was a form of radical protest against the existing order of the world: 'monks withdrew from the world to show how they imagined a perfectly Christian life should be', as an earthly sign of the heavenly kingdom.[27]

The early monastic code writers – from Saint Augustine to Saint Benedict – were the authors of the first rules that provided 'comprehensive rationalizations of behaviour and attitudes'.[28] When hermits turned into monks, 'the time for work and the time for prayer started to be organized; since these times are shared, they cannot be chosen on an individual basis'.[29] The hermits-turned-monks could no longer do as they pleased. Monastic rules turned the hermit's uncontrolled escape from the world into a controlled cloister that was closely monitored and tightly regulated. Monasticism became an institutionalized utopia. These rules created a form of life, with its own way of seeing and doing things, and with its own form of moral order. Obedience to authority was a central feature of this new form of moral order. Only hermits could do without obedience or authority, but as soon as groups began to form to live as monks, modes of authority became indispensable. When eremitism yielded to cenobitism, it also yielded to authority.

The monastic rules constituted a total and comprehensive code of conduct for the monks. To belong to a monastery was to be part of a consecrated *order*. The monastic code not only reshaped the monk's life, but it also reshaped his sense of time. The monk's time, structured symbolically, 'no longer matched with the one that regulates the universe of ordinary life'.[30] In the words of Paul, the monks were 'redeeming the time, because the days are evil'.[31] The monastic community was to be a perfect union in perfect time. At the heart of it was the division between physical work and spiritual prayer. When

---

[26] MacIntyre, *After Virtue*, 197. Saint Benedict was the author of the most widely used monastic code in Western Christendom.
[27] Pace, 'Seguy and the Monastic Utopia', 279.
[28] Abbruzzese, 'Monastic Asceticism and Everyday Life', 10.
[29] Abbruzzese, 'Monastic Asceticism and Everyday Life', 9.
[30] Abbruzzese, 'Monastic Asceticism and Everyday Life', 7.
[31] Letter to the Ephesians 5:16.

the hermits first went out to the desert, they thought that they could devote themselves totally to prayer alone. They initially, and naively, 'thought that they did not need to work', for 'God would provide for their survival', but the early Desert Fathers soon realized that 'they could not live as angels and that work was a necessity for their material or biological survival'.[32] Consequently, time for prayer and time for work – *ora et labora* – were both institutionalized in the monastic rules when the first monasteries were founded. Although work responded to certain material necessities, it was also presented as a moral demand that aided the task of contemplation. Work was needed to control the desires of the flesh. The monks aimed to achieve a total control of their natural impulses by living a methodical life, which involved the routinization and rationalization of work and prayer. The routine of work and the rhythm of prayer, as defined by the rules, constituted the regular life of the monks. Monastic rules brought regulation, and hence regularity, into the lives of the monks.

The monastic life may be totalitarian, but it need not be oppressive. In fact, monasticism is a paradigmatic example of how a form of life can be totalitarian and free, so long as there is identification. Identification is doing all the work of freedom here. By setting themselves apart, spiritually and physically, from the private sphere of the family and the public sphere of the polity, the monks find their identification elsewhere. They identify with something else entirely, that is, with something entirely otherworldly. Mystics may enjoy sparks of momentary ecstasy, but for the vast majority of monks, this process of identification is 'understood as a laborious, lifetime quest'.[33] The distinctive vow that monks make, which other religious orders do not, is the vow of *conversatio morum*, the conversion of life, to live the rule. In monks, we find a conjoining of the joy of freedom with the vow of obedience. For them, freedom consists 'in the self-imposition of rules',[34] which is really the self-identification with the rules that are imposed by the monastic code. The self-identification is pronounced through the profession of the monastic vows at the time of admission. Freedom is to be found, not in rebellion, but in obedience: 'Obedience becomes perfect when the one who commands and the one who obeys come to share one mind ... A totally obedient community would be one in which no one was ever compelled to do anything'.[35] The freedom that the monks seek is not one of independence, but identification. A monk enters a monastery because he identifies with the monastic life. Insofar as

---

[32] Jonveaux, 'Redefinition of the Role of Monks in Modern Society', 72.
[33] Siedentop, *Inventing the Individual*, 96.
[34] Siedentop, *Inventing the Individual*, 98.
[35] McCabe, *God Matters*, 228–9.

there is identification, there is freedom within the walls of the monastery. However, if the identification ceases for any particular monk, the walls of the monastery cannot but appear like prison walls to him. He may remain there, but he will be anything but free. Likewise, insofar as there is identification, there is freedom in obedience to the monastic code. The monk obeys that which he identifies with. However, if the identification ceases, the monastic code cannot but appear like an external imposition on him. When that happens, it is probably time for him to leave.

We have now reached the end of the long road from Paul to the monastic ideal. We have examined how the values of law, love and freedom that were first raised by Paul in his letters to his scattered Christian communities (see Chapter 1) were explored and transformed in practice by subsequent Christians. These values were brought together and reconfigured in the figure of the martyr, and later, in the figures of the eremitic hermit and the cenobitic monk. Paul was neither a hermit nor a monk. Nonetheless, both hermits and monks claimed the imprimatur of Paul. Indeed, any Christian movement after Paul has to claim the imprimatur of Paul, given the status of Paul as the 'second founder' of Christianity. It is unclear whether Paul would have actually approved of what the monks did. What is most striking about the transformation of ideas from Paul to the monastic ideal is in the role of law. Although Paul never crossed the Rubicon into antinomianism, he clearly saw law as a stumbling block to religious life. He was not a fan of law, to put it mildly. This lukewarm attitude to the role of law in religious life disappeared when the monk came on the scene. Law changed from being the stumbling block to being the building block of religious life. Law, with the order and regularity that it brings, is central to the religious life of the monk. This nomian change is 'revolutionary', in the two senses of the word. It is revolutionary in the sense that it is a dramatic turn away from Paul's dim view of the law. But it is also revolutionary in the sense that it is a re-turn to the original Jewish view of the law as constitutive of one's relationship to God and neighbor, which is the view that Paul was reacting against to begin with. If there is a lesson here, one of the lessons must surely be that the more things change, the more they stay the same.

FROM ANCIENT TO MEDIEVAL MONASTICISM

As the Church grew in power, prestige and privilege, monasteries grew along with it from the ancient to the medieval period. 'The High Middle Ages were above all a period of expansion in Christian monasticism'.[36] Monasteries grew

---

[36] Collins, *Weberian Sociological Theory*, 52.

in number and size. Despite the vow of poverty, the monasteries also grew in wealth. To be sure, this growth in wealth was compatible with the vow of poverty, strictly speaking. Wealth was depersonalized in the monastery. The wealth of the monastery was distinguished from the poverty of the monks. The vow of poverty required a monk to be as poor as a church mouse, albeit in a rich church. The device that was used to accomplish this result would be familiar to lawyers: the invention of corporate personality as a separate entity, which allowed monasteries to hold property, without burdening the conscience of the monks. This device required the drawing of a very fine line and provided for an unstable compromise.

The more wealth accumulated, the more the practice of monasticism appeared to depart from the promise of monasticism. The gap between practice and promise could only be tolerated to a certain degree before reform movements would emerge to demand that the practice fulfill its promise. Within monasticism, there were cycles of reform to return the practice to its promise. The reform of the Benedictine Order resulted in the creation of the Cistercian Order. The reform of the Cistercian Order, in turn, resulted in the creation of the Order of Cistercians of the Strict Observance. Thus, monastic orders proliferated. The cycles of reform were the inevitable consequence of the growth in wealth, which was the inevitable consequence of the work habit of the monk, which combined a strict regimentation of labor with an equally strict restriction on the consumption of the fruits of one's labor. Under such conditions, wealth would accumulate as a matter of course. Notwithstanding the actual accumulation of wealth in monasteries, the active pursuit of wealth, like that of a merchant, remained 'a pudendum which was to be tolerated',[37] but neither endorsed nor encouraged. The actual accumulation of wealth in monasteries was an accidental accumulation.

Aristotle famously said that the end of human association was 'life and the good life'. In monasteries, the production and accumulation of goods was necessary for life, but it did not constitute the good life for the monks. Physical labor was needed to satisfy the demands of life, but it was not the high life. The high life consisted in the High Mass, that is, liturgical worship. Physical labor was a prelude to liturgical worship. While labor and liturgy together made up the activities of the monk, labor had to be confined in order to free up time for the more important task of liturgical worship. The monks had to work, but they should not work too hard, for work had to be balanced with prayer. They had to work smart. Hence, labor was confined by working more efficiently, through the innovative use of equipment and the adoption of

[37] Weber, *Protestant Ethic*, 35.

systematic and rationalized work practices. Once the requirements of labor were satisfied and life taken care of, the monks could then turn to what truly mattered. The highest form of monastic productivity was not the increase in grains, but the 'increase of the *thesaurus ecclesia* [the spiritual treasure of the church] through prayer and chant'.[38] Therein lay the good life.

There was one particular aspect of lay life that the monks were required to renounce once and for all: the reproduction of life. Alongside liturgy, monks labored in the production of goods, but not the reproduction of life. Although monks opted out of lay life, lay life, including its reproduction, was not denuded of value. In this regard, the monk was markedly different from the stoic.[39] For the monk, the monastic form of life was a choice, which involved the sacrifice of a good for a greater good. Monks gave up something of value for something of greater value. The relationship between monastic life and lay life was set in the context of ecclesiastical mediation, in which 'some, more dedicated members could win merit and salvation for others who were less so'.[40] Monks prayed for all, just as the warrior fought for all. Monks lived a special form of life, which became 'the privileged locus of the sacred'.[41] The laity relied on the monks for prayers, while the monks relied on the laity for the continuation of life on earth. It was a relationship of mutual dependence. Thus was the state of medieval monasticism before the Reformation turned it topsy-turvy.

REFORMATION: 'NOW EVERY CHRISTIAN HAD TO BE A MONK ALL HIS LIFE'[42]

The Reformation turned life topsy-turvy when it turned the hierarchy of monastic and lay life on its head. It eliminated monasticism as a higher form of life and folded it into lay life. Thenceforth, there would be no more high life and lay life; only ordinary life. Ordinary life would be where all the action is. The dethroning of monasticism began with the rejection of ecclesiastical mediation. Salvation could not be earned, not even by the Church. Access to the divine was to be direct and immediate, that is, unmediated by

---

[38] Weber, *Protestant Ethic*, 106.
[39] Taylor, *Sources of the Self*, 218.
[40] Taylor, *Sources of the Self*, 215.
[41] Taylor, *Sources of the Self*, 217.
[42] Weber, *Protestant Ethic*, 74. Given our patriarchal history, most of the characters in this historical narrative, and most of the pronouns used in quotes, are male. To avoid whitewashing our patriarchal past, I have refrained from retrofitting them to make them appear gender-inclusive retroactively.

the Church with its sacraments, sacred sites and holy orders. For the reformers, the individual stood alone before God. 'There could be no such thing as more devoted or less devoted Christians: the personal commitment must be *total* or it was worthless'.[43] In living the Christian life, there could not be half-hearted laity and whole-hearted monks. All had to be wholehearted. It was the great leveling *up*. What was required was 'a thoroughgoing Christianization of the whole of life'.[44] From this perspective, monasticism seemed misguided. Monks were barking up the wrong tree. Having made this realization, Luther ceased to be a monk and married a nun. Earlier, Luther left the world to enter the monastery; now, Luther left the monastery to enter the world. However, instead of leaving the monastic ideal behind, Luther brought seeds of the monastic ideal with him from the monastery into the world.

The monastic ideal was not abolished, but it was instead transformed and absorbed into ordinary life. The reformers did away with the Aristotelian distinction between 'life and the good life'. Instead, the good life was to be found in life itself, that is, in labor in the double sense of the production of goods and the reproduction of life. In short, the Christian life would be workaday: doing one's work every day in ordinary life. Ordinary life was not to be transcended, but lived. The reformers substituted the Catholic notion of a vocation with the Protestant notion of a calling. The Catholic vocation referred to the higher forms of life, notably, the life of a monk. In contrast, the Protestant calling referred to one's work in the world in ordinary life. The existence of the Catholic vocation was a slur on the Protestant calling. In the eyes of the reformers, all callings were equal. Luther's doctrine of 'the priesthood of all believers' laicized the clergy as much as it clericalized the laity, with the result that all lay offices were rebranded as different forms of divine calling.[45] The flattening of life and the equalization of work were accompanied by the specialization of labor. Labor in a calling, especially the division of labor in a specialized calling, was an expression of the love of neighbor, for it required 'every individual to work for others'.[46] Alongside the production of goods, there was the reproduction of life. While monks could afford to be celibate, when the monastic ideal was popularized, the populace could not be celibate as the actual monks were. Widespread celibacy would have made the society go extinct. Society needed to reproduce itself. In the

---

[43] Taylor, *Sources of the Self*, 215.
[44] Weber, *Protestant Ethic*, 77.
[45] Witte, *Law and Protestantism*, 7.
[46] Weber, *Protestant Ethic*, 41.

place of celibacy, sexual fidelity was emphasized, along with a strict code of sexual conduct.

This emphasis on working in a calling gave rise to what Weber famously named the Protestant work ethic. The Protestant work ethic combined industry with frugality. Industry aimed to strip life of idleness: hence the maxim, the idle mind is the devil's workshop. 'Every hour lost is lost to labour for the glory of God'.[47] One of the favorite parables of the Puritans was the Parable of the Talents, in which the servant who hid his talent in the ground and did nothing about it was rebuked as 'wicked and slothful' and cast into 'the outer darkness: there men will weep and gnash their teeth'.[48] Talents, whether in the contemporary sense of natural endowment or the archaic sense of monetary wealth, ought to be multiplied in the world — not for the pleasure of the self, but for the greater glory of God. In this way, industry intersected with frugality, for frugality was the sign that the achievement was not for the pleasure of the flesh but solely for the glory of God. As industry stripped life of idleness, frugality stripped life of self-indulgence. Industry called for the intensification of labor, but frugality prohibited the consumption of the fruits of one's labor. Just as under the monastic ideal, wealth accumulated in the monastery, so under the monastic ideal writ large, capital accumulated in the world.

The Protestant virtue of frugality replaced the Catholic virtue of poverty. For Catholics, the virtue of poverty was closely linked to the work of charity. Poverty was spiritually fruitful because, when undertaken voluntarily, its asceticism conferred spiritual benefits upon its practitioners; however, even when it was involuntary, it nonetheless provided an opportunity for the well-to-do to help the poor and thereby accumulate works of charity.[49] Mendicant and itinerant friars, whose poverty was voluntary and whose lives and livelihood relied on charity, played an important role in the Catholic spiritual economy. The Catholic spiritual economy, of which the friars were an integral part, crashed when the Protestants rejected the salvific effect of works of charity in favor of *sola fide*, justification by faith alone. The doctrine rejected both 'the spiritual idealization of poverty' and 'the spiritual efficaciousness of charity'.[50] Poverty, whether voluntary or not, imposed a burden on the community, which did more harm than good. In fact, it did not do anyone any good. Protestants looked upon mendicancy with disdain. Mendicancy became indistinguishable from vagrancy; and mendicants were

---

[47] Weber, *Protestant Ethic*, 104.
[48] Gospel of Matthew 25:14–30.
[49] Witte, *Law and Protestantism*, 20.
[50] Witte, *Law and Protestantism*, 20.

no better than vagrants and vagabonds. Beggars became an eyesore, and begging was banned. For the Protestants, what was virtuous was not poverty, but frugality. The Protestants promoted the value of self-sufficiency coupled with modesty. Everyone should have a job and do it well. In other words, everyone should be respectably middle class. Mandatory education for all children became the means to create this new class of productive Protestants. The new compulsory school curriculum combined biblical teaching with vocational training. The purpose of education was directed to preparing each and every Christian to fulfill their respective calling in the world – to get a job.[51]

In contrast to ancient and medieval Christianity, whose model of the perfect Christian was, successively, the martyr, the hermit and the monk, the model of the perfect Christian in reformed Christianity was 'the sober, middle-class, self-made man'.[52] The world was to be the new site of the monastic ideal. 'The Protestant ethic represented both a transformation and an extension of medieval monasticism: it carried asceticism out of monastic cells into everyday life'.[53] Instead of a small spiritual elite pursuing the monastic ideal within the confines of monasteries, the Protestant ethic required everyone to pursue the monastic ideal within the confines of their everyday jobs. The lay faithful could no longer rely on the consecrated order for spiritual graces, and the consecrated order could no longer rely on the lay faithful for material donations. Every Christian was responsible for his or her own livelihood in this world and for salvation in the afterworld. All and sundry had to live a life of *ora et labora*. This expansion of the monastic ideal led to the re-evaluation of law, love and freedom in the life of the individual and the ordering of the society.

At the level of the individual, the totalitarian demands of monastic life were extended to everyone: what was demanded of all believers was no longer 'single good works, but a life of good works combined into a unified system ... at every moment and in every action'.[54] The Catholic theology of good *works* was transformed into the Protestant theory of good *work*: the Protestants 'discovered in work the primary and elemental form of social discipline, the key to order, and the foundation of all further morality'.[55] Continuous control had to be exercised over the whole of one's life. This systematic control was in contrast to the leniency that was permitted to the Catholic laity. The laity was permitted laxity. For the Catholic laity, there was 'the very human Catholic cycle of sin, repentance, atonement, release,

[51] Witte, *Law and Protestantism*, 19.
[52] Weber, *Protestant Ethic*, 109.
[53] Silber, 'Monasticism and the Protestant Ethic', 105.
[54] Weber, *Protestant Ethic*, 71.
[55] Walzer, *The Revolution of the Saints*, 211.

followed by renewed sin',[56] mediated through the sacraments and the intercession of saints. The sacrament of confession, in particular, provided the Catholic laity with a safety valve to get periodic spiritual release from sin, coupled with psychological release from guilt. With the abolition of the sacrament of confession in the Reformation, reformed Christians would be permitted no such laxity. Like the monks before them, their practice was severe and spirit strict. We have come full circle here. Hermits began by withdrawing from the world into solitude, before they were cloistered together as monks in monasteries, thus giving rise to the monastic ideal. With the Reformation, the monastic ideal finally returned to the world, from which the hermits first fled. Just as Luther left the monastery to go into the world, so the monastic ideal 'strode into the marketplace of life, slammed the door of the monastery behind it, and undertook to penetrate just that daily routine of life with its methodicalness, to fashion it into a life in the world, but neither of nor for this world'.[57]

The return to the world was not the only full circle that the Reformation effectuated. The other full circle was the role of the law in the life of the believer. The first in the Judeo–Christian tradition who most acutely and accurately perceived the possibility of hallowing everyday life through obedience to the law was the Pharisee. The Pharisee prescribed 'a way of living the law which thoroughly permeated the details of everyday life'.[58] In this regard, the Pharisee was merely being faithful to the covenant between God and Israel, and working out the covenantal logic to its inexorable conclusion. Later Puritans such as the Calvinists, in contrast to the earlier Protestants, were particularly drawn to the religious life of the ancient Israelites in the Old Testament. As Protestantism developed into Puritanism, there was a return to law. In contrast to Luther's Protestantism, Calvin's Puritanism, as the second generation of Protestantism, tended to be more 'practical and social, programmatic and organizational', with a focus on 'covenants, assemblies, congregations and holy commonwealths'.[59] In the early heady days of Protestant defiance against Rome, it was easy for the Protestants to be swept up in the radical rhetoric of eradicating ecclesiastical law, but once they regained their composure, they soon realized that they needed law.[60] Law was necessary to control one's impulses and order one's life. The ordering of life required the authority of law.

[56] Weber, *Protestant Ethic*, 71.
[57] Weber, *Protestant Ethic*, 39.
[58] Taylor, *Sources of the Self*, 221.
[59] Walzer, *The Revolution of the Saints*, 26.
[60] Witte, *Law and Protestantism*, 23.

The authority of law was not only needed to order an individual's life; it was also needed to order the social life of whole communities who were dedicated to this new brand of reformed Christianity. The Puritan reformers wanted to reform, not only the self, but also society. Everything, including human society, exists for the greater glory of God; and God wills that 'social life shall be organized according to His commandment'.[61] In the recitation of the Lord's Prayer, the Christian prays for His will to 'be done on earth as it is in heaven'. Hence, it is the duty of the Christian to order this world according to the divine will. A Christian society is an orderly society. Even the unbeliever has to be ordered, for disorder 'continuously stinks in God's nostrils'.[62] A state of disorder is one in which 'licentious desires and the hold of intemperate practices make impossible all discipline and steadiness of life'.[63] Disorder is the heart of darkness. When staring at disorder, the Puritan could only exclaim what Kurtz exclaims in the Heart of Darkness: 'The horror!' Order had to be imposed. How? Law! Hence, 'all the more emphasis was placed on those parts of the Old Testament which praise formal legality as a sign of conduct pleasing to God'.[64] The Puritans identified themselves as the people of God's law: 'They could as a people feel constituted by God's law, exactly like the people portrayed in the Old Testament, just because they felt so strongly the imperative to rectify the disorder in the world'.[65]

For the Puritans, the Bible contains 'the best summary of natural law' and provides 'the surest guide for positive law'.[66] Protestant jurists adopted and adapted the Ten Commandments in the Bible as the jurisprudential framework for organizing and structuring the content of various substantive areas of positive law, such that each Commandment would act as the foundation for an area of law. For example, the Commandment 'Thou shalt not steal' was the foundation of the law of property; the Commandment 'Thou shalt not bear false witness' was the foundation of the law of evidence; and so on. As the church on earth consists of both saints and sinners, the law is needed to educate the saint and coerce the sinner.[67] The intermingling of saints and sinners is further complicated by the fact that no one actually knows whether he or she is a saint or a sinner, for 'the more a person thinks himself a saint, the more sinful he in fact becomes', and 'the more a person thinks herself a sinner,

---

[61] Weber, *Protestant Ethic*, 64.
[62] Taylor, *Sources of the Self*, 228.
[63] Taylor, *Sources of the Self*, 229.
[64] Weber, *Protestant Ethic*, 110.
[65] Taylor, *Sources of the Self*, 230.
[66] Witte, *Law and Protestantism*, 10.
[67] Witte, *Law and Protestantism*, 11.

the more saintly she in fact becomes'.[68] In present-day jurisprudential terms, one could say that the law is needed for Holmes's bad person,[69] Raz's good person[70] and Hart's puzzled person.[71] All stand in need for the kind of order and regularity that only the authority of law can bring.

The disciplined form of life was the Puritan's response to the reality of the Fall. Their pious rigor and routine stopped the slide into evil and injected a sense of order into their lives. The Fall brought terror into human lives. It made humans anxious and restless. If the flaw which led to the Fall was disobedience, then its remedy must surely lie in obedience, perfect obedience. If the fault of Adam and Eve was unrestrained desire for the forbidden fruit, then its antidote must surely be restraint, absolute restraint. That was the reason why God gave the ancient Israelites the Ten Commandments. In order to restore the human community to the bond of fellowship with one another and with God, what is required is not only moral will, but also political will, for what is needed is nothing less than a complete legal order. Hence, the centrality of the covenant in constituting the holy commonwealth, for the covenant brings control and consolation to the community. Entering into the covenant conveys to the members of the covenantal community the dual sense of choosing and being chosen, which implies that the required obedience and restraint is not only necessary, but also ultimately voluntary. However, the backhandedness of all this is that those who refuse to enter the covenant would have to be forced to do so nonetheless. In Rousseau's aphoristic phrase, they would have to be 'forced to be free'.

The high valuation placed on order by the Puritans matched that of the monks. The difference was that the Puritanical order was not limited to a cloistered community, but extended to the community at large. Like the monks, the Puritans placed a similarly high value on law as a mode of authority to preserve order. There would be freedom under law, not because individuals would be independent to pursue what they wanted, but because individuals would identify with the communal order as a manifestation of divine will and see their place within it. It would be a collective form of freedom born out of an intense identification with the collective. Just as monks constantly lived under the gaze of other monks, in many Puritan communities, neighbors constantly lived under the gaze of other neighbors. The world became a monastery. I would obey the law because that was how I expressed

---

[68] Witte, *God's Joust, God's Justice*, 54.
[69] Holmes, 'The Path of the Law', 459.
[70] The good person would be a member of Raz's society of angels: Raz, *Practical Reason and Norms*, 159.
[71] Hart, *The Concept of Law*, 39–40.

love for my neighbors, and that was how I could become one with the community of the saved. The community, of course, consisted of the saved and the damned, but everyone wanted to think, wishfully, that they belonged to the community of the saved. Such a community could be, and many were, intolerant of differences, with occasional hysterical outbursts against perceived deviance, the most notorious of which were the Salem witchcraft trials. As dubious as they might sound to us today, the Salem trials were legal trials, held in open court.[72]

The Salem witchcraft trials were a dramatic example of the moral panic that gripped the covenantal community. The Puritans saw the work of the devil everywhere. The paranoia justified, all the more, the need for discipline and order: 'the chain of being had been transformed into a chain of command'.[73] The covenant combined command and consent, God's willfulness and human willingness, God's sovereign will and human's willing obedience, which bound the covenantal community together more tightly than ever before.[74] Just as the monks were monitored in a system of mutual surveillance, so the Puritans were kept track of in a system of collective watchfulness: 'the admonitions of the brethren were anxious, insistent, continuous', for 'they felt themselves to be living in an age of chaos and crime and sought to train their conscience to be permanently on guard'.[75]

This development of Protestantism into Puritanism might seem ironic in a reform movement which started with the pitting of law against faith, and called for the setting aside of salvation by law in favor of salvation by faith alone. This ironic development is notable for two reasons. First, it shows how the place of law in religious life remained as much an unresolved question for the reformers as it was for Paul. Second, it shows how, the more things change, the more they stay the same. Paul reacted against the legalism of the Pharisees. In working out the Pauline puzzle, the monks returned to the law as part of the monastic ideal. From the Pharisees to Paul to the monastic ideal, the law came full circle. Luther reacted against the legalism of the Papists. In working out the Lutheran puzzle, the Calvinists returned to the law as part of the Protestant ethic. From the Papists to Luther to the Protestant ethic, which was really the monastic ideal writ large, the law again came full circle.

---

[72] Baker, *A Storm of Witchcraft: The Salem Trials and the American Experience*.
[73] Walzer, *The Revolution of the Saints*, 166.
[74] Walzer, *The Revolution of the Saints*, 167.
[75] Walzer, *The Revolution of the Saints*, 301.

FROM PURITANISM TO (AMERICAN) CONSTITUTIONALISM

The reformers carried the monastic ideal from the monasteries into the world. In structuring their societies in the world, they brought the same ideal into their project of modern constitutionalism. There have been numerous studies on what makes constitutionalism work. Many stars have to align in order for it to work, but I will just focus on one factor here. To find out what makes constitutionalism work, we need to find out what makes the people tick. Constitutionalism requires fidelity to the constitution. We need to find out what makes the people tick, such that they will stick to the constitution through thick and thin. At bottom, 'fidelity *to* the Constitution requires faith *in* the Constitution'.[76] Faith, here as in elsewhere, can be argued for, but cannot be proven.[77] How, then, is such a faith engendered or engineered in the subject? We need to consider the position of the person subject to the constitutional order, and the frame of mind and mode of life that is required of that person. It is an inquiry into the constitutional ideal from the perspective of the constitutional subject. The claim that I want to advance here is that the constitutional ideal is, at least partly, shaped by the monastic ideal.

A creation myth is an imaginative reconstruction of the natural state, while a national myth is a reconstruction of the political state. Mythology allows for worldly history to be recast in cosmic terms. The function of myths is not so much logical as it is typological. Myths do not describe reality; rather, they transfigure reality to provide 'moral and spiritual meaning to individuals or societies'.[78] Mythological and historical narratives work together to provide the moral framework for constitutionalism. The American constitutional experiment supplies the paradigmatic example of how mythological and historical narratives could be brought together to create a moral vision for the constitutional project. The early settlers and later revolutionaries viewed their political history as an extension of the biblical story, and their constitutional project as nothing less than covenantal. The Edenic narrative opens with, 'In the beginning ... '[79] According to Locke, 'In the beginning, all the world was America'.[80] In America, the early settlers found a state of nature to begin anew and start afresh.

'America came to be thought of as a *paradise* and a *wilderness* with all of the rich associations of those terms in Christian and biblical traditions'.[81] The ancient

---

[76] Balkin, *Constitutional Redemption*, 2.
[77] Balkin, *Constitutional Redemption*, 6.
[78] Bellah, *The Broken Covenant*, 3.
[79] Book of Genesis 1:1.
[80] Locke, *The Second Treatise of Government*, §49.
[81] Bellah, *The Broken Covenant*, 6.

Israelites journeyed through the *wilderness* to reach the *paradise* of the Promised Land, promised pursuant to a covenant. The hermits withdrew into the *wilderness*, while the monks created a cloistered *paradise*. Hermits withdrew into the *wilderness* to experience an individual conversion, while monks created the cloistered *paradise* to establish a collective form of life. The transition from eremitism to cenobitism was a move from the individual to the collective, from the personal body to the body politic. Individual conversion and collective covenant work hand in glove.[82] The experience of conversion needs to be stabilized through a covenant, just as the result of revolution has to be entrenched through a constitution. The move from conversion to covenant in the religious domain mirrors the move from revolution to constitution in the political domain. If conversion and revolution are about breaking away from the past, then covenant and constitution are about securing the future. The future could only be secured – the experience of conversion stabilized and the result of revolution entrenched – through the kind of institutionalization that a constitutional order provides.

The opening words of the American constitution begin by creating a trans-temporal and trans-generational subject called 'We the People', bound not by blood or kinship, but by a vision of the constitutional order. 'We the People' exists in the mind's eye, which is the most important sight of all. The People is singular and elastic: it extends back in time to the foundational moment, and it is projected into the indefinite future till the end of time. The People is the self in self-government. The People, as a single entity, has a changing composition, as each generation succeeds another across time. Hence, 'to participate in constitutional governance is to participate in an intergenerational project'.[83] The constitutional project transforms individual selves into a collective self, and disparate persons into a people. Without this affective and effective transformation, there is no self in self-government. For constitutionalism to work, the individual I have to identify with the collective We. Accomplishing this feat is no easy task.

The ideology of Puritanism helped to accomplish this constitutional feat in America. The Puritans in the New World, especially in New England, saw themselves as God's new chosen people, just as the ancient Israelites were God's old chosen people. They were part of God's plan in the history of the world, in the journey from the cosmological beginning to the eschatological end. They saw themselves as being called by God to be 'a city on the hill', 'a light to the nations', and 'a model of Christ's kingdom among the heathens'.[84]

---

[82] Bellah, *The Broken Covenant*, 19.
[83] Kahn, *Legitimacy and History*, 4.
[84] Winthrop, 'A Model of Christian Charity', 75, 93; Scottow, 'Narrative of the Planning of Massachusetts', 4:279.

This mission was a matter of life and death: God had promised them peace and prosperity if they succeeded in their covenantal task; death and damnation if they failed.[85] In the immediate aftermath of the Revolution, the cultural image of Puritanism in New England came to dominate the construction of the new American national identity.[86] After the chaotic revolutionary years, the Puritanism of New England provided a vision of stability, regularity and order, with its emphasis on 'self-restraint and attention to duty'.[87] The Puritans of Massachusetts, for example, were often contrasted with the Virginians. In contrast to the self-interested Virginians who migrated to the New World to amass private wealth, the Puritans of Massachusetts migrated to the New World to create the new and true Christian commonwealth. While the Virginians descended into 'disorder and misrule' and 'dissolved into every irregularity of life',[88] the Puritans of Massachusetts led well-ordered lives, even in the face of trials and tribulations. To keep the faith, they 'suffered hardship and braved death'.[89] The Puritans wanted to create a truly new world in the New World. This vision of the brave new world began as a theological idea, which grew into a political ideology, and crystallized into constitutional form.

The Puritans of Massachusetts created a commonwealth, whose constitution states that the people 'form themselves into a free, sovereign, and independent body politic, or state by the name of the Commonwealth of Massachusetts'.[90] The commonwealth is simultaneously a physical place and a moral space, with physical borders and moral boundaries. While the commonwealth is located in a specific place, it must 'transcend place if it is to constitute itself as a self-sufficient or sovereign juridical structure'.[91] The complex moral world of the commonwealth is built on a structure of law, for 'the primary way in which the commonwealth commands its subjects is through the medium of law'.[92] The law of the commonwealth is not the law of an unruly mob, but the law of a unified body. Civil law unifies the civic body. One is a member of the civic body in virtue of being absorbed into it by its laws. Unlike slaves, members of the civic union are 'bound not by physical chains but by law'.[93] The former is the paradigm of the unfree, while the latter is the paragon of freedom.

[85] Witte, *God's Joust, God's Justice*, 152.
[86] Adams, *The Specter of Salem*, 44.
[87] Adams, *The Specter of Salem*, 45.
[88] Adams, *The Specter of Salem*, 52.
[89] Adams, *The Specter of Salem*, 54.
[90] *Constitution of Massachusetts 1780*, Part the Second.
[91] Brett, *Changes of State*, 7.
[92] Brett, *Changes of State*, 142.
[93] Brett, *Changes of State*, 143.

The New England Puritans placed covenantalism at the heart of their theology. Their theology fitted God's word into a covenantal framework. Logos became nomos. The covenant was God's special constitution for his chosen people. It defined 'each person's role in the unfolding of God's providential plan', thereby creating 'the conditions for perfect communion with God and perfect community among persons'.[94] The covenant bound both parties: God and the people. Each had to keep its side of the bargain. The divine, no less than the human, had to fulfill its covenanted obligation. Human worship was offered in exchange for divine protection. The Puritan covenantal theology transformed God's gift of grace into a bargained contract, and God's covenantal faithfulness into a contractual obligation.[95] Having secured covenantalism in the theological sphere, the Puritans extended it to cover the political sphere as well. In the political sphere, covenantalism morphed into constitutionalism. The ancient covenant re-emerged as the modern constitution. The covenantal logic would govern both divine and human relations. From the legalistic foundation of the covenant, the Puritans constructed, not only a theology, but also a political theory, which should more properly be called a political theology.

The Puritans entered into covenants with one another and with God to constitute their communities. Theirs was a covenanted constitutional community. The covenants dictated the terms of their relationships with one another in their polity and with God in their destiny. The covenants, however, needed to be enforced. The enforcement of the covenants required the force of law in a communal setting. Just as, in the earlier centuries, the cenobitic monks were suspicious of the eremitic hermits, so the intensely communal Puritan communities were suspicious of individuals who were not rooted in any community. No human is an island, and no person should be a law unto himself or herself. Just as a monk needed a monastic community, so a puritan needed a puritanical community. Both the monastic community and the puritanical community were extremely nomian communities. They lived their lives according to law, including highly intrusive laws. For the Puritans, this form of social control was born of both 'human necessity and divine destiny': every person should belong to a family, a church and a polity, for 'every person needs the association of others to exhort, minister, and rule with law and with love'.[96] The strictures of positive law are required to enforce the structures of natural law.

---

[94] Witte, *God's Joust, God's Justice*, 145.
[95] Witte, *God's Joust, God's Justice*, 147.
[96] Witte, *The Reformation of Rights*, 15, 295.

Puritan communities were subject to heavy regulation and tight control. They needed to keep an eye on one another in order to ensure that their community as a whole was pleasing to God, for nothing less than their salvation depended on that. Their social covenant with one another was bound up with their divine covenant with God. The covenant with God required them to reform and restructure their society in line with the terms of the divine compact. It required them to live their lives and carry themselves in a certain way. Their social covenant with one another was a means of fulfilling their divine covenant with God, by creating institutions that comported with the divine compact. The terms of the covenants endowed a multitude of mundane matters with cosmic significance. Like the medieval monks before them, 'the New England Puritans devised elaborate legal codes and subjected the most minute detail of daily affairs to close statutory regulation'.[97] The covenants placed 'each community under a solemn divine probation' and rendered them 'instruments of God's providential plan': consequently, 'for them to be lax in zeal, loose in discipline, or sumptuous in living' would be a breach of both the divine and the social covenants.[98]

The Puritan theology of covenantalism was carried over into the American theory of constitutionalism. It was carried over, not in its original form, but in a vestigial form: republican writers 'transformed the Puritan idea of the elect nation into a revolutionary theory of American nationalism', and 'recast the Puritan ideal of the covenant community into a theory of public virtue, discipline, and order'.[99] John Adams, the Massachusetts lawyer who later became American President, considered the Puritans to be 'illustrious patriots', and embedded 'some of this early Puritan covenantal theory into the 1780 Massachusetts Constitution, which he drafted and defended at great length'.[100] Following the American Revolution, these Puritan-inspired institutions grew into full-fledged state and federal institutions within the new constitutional republic. The American experiment in constitutionalism 'points back directly to its puritanical origin', and as with many other supposedly modern political innovations, this piece of innovation too is really 'the modern political fruits of ancient religious beliefs'.[101]

Just as Puritan covenantalism was carried over into American constitutionalism, so the Puritan vision of the equality of all believers was carried over into the American dream of the equality of all citizens. In the religious realm, the

[97] Witte, *Reformation of Rights*, 317.
[98] Witte, *God's Joust, God's Justice*, 153–4.
[99] Witte, *Reformation of Rights*, 18.
[100] Witte, *Reformation of Rights*, 277–8.
[101] Witte, *Reformation of Rights*, 326, 335.

Puritan reformers flattened the religious world by demolishing the higher forms of life and collapsing them into ordinary life. In the political realm, the American revolutionaries carried out an analogous flattening of social hierarchies. When the Puritans became Americans, they carried the same zeal from Reformation to Revolution. The political aristocracy of the old world that the American revolutionaries overthrew was parallel to the spiritual aristocracy that the Puritan reformers overthrew earlier. When the American revolutionaries rebelled against the monarchy, they were rebelling against, not only the king per se, but also an entire 'form of governance and structure of social relations', in which 'the king sat at the top of an elaborate system of social hierarchy with intricate gradations of social rank'.[102] The revolutionaries flattened this social hierarchy by establishing, however imperfectly at first, 'a new realm of republican citizens, who recognized no king or nobility, but who were equal in political and social rank'.[103] American constitutional discourse is, to this day, still working out the full implications of this flattening of social hierarchy and the associated commitment to radical equality. Think, for example, of the recent constitutional controversies regarding blacks, women and gay people.

The revolutionaries created this brave new world of equal subjects under the rule of law, with the Constitution as the supreme law. Both the American revolutionaries and the Protestant reformers created societies of the book, of the Constitution and the Bible respectively. In both cases, the 'highest law is found in a historically given text'.[104] The text is the be all and end all. All actions have to be sanctioned by the text. Citizens and Christians swear to uphold the sanctity of their foundational texts, sometimes to the point of death. Hence, interpretive disagreements in law and religion always carry within them the potential of erupting into violence, the bloodiest of which are full-blown civil and religious wars. The intensity of these interpretive disputes is partially attributable to the two types of questions that citizens and religious believers ask of themselves: what is true *of* the text and how can they be true *to* the text? Applying Taylor's terminology, religious believers achieve 'fullness' through a religious text that points toward the transcendental truth of the rule of God, while citizens in a constitutional state achieve 'fullness' through a legal text which points to the immanent truth of the rule of law.[105] The Constitution transforms disparate individuals into citizens,

---

[102] Balkin, *Constitutional Redemption*, 21.
[103] Balkin, *Constitutional Redemption*, 21.
[104] Kahn, *Legitimacy and History*, 1.
[105] Taylor defines 'fullness' as follows: 'We all see our lives, and/or the space wherein we live our lives, as having a certain moral/spiritual shape. Somewhere, in some activity, or condition,

a sovereign people in a sovereign state. The Bible transforms mere mortals into a people of God, a people set apart, whether as 'the house of Israel' in the Hebrew Bible or 'the body of Christ' in the Christian Bible. In that transformation, the individual achieves a sense of 'fullness' by becoming a part of a larger whole, of something greater than themselves. Hence, any threat to the text, or their understanding of the text, is a threat to their individual and collective identity, their source of 'fullness'. In biblical and constitutional disputes, the stakes are high.[106]

Just as the Bible defines the Puritan, so the Constitution defines the American. Submission to its law marks one as a member of the community. By submitting myself to the Constitution, I become a part of the constitutional community of the modern state, just as submission to the law of Moses made a person a part of the covenantal community of ancient Israel. Law leads to love as union with my fellow citizens today, my predecessors in the past and my successors in the future. We become one across time. Submission to the same law allows 'people to see the actions and the ambitions, the hopes and the achievements, of people who lived long ago as their actions and ambitions, as their hopes and achievements', just as 'in the Passover Seder, Jews living today tell themselves that *they* were slaves in Egypt, that God brought *them* forth from the house of bondage'.[107] A similar sentiment is expressed when Americans living today speak of *their* constitution, and tell themselves how, through *their* constitution, *they* are creating a more perfect union with the progressive inclusion of blacks, women and gay people as equal members of 'We the People'. If you identify with the law in this way, you have achieved freedom through identification. The law lives in you, and you in the law. I do not mean this statement to sound unnecessarily mystical and mysterious. What I mean here is simply that the law is part of how you experience the world and conduct yourself in the world; hence you live in the law. Conversely, you also feel that you have a say in the law, and you are committed to upholding it and making it work; hence the law lives in you. Law thus

---

lies a fullness, a richness; that is, in that place (activity or condition), life is fuller, richer, deeper, more worthwhile, more admirable, more than what it should be. This is perhaps a place of power: we often experience this as deeply moving, as inspiring': Taylor, *A Secular Age*, 5.

[106] There is, of course, the question of authoritativeness: who is to say, finally if not infallibly, what the text means. In the domain of biblical interpretation in the Catholic Church, the answer is the Pope. In the domain of constitutional interpretation in the United States, the answer is the Supreme Court. For a fuller exploration of these issues, see Neoh, 'Text, Doctrine and Tradition in Law and Religion', 175.

[107] Balkin, *Constitutional Redemption*, 31.

becomes for you a way of life, freely chosen and freely lived. Free because you identify with it.

The modern legal order requires of its subjects a great deal of 'voluntary subjection and self-control'.[108] Today, the disciplined subject is assumed as a given, and its long and checkered history forgotten. However, it was not a given. The disciplined subject was created through a long and laborious process, stretching from monasticism to Puritanism. What the monks did in the cloister the Puritans did out in the open. What the Puritans required of the Christian would later be required of the citizen: 'the same sense of civic virtue, of discipline and duty', based upon the novel view of 'politics as a kind of conscientious and continuous labour' to create the holy commonwealth.[109] The monks and Puritans rejected the laxness of the fallen world in favor of a systematic and methodical existence, which required the continuous exercise of control over the self. The effort, initially confined to monks in monasteries, later expanded to entire congregations, and eventually to whole populations. The vision of the utopian elite became generalized. Once the habit of self-control was inculcated and firmly entrenched, the sense of moral urgency faded, and the existence of the disciplined subject of the modern legal order is taken for granted. The time for Puritanism might be over, but its legacy lives on. Just as Puritanism overthrew monasticism, so secularism overthrew Puritanism. The son might have killed the father, but as is often the case, the spirit of the father lives on in the son.

LAW, LOVE AND FREEDOM FROM MONASTICISM TO CONSTITUTIONALISM

The monastic-turned-constitutional ideal unites *law as authority* with *love as union* and *freedom as identification*. It brings together one half of the bipolarity of law, love and freedom that was laid out in Chapter 2. From this configuration of values, we can make three claims about the linkages of these values.

First, law constitutes freedom. Law as authority constitutes freedom as identification. According to Finnis, the central case of law is the law 'of a complete community, purporting to have authority to provide comprehensive and supreme direction for human behaviour in that community'.[110] Authority is 'required for the realization of the common good'.[111] Authority is

---

[108] Walzer, *The Revolution of the Saints*, 302.
[109] Walzer, *The Revolution of the Saints*, 2.
[110] Finnis, *Natural Law and Natural Rights*, 260.
[111] Finnis, *Natural Law and Natural Rights*, 246.

necessary to realize the common good in a common life. Law provides a source of authority, with which one can identify, and to which one can submit. Freedom is to be found in identification with the law, under whose authority one submits. True freedom is freedom under law. The content of the law may differ, but the idea stays the same. Before Paul, the Pharisees advocated this idea in relation to the law of Moses. After Paul, the monks advocated this idea in relation to monastic law; the Puritans advocated it in relation to biblical law; and the constitutionalists advocated it in relation to constitutional law.

The monks and the Puritans 'admitted as compatible with this collective freedom the complete subjection of the individual to the authority of the community'.[112] Not much importance is accorded to individual independence: the monk is absorbed entirely into the monastic community and the Puritan into the puritanical community. To participate in these forms of life, the individual has to con-form. What is required to attain this sort of freedom is an identification of the self with elements outside the individual self. For the solitary self to escape its solitude, the self has to identify with the collective law, whether the collective law is Mosaic or monastic, covenantal or constitutional. Identification expands the boundary of the self. Identification brings the hitherto external object into the orbit of the self. If I identify with something, that thing becomes a part of who I am. 'An act is free if the agent identifies with the elements from which it flows', for 'freedom is the acting out of that identity'.[113] Where there is identification, there is freedom. It is in this sense that one could say that the Pharisees and the Puritans are, in their own way and through their own forms of identification, free.

Under this ideal of freedom as identification, freedom is attained, not by escaping from authority, but by identifying with it and integrating oneself into it. It is attained by making the external world 'part of oneself, no longer alien [or] obstructive, no longer a frontier [or] a field of force which hems one in'.[114] For freedom consists in one's ability for self-expression, and one's self-expression is the expression of one's identity, that is, one's identifications. It is the freedom to express oneself within a form of life, under the law appropriate to that form of life. Monastic law defines the monastic form of life, just as constitutional law defines the constitutional form of government. Within a particular form of life, one could still be free even if someone else makes the decision on the direction of one's life, so long as one identifies with

---

[112] Constant, 'The Liberty of the Ancients Compared with that of the Moderns', 311.
[113] Bergmann, *On Being Free*, 37.
[114] Berlin, 'Two Concepts of Freedom: Romantic and Liberal', 184.

the person or process that stands behind the decision. A monk or a citizen could still be free even if they are bound by the decision of the monastic abbot or the constitutional court, so long as the monk or the citizen identifies with the monastic law or the constitutional law that justifies the exercise of authority by the abbot or the court. To be free is to identify with a certain kind of moral order.

Obedience to the authority of law is demanding. It requires citizens to renounce at least some of their desires and control their impulses in order to act in conformity to the requirements of the law. It demands discipline. In despotism, the demand is enforced coercively. The discipline that would have been imposed coercively under despotism would have to be self-imposed in a free society: the despotic coercion would have to be replaced with 'a willing identification with the polis on the part of the citizens, a sense that the political institutions in which they live are an expression of themselves' and are 'extensions of themselves'.[115] In identifying with the authority of law, the individual self identifies with the whole, such that each becomes an indivisible part of the whole. In this regard, the Puritans and the Pharisees, the monks and the constitutionalists, are like Berlin's musician. In a concert, the musician identifies, not only with the symphony, but also with the orchestra: 'the more undeviating the adherence to the rules for concerted playing, the more fully satisfied the players feel, the fewer obstacles at that moment do they find in the universe about them'.[116] By being absorbed in and by the performance, the musician becomes part of the whole, and there is music in the air.

Second, love is impossible without law. Love as union is impossible without law as authority. Law unites us in a common life, without which we run the risk of reverting to fighting each other in the Hobbesian state of nature. A common life is impossible without a common law. As the Puritans never ceased to remind themselves, humans are fallen. Like Hobbes, the Puritans were wont to emphasize the depravity of humanity. The Hobbesian state of nature is a fallen world. The humans in that world are quarrelsome. The Hobbesian state of nature is a world where interpersonal feud could easily turn bloody, with one son, Cain, killing another, Abel. To attain peace, we need to get out of this deplorable condition. Hobbes's solution lies in the creation of a common, coercive, compelling power that could rule with authority. The authoritative ruler is known idiomatically as the Leviathan, but is technically called the sovereign. Chapter 1 has painted the picture of the Hobbesian state of nature in relative detail, and Chapter 2 has

---

[115] Taylor, 'Cross-Purposes: The Liberal-Communitarian Debate', 165, 171.
[116] Berlin, 'Two Concepts of Freedom: Romantic and Liberal', 185.

shown a close connection between the institution of law and the creation of the Leviathan. I shall not repeat those arguments here. Suffice it to say that, emerging from the state of nature into the state of civil society, law saves us from ourselves. Without the authority of law, we would be at the constant risk of collapsing back into the state of nature, where no humane relationships could ever survive, let alone relationships of love. Law stabilizes social relations. Law as authority makes the condition of love as union possible.

Law does not just enable love; law itself may be an expression of love. Submission to the authority of law may, itself, be an expression of love as union. The Puritans knew this; the monks before them knew it too. The expression of love through submission to law works vertically in one's relation with God as well as horizontally in one's relation with one another. Submission to the law of God is central to the love of God. Loving God involves absolute submission to his will, as embodied in his law, or in the Puritan's case, in the divine covenant. To love God is to 'cling to him',[117] even if it requires the killing of one's son, as demonstrated in Abraham's sacrifice of Isaac.[118] The love of God – the desire to be one with him – supplies the motivation for obedience. 'If you love me', says Jesus, 'you will keep my commandments'.[119] By obeying God's law, the human subject becomes one in mind and heart with the divine lawgiver. Hence, the monks could say with Paul, 'It is no longer I who live, but Christ who lives in me'.[120]

The expression of love through submission to law works horizontally, too, in one's relation with one another. For the Puritans, the horizontal logic of law and love works through the social covenant. It was this logic that was subsequently carried over from covenantalism to constitutionalism, for the operation of this logic does not necessarily rely on God. Submission to the authority of law is an expression of the love of neighbor, whether the neighbor is the fellow monk who lives in the next cell, or the fellow believer who lives down the street, or the fellow citizen who lives across the continent. The authority of law unites individuals and binds them together, as a community of monks, or a community of the elect, or a community of citizens. Submission to the authority of law is an expression of civic friendship. In a complex society with its coordination problems, the only way of expressing the love of neighbor is through obedience to the authoritative plan for the common good, which we call law. Law is needed for the pursuit of the common good, within which

---

[117] Arendt, *Love and Saint Augustine*, 19.
[118] Neoh, 'Law and Love in Abraham's Binding of Isaac', 237.
[119] Gospel of John 14:15.
[120] Letter to the Galatians 2:20.

individuals can pursue the good life. At times, I may disagree with the law, but in matters where a collective decision has to be made one way or another, my submission to the collective judgment as embodied in the law, in spite of my disagreement with it, is an expression of my desire to continue living with my fellow citizens in the one constitutional community. The authority of law gathers the multitude under a common plan.

Loving should not be confused with liking. I might not like what I love. Here, the experience of love is that of union. I could love my family, although I might not like them very much, which is not at all unusual. Analogously, a monk could love his fellow monks without necessarily liking them. In the context of the state, I may not know most of my fellow citizens, and may not like them when I do meet them, but love enters in 'because my bond to these people passes through our participation in a common political entity'.[121] The common political entity creates a we-identity that is more than the sum of you and me. It is a new identity, which creates matters of concern, not just for you and for me, but for us. In this respect, states are like families. Both are united in a common entity, and both experience love as union, which partially explains the traditional idea of the family as a microcosm of the state, and the nation as one big family. Although the family has been the dominant point of comparison with the state, one could draw a similar analogy between the state and the monastery to make the same point, just as Thomas More did in his Utopia, which was set in 'designed towns with ultra and pan-monastic structures in the middle of an Edenic countryside'.[122]

Third, love sets us free. Love as union sets us free, not as an individual, but as part of a larger whole. If I am of one mind and one heart with the collective, whatever the collective does, I do too. Hegel posits love as 'the dissolution of the opposition between self and other, so a finding of oneself in the other'.[123] Rawls points out that those who love acquire attachments, which enable them to overcome the 'separateness of persons and of the ends they pursue'.[124] Nozick argues that those who love are 'united to form and constitute a new entity in the world, what might be called a *we*'.[125] The union of love alters the constitution of the self to include the other. It unites 'the most radically separated beings, namely individual persons'.[126] Love unites individuals into a *we*, to create a *koinos bios*, a common life, either within the walls of the

---

[121] Taylor, 'Cross-Purposes: The Liberal-Communitarian Debate', 166.
[122] Seguy, 'A Sociology of Imagined Societies: Monasticism and Utopia', 302.
[123] Bernstein, 'Love and Law: Hegel's Critique of Morality', 415.
[124] Mendus, 'The Importance of Love in Rawls's Theory of Justice', 68.
[125] Nozick, 'Love's Bond', 418.
[126] Tillich, *Love, Power and Justice*, 26.

monastery or within the boundaries of the nation. It turns an individual into a monk in a monastic community and a citizen in a constitutional community.

Communal love could be directed toward one another or toward a common object of love. Augustine argues that it is both, but in a sequential manner. Although Augustine affirms the love that members of a community have toward one another, that love is a second step. The first step – the first love that founds a community – is not inward, but outward: it is directed, first, toward a common object of love.[127] According to Augustine, a community is 'a gathering of rational beings united in fellowship by a common agreement about the objects of its love'; hence, 'the better the objects of its united love, the better the people, and the worse the objects of its love, the worse the people'.[128] Love is that which 'unifies a multitude of human agents into a community of action and experience sustained over time', through which 'we become a "multitude" no longer, but a "people", capable of common action, susceptible to common suffering, participating in a common identity'.[129] A community comes into being through, and is sustained by, shared objects of love, and is to be evaluated in terms of the objects of its love. For our present purposes, the key point here is less about Augustine's portrayal of the two-stepped process in the formation of communal love than it is about the centrality of love overall in the formation of community.

Love is a motion toward the desired object, to become one with it.[130] Hence, love is both motion and emotion. Humans overcome their existential isolation through love, whether through the love of God or the love of the nation. To overcome its existential loneliness, the self desires to belong to something outside itself and become entirely absorbed by the object of love. It is in this sense of love as union that the monks and the Puritans could claim to be of one mind and heart with one another and with God. This view of love as union is of a piece with freedom as identification. One identifies with the object of love. There is a sense of wholeness – a merging of identity – with the object of love. By being in union with the whole, be it the monastery or the nation, there is freedom even in obedience. Out of love, I may have to deny a multitude of desires. I may be called upon to make numerous sacrifices. All these I will do happily if I am in love, that is, if I am one with the object of my love. I will identify with its cause in the most intimate way imaginable. Whatever

---

[127] O'Donovan, *Common Objects of Love*, 26.
[128] Augustine, *City of God*, Bk XIX, §24.
[129] O'Donovan, *Common Objects of Love*, 1, 21–2.
[130] Arendt, *Love and Saint Augustine*, 9.

sacrifices I make, whatever desires I deny, I do them freely. Without love, I am coerced. With love, I am free. Hence, love sets me free.

Rousseau famously asks us to identify, not with this-and-that will, but the General Will. The General Will is the 'common self', or *moi commun*, in which the self is 'inflated into some super-personal entity – a State, a class, a nation, or the march of history itself'.[131] In the *The Social Contract*, Rousseau uses the notion of the General Will to construct a form of association, in which one, while uniting with the whole, may still obey oneself alone.[132] The trick lies in the identification of the individual self with the whole community. Each becomes an indivisible part of the whole. Law, love and freedom transform disparate persons into a unified people. The composition of the people may change over time, but the people itself persist through time. The people are united by the authority of law, in a structure, whether state or monastery, which they identify with freely. The result is love as union, which holds the people together. Hence, 'we cannot understand the character of the relationship between self and polity without first understanding love'.[133] Love explains why a person is willing to die for the people. Just as Paul could say, 'it is no longer I who live, but Christ who lives in me',[134] so a citizen could say, 'it is no longer I who live, but the state that lives in me'. The state is not just about budgets and balance sheets; it is ultimately a matter of life and death. The state presents the citizen with a higher calling, in which the citizen may be asked to make the ultimate sacrifice. The social contract alone cannot explain this curious feature of political life. Here, we are not dealing with political bargain, but existential meaning. It is about what we will do for love. A citizen is willing to die for the state because the relationship between the self and the state is not contractual, but existential. The self and the state, the person and the polity, are united in love. Love cannot be relegated to the private domain, as some liberal theories are wont to do. Love is public, through and through, not least because it is love that holds the public sphere together. Love defines a political community, which demarcates the jurisdiction of law. So law, love and freedom abide, these three; but the greatest of these is love.

---

[131] Berlin, 'Two Concepts of Liberty', 134.
[132] Rousseau, *Social Contract*, Bk 1, ch 6.
[133] Kahn, *Putting Liberalism in Its Place*, 9.
[134] Letter to the Galatians 2:20.

5

Counter Narrative: From Antinomianism to Anarchism

The bipolarity within law, love and freedom that was left unresolved by Paul produced a fork in the road: one path leads from monasticism to constitutionalism and the other leads from antinomianism to anarchism. The former creates a form of life that combines law as authority, love as union and freedom as identification; while the latter creates a form of life that combines law as resistance, love as attention and freedom as independence. The former constructs an ordered form of life, against which the latter reacts. Hence, the former is the prior narrative, while the latter is the counter narrative. Having charted the first path in the preceding chapter, this chapter will chart the second path. As with the first path, Paul will, again, be the starting point and the Reformation the turning point in the story.

PAUL AND THE ANTINOMIAN IDEAL

Standing at the cusp of the Judeo–Christian tradition, Paul struggled to articulate the relationship between Jewish law and Christian love for his new Christian community. In his Letter to the Romans, Paul proclaims, loudly and proudly, that Christ is the end of law. The new Christian community promises to be a community sustained not by law, but by love. However, despite their best efforts to reach for the moon, the early Christians were still trapped in this sublunar world. In the sublunar world, life always falls short of its promise. An earthly community, even one as otherworldly as the early Christian community, needs law to govern behavior and mediate interpersonal conduct. Unlike Jesus, Paul was a pastor who had to build actual ecclesiastical communities in the here and now, which have to last into the indefinite future until Jesus comes again. Paul has to make his theology workable, which means that Paul needs to fit law in somehow within his theology, no matter how ill-fitting it may be. As a result, one could find in

Paul's letters statements that are pro-law and anti-law, often side-by-side.[1] By cherry-picking from Paul's letters, one could portray Paul as the strict legalist or the radical antinomian.

Some sophisticated intellectual manoeuvres are required to reconcile the nomian and the antinomian elements in Paul.[2] One way to approach Paul is to place him in the context of the various disputes that he was engaging in, which is the approach I adopted in the previous chapter. I propose to adopt the same approach in this chapter. In the prior narrative, I described how Paul had one eye toward Jerusalem and another eye toward Rome. In this counter narrative, I want to shift the camera and redraw the landscape. As pastor, Paul was called to mediate between two rival groups in Corinth: the nomian quasi-Jewish Christians (sometimes called the Judaizers) and the antinomian proto-Gnostic Christians (sometimes called the libertine pneumatics).[3] Again, Paul had to fight on two fronts. He had to fight off quasi-Jewish nomianism, on the one hand, and proto-Gnostic antinomianism, on the other. Being the astute pastor that he was, Paul straddled very carefully the middle ground. He carved out the middle ground by making some concessions to both sides of the divide. Hence, one can find both elements in his letters. In this chapter, I will pursue the antinomian strand.

Gnosticism, as an ism, was a second-century Christian heresy. A full-blooded Gnostic was a creature of the second century. Therefore, what we had in Corinth in Paul's time was proto-Gnosticism, that is, the first tentative beginnings of what would develop later into full-scale Gnosticism.[4] To make the chronology clearer, one could chart the flow of ideas in the following way. Proto-Gnostics in Corinth in Paul's time posed a distinct answer to the perennial question of what makes a perfect Christian. Their answer was not quite heretical yet, for the ascription of heresy would come later with the entrenchment of orthodoxy. The gospels had not yet been written, and things were still rather fluid at this stage. In any case, Paul responded to the proto-Gnostics in his letter to the Corinthians, conceding some ground to them. Later, full-blooded Gnostics in the second century would come to occupy that ground and erect a whole structure of thought on it. The second-century Gnostics read Paul's letters and integrated them within a set of esoteric theological doctrines, which was at variance with the emerging orthodoxy.

---

[1] Gager, *Reinventing Paul*, 9.
[2] For example, E. P. Sanders effectuates this reconciliation by arguing that, for Paul, following the law of Moses is *good*, but having faith in Christ is *better*: see Sanders, *Paul, the Law and the Jewish People*, 137–40.
[3] Dunn, 'Reconstructions of Corinthian Christianity and the Interpretation of 1 Corinthians', 301.
[4] Wilson, 'How Gnostic Were the Corinthians?', 74.

The severity of the threat that Gnosticism posed to the emerging orthodoxy in the second century was evidenced by the intensity of the polemical attacks against Gnosticism at that time. Those who led the attack against Gnosticism – and won – came to be known as the early Church Fathers, such as Ignatius of Antioch and Irenaeus of Lyons. The Gnostics and the Church Fathers were engaged in the age-old struggle to define Christianity. Then, as now, what it means to be a Christian is far from clear and nowhere near settled.

What is of interest to us here is not ancient Gnosticism per se, but the Gnostic type.[5] Gnostics draw sharp divisions: between materiality and spirituality, and between the spiritually strong and the spiritually weak. I will deal, first, with the former division. The sharp contrast between materiality and spirituality leads Gnostics to depreciate the body and devoid it of value. This repudiation of the body could lead to two extreme consequences: severe punishing of the flesh *or* libertine indifference to matters of the flesh. When dealing with bodily appetites, there are two options: starve or sate. The practical consequence of this can be either asceticism or libertinism.[6] Gnostics who pursue the former course become ascetic Gnostics, while those who pursue the latter course become antinomian Gnostics.[7] Paul's letter to the Corinthians provides textual evidence of antinomian, not ascetic, tendencies in Corinth, which leads to the conclusion that the Corinthian proto-Gnostics were antinomian Gnostics.[8] The antinomian Gnostics are also called libertine pneumatics because they view themselves as spiritual beings who can take liberties with their bodies. What you do to your body makes no difference to the spirit, which is free. For pragmatic reasons, one may choose to maintain an outward material compliance with the law, yet preserve inward spiritual freedom, for even the most restrictive law does not touch one's inner being. Outward compliance, done out of choice, is compatible with inward freedom. The antinomianism is primarily spiritual, not material.

Take the circumcision controversy as an example. Circumcision is a mark on the body of the Jew that sets him apart as a Jew. The requirement of the law is inscribed, literally, on his penis. In contrast to the Jews, for the Gnostics, as for Paul, circumcision is neither here nor there: 'neither circumcision nor uncircumcision counts for anything',[9] for, in Christ, 'there is neither Jew nor

---

[5] For an elaboration of the distinction between Gnosticism and the Gnostic type, see Lee, *Against the Protestant Gnostics*, 6.
[6] Bultmann, 'The Problem of Ethics in the Writings of Paul', 7, 21.
[7] Yamauchi, *Gnostic Ethics and Mandaean Origins*, 25.
[8] Horrell and Adams, 'The Scholarly Quest for Paul's Church at Corinth: A Critical Survey', 18.
[9] Letter to the Galatians 6:15.

Greek'.[10] The circumcision of the flesh is adiaphorous, for 'in the spirit such marks do not exist'.[11] Jesus is human in the flesh, but Christ is divine in the spirit. The Crucifixion kills Jesus in the flesh, but the Resurrection restores Christ in the spirit. Unlike Peter who met Jesus in the flesh, Paul had only met Christ in the spirit. Having encountered Christ in the spirit on the road to Damascus, Saul died and Paul was born. Following Christ and Paul, the Gnostics, too, partake in the 'flight from the body to the spirit'.[12] The Gnostics denude the physical world, including the physical body, of all value, and withdraw into the spiritual self. The body represents the 'outer, physical reality', while the spirit represents the 'inner, spiritual reality'.[13]

This spiritual view of the self dovetails with the second Gnostic division between the spiritually strong and the spiritually weak. Only the spiritually strong ('the pneumatics') have access to the secret higher wisdom ('gnosis'). In the words of Jesus, 'many are called, few are chosen'.[14] The pneumatics see themselves as the chosen few. They are not the hoi polloi. As the chosen few, they are the perfect Christians. As the strong, they say of the law what Nietzsche would later say of morality: the law is for the weak; the strong has no need for the law. Sociologically, 'the rapid growth of the Gnostic movement can be explained as a reaction against the popularizing of Christianity': as the Church became increasingly popular among the masses, and as it adopted more disciplinary mechanisms to manage the masses, a segment of Christians began to yearn for something more exceptional, in the full sense of the word 'exceptional' – they wanted to be different from and better than the masses, and thereby, be excepted from the religious discipline that applied to the masses.[15] Weber likens Gnosticism to intellectualism and calls the Gnostics the 'intellectual aristocrats'.[16]

Notwithstanding its heterodoxy, full-blooded Gnostics claim Pauline pedigree as rigorously as the prevailing orthodoxy. Victors write history, especially church history. Although the victorious orthodoxy labels Gnostics as heretics, it goes without saying that the Gnostics themselves would never see their own views as heretical. They claim to be Christians, if not the perfect Christians. They seize upon certain Pauline statements as support for their position. For example, in 1 Corinthians 6:2–3, Paul says:

[10] Letter to the Galatians 3:28.
[11] Boyarin, *A Radical Jew*, 23.
[12] Boyarin, *A Radical Jew*, 37.
[13] Boyarin, *A Radical Jew*, 53.
[14] Gospel of Matthew 22:14.
[15] Lee, *Against the Protestant Gnostics*, 33.
[16] Weber, *The Sociology of Religion*, 131.

> Do you not know that the saints will judge the world? ... Do you not know that we are to judge angels? How much more, matters pertaining to this life!

According to the antinomian Gnostics, the saints referred to in this passage are the spiritually strong to whom the secret wisdom ('gnosis') has been revealed. The Gnostics are the saints. They will judge all things, even angels, for Paul says that the saints will judge angels. Insofar as the devil is nothing but a fallen angel, they will judge the devil too. They possess what they call spiritual or pneumatic freedom. They are freed from the law, and hence, free to live as they please. To be sure, such freedom from the law is perfectly compatible with an outward compliance with the law. To be truly free from the law means being able to deal with it as one sees fit. It means that one is free to comply with the law, and free to disregard it. It does not require compliance, but neither does it require transgression. True freedom from the law requires compatibility either way, with either compliance or transgression. Their freedom from the law is derived from a deeper spiritual freedom of cosmic proportions. 'The pneumatics, no longer subject to the cosmic powers, therefore are free from the sexual, ethical and dietary practices the law prescribes'.[17] As materiality no longer has any power over them, they are free to regard the things of this world with indifference.[18] They can do with them what they will. Having perceived the noumenal reality, the phenomenal no longer matters.

A few lines later, in 1 Corinthians 6:11–12, Paul says:

> You were washed, you were sanctified, you were justified in the name of the Lord Jesus Christ and in the Spirit of our God. All things are lawful for me.

In the Letter to the Galatians 5:18–25, Paul reiterates the same point in even clearer terms:

> If you are led by the Spirit you are not under the law ... against such there is no law. And those who belong to Christ Jesus have crucified the flesh with its passions and desires. If we live by the Spirit, let us also walk by the Spirit.

Again, the antinomian Gnostics seize upon these passages to claim that, for those who are washed, sanctified and justified by the spirit – in short, spiritualized – all things are lawful. Again, the Gnostics believe they are the ones to whom Paul is referring in this passage. As spiritual beings, materiality no longer has any hold over them and what they do with the flesh no longer matters. The true Christian message is a gospel of liberation from the scourge of the flesh and the yoke of the law. It is a gospel of freedom of the most radical

---

[17] Pagels, *The Gnostic Paul*, 67.
[18] Pagels, *The Gnostic Paul*, 67.

sort. Valentine claims that the Gnostics 'stand at a height above any power; therefore they are free to do anything, having no fear of anyone in any way'.[19] Hence, libertine pneumatics 'freely attend pagan meals, festivals and (if Irenaeus is to be believed) engage freely in diverse sexual practices'.[20] The antinomian undertone in Paul's message is given full blast by the Gnostics.

The interpretive challenge for the Gnostics is that Paul is not entirely against the law. As discussed in Chapter 1, there are as many pro-law passages as there are anti-law passages in Paul's letters. To account for the pro-law passages in Paul's letters, the Gnostics ascribe to Paul a kind of bivocality: they argue that Paul taught 'in two ways at once',[21] with one message for the many and another message for the few. Paul has a dual responsibility to both constituencies. The pro-law passages are for the many who are weak, while the anti-law passages are for the few who are strong. Just as there are two testaments, so there are two paths to salvation: one for the many and another for the few. The former relies on law, while the latter transcends it. The bivocality of Paul is well illustrated in his response to the dietary debate. The issue at stake is whether Jewish dietary laws apply to Christians. Paul responds, cryptically, that 'nothing is unclean in itself; but it is unclean for anyone who thinks it unclean'.[22] The Gnostics interpret this verse to mean that, for the strong, the dietary laws do not apply: 'nothing is unclean'. The dietary laws are only for the weak: 'it is unclean for anyone who thinks it unclean'. Hence, the Gnostics 'do not hesitate to eat meat offered to idols, considering that they cannot in that way [or in any way, for that matter] be defiled'.[23] However, Paul is ever mindful of his dual responsibility to the strong and the weak. The strong are not to despise the weak: 'as for the man who is weak in faith, welcome him'.[24] The strong should not use their liberty to scandalize the weak: 'we who are strong ought to bear with the failings of the weak',[25] therefore the strong should not 'eat meat or drink wine or do anything that makes your [weaker] brother stumble'.[26] Consequently, to the strong, Paul says: 'the faith that you have, keep between yourself and God'.[27] In effect, on the Gnostic interpretation, Paul is telling the strong that they are free to do

---

[19] Valentine, as quoted in Pagels, *The Gnostic Paul*, 66.
[20] Pagels, *The Gnostic Paul*, 45.
[21] Pagels, *The Gnostic Paul*, 5.
[22] Letter to the Romans 14:14.
[23] Pagels, *The Gnostic Paul*, 45.
[24] Letter to the Romans 14:1.
[25] Letter to the Romans 15:1.
[26] Letter to the Romans 14:21.
[27] Letter to the Romans 14:22.

what they want, but they are to keep it secret. It is thus unsurprising that Gnosticism developed into a secret sect within the Church, like a secret elite fraternity.

This kind of thinking is dangerous stuff, especially to a bishop like Irenaeus who has to run a church: 'so long as their presence is tolerated, Irenaeus warns, they incite confusion and controversy: they call into question the authority of church leaders, and disturb the faith of simple believers'.[28] The church is not all spirit. The church is also a community of believers that is housed within an ecclesiastical structure. A structure is an artifice that lasts. The artifice is both physical, in the shape of a church building, and social, in the form of an institutional hierarchy of persons. The structure is built and sustained across generations, especially when the anticipated second coming of Christ did not happen with the haste that the first generation of Christians thought it would. Faced with the realities of life, the church soon resorts to the language of law: canon law. At its best, canon law is supposed to be 'a bridge between theology and norms for practical action' in building the church on earth.[29] Irenaeus held up a common 'creed, clergy and canon' as the hallmark of the Church, which he thought was absolutely necessary in order to hold the diverse groups of Christians together within the one Catholic (that is, Universal) Church.[30] Irenaeus could not tolerate the lawless existence of secret sects within his unified and universal Church.

Notwithstanding this resort to law, the antinomian challenge remains an inbuilt feature of Christian thought, as it has been from its very inception. The Pauline compromise may provide a temporary truce, but it is not a permanent solution. The antinomian spirit would come back, again and again, to haunt subsequent generations of Christians. The antinomian spirit would return later to haunt the Reformers. The Calvinist doctrine of predestination was particularly susceptible to antinomianism: 'If one knew, as a certainty, that one was elected to be saved – and that this was God's will – then it could follow that one would be saved whatever one did: the "saints" might live henceforth outside the "moral law"'.[31] Simply put, 'the elect must be saved, do what they may'.[32] Whether in Gnostic or Reformed antinomianism, 'the notion of the abrogation of the law and the notion of elected

---

[28] Pagels, *The Gnostic Paul*, 160.
[29] Coughlin, *Canon Law A Comparative Study with Anglo-American Legal Theory*, 49.
[30] Pagels and King, *Reading Judas*, 9, 102.
[31] Thomson, *Witness against the Beast*, 12.
[32] Thomson, *Witness against the Beast*, 14. The Reformers found various ways of hedging to avoid this radical conclusion, such as by arguing that 'if a "saint" led a scandalous life, then this was evidence that he or she was none of the elect': at 12.

"sainthood" tended to go together'.[33] The antinomian challenge reflects the inherent instability in the Christian attitude toward law. 'Should Christianity be understood as a fundamentally juridical religion? Or is Christianity founded on the rejection of Jewish legalism, and on an assertion of values transcending or even opposing those of law?'[34] This pointed question admits of no precise answer.

ANTINOMIANISM: LAW, LOVE AND FREEDOM

Because the above question admits of no definite answer, the same religion could give rise to radically divergent ideals: the monastic ideal versus the antinomian ideal. In contrast to the monastic ideal, the antinomian ideal brings together its own distinctive configuration of the values of law, love and freedom.

Freedom as Independence: The antinomian ideal places a high premium on freedom as independence. The notion of pneumatic freedom that the antinomian Gnostics champion for themselves places their independence of and from the world front and center. In escaping from the physical world into the spiritual self, the Gnostics seek to be freed from the world, while living in the world. The latter qualification is important because death is another way to escape from the physical world. Insofar as they want to continue living in the world, they have to find a way to be freed from the world while remaining in it. For the Gnostics, being freed from the world means being independent of it, which in turn means being indifferent to it and being able to deal with it *ad libitum*. Hence, 'all (material) things are lawful' for those who are (spiritually) free. To be spiritually free is to be over and above the material world. Hence, 'the saints will judge the world'.

Love as Attention: In contrast to the monastic ideal which values love as union, the antinomian ideal presents love as attention. Hence, the emphasis placed on gnosis: the wisdom that enables one to see the true spiritual nature of things, stripped of their material illusions. One could only love by seeing things as they truly are. Separateness, not union, is the basis of this kind of attentive vision. It requires an appreciation of the distinctness of persons. Consequently, the Gnostics have no qualms about drawing sharp divisions between individuals, such as between the spiritually strong and the spiritually weak. Having accurately

---

[33] Thomson, *Witness against the Beast*, 17. The problem for the Reformers was that the solifidian position (*sola fide*: by faith alone; or faith *without* the law) could slip easily into an antinomian one (faith *against* the law). The Reformers struggled to find 'some doctrinal foothold halfway down' this logical slippery slope: at 16.

[34] Simmonds, 'Judgment and Mercy', 52.

perceived the predicament of the spiritually weak, the spiritually strong can then attend to the weak out of love. This kind of love is the result of attention. The weak are not prepared for freedom; as a result, the Gnostic expression of freedom may scandalize them and jeopardize their weak faith. Therefore, the Gnostics are prepared to modify their expression of pneumatic freedom 'for the sake of the weak', like Christ who is willing to give up his divinity to take up the human form 'for the sake of man'.[35] Following Christ, Paul too is willing to give up his pneumatic freedom for the sake of the unfree. Paul expresses this kind of love eloquently when he says: 'For though I am free from all men, I have made myself a slave to all ... To the Jews, I became as a Jew ... To those under the law, I became as one under the law ... To the weak, I became weak ... I have become all things to all men'.[36] All persons are different. Hence, the Gnostics have to apply different strokes for different folks.

Law as Resistance: For the Gnostics, the law is the ladder that one can kick away once one has reached the top. Reliance on the law is a means of support for the weak, while resistance against the law is a means of freedom for the strong. As Paul says in his Letter to the Galatians, 'the law was our schoolmaster ... but after faith has come, we are no longer under a schoolmaster'.[37] At an earlier stage of spiritual life, when one is still under pupillage, the law could serve a pedagogic function to inculcate virtuous habits. At this stage, law serves as a ladder. However, spiritual growth means outgrowing the need for law. It means reaching a stage where you no longer rely on the law to tell you what to do. By being independent of the law, one moves from pupillage to mastery. One becomes the master of oneself, instead of allowing the law to be a master over oneself. At this stage, one kicks the ladder away. Fuller, too, uses the image of the ladder to differentiate between the morality of duty and the morality of aspiration: 'duty is the bottom rung and aspiration goes on upwards ad infinitum'.[38] One could also draw an analogy with the rules of grammar in the art of writing. When one begins to learn a language, one starts by learning the rules of grammar. Once one has mastered the rules of grammar, one can then bend the rules strategically to move from prose to poetry.[39] Hence, according to the Gnostics, it is the faithless who should be lawful, while the faithful could be lawless.[40]

[35] Pagels, *The Gnostic Paul*, 160.
[36] 1 Corinthians 9:19–22.
[37] Letter to the Galatians 3:24–5.
[38] Bankowski, 'Law, Love and Legality', 212; Fuller, *Morality of Law*, 5.
[39] Bankowski, 'Law, Love and Legality', 210.
[40] Law is needed primarily for the faithless. In addition, law is also needed as an insurance policy for the faithful. 'For a believer might always fall away from the faith, and hence fall within the

As the faithful, the Gnostics could express their transcendence of the law by transgressing it, just as a son at the cusp of majority and maturity might transgress his limits in a strategic and calculated way as an expression of his newfound independence, or just as a poet might transgress the rules of grammar strategically to produce poetry. The ecstatic existential feeling of freedom in pushing one's boundaries could only be felt insofar as there are boundaries to be pushed. Law provides those initial boundaries. The complex interplay between compliance and transgression leads to transcendence. In this picture, the value of law does not lie in authority, but resistance. Law is valuable insofar as it provides a means of resistance. In the Sermon on the Mount, for example, Jesus appeals to the spirit of the law to rebut the letter of the law in overturning six norms of the law of Moses. In that sense, Jesus could claim that he has not abolished the law, but fulfilled its purpose, and thereby transcended it.[41]

REFORMATION

Just as the Reformation is the turning point from monasticism to constitutionalism, so the Reformation too is the turning point from antinomianism to anarchism. The Reformation expanded the monastic ideal by bringing it out of the monastery into the world. In the prior narrative, I showed how the monastic ideal was then transposed into the state through the project of modern constitutionalism. In this counter narrative, I will show how the expansion of the monastic ideal following the Reformation triggered an antinomian response in the form of anarchism. The transformation of the monastic ideal into constitutionalism triggered a tit-for-tat transformation of the antinomian ideal into anarchism. The latter transformation was a response to the former. Hence, the former is the subject of the prior narrative, while the latter is the subject of the counter narrative.

Prior Narrative: Paul → Monasticism → Reformation → Constitutionalism
Counter Narrative: Paul → Antinomianism → Reformation → Anarchism

Monasticism and antinomianism are, in the first instance, theological ideals, while constitutionalism and anarchism are, on the surface, political ideologies. As Schmitt argues in *Political Theology*, there are two ways in

---

rule of the law once more': E. P. Thomson, *Witness against the Beast*, 16. For the faithful, law remains relevant as 'insurance against backsliding': at 17.

[41] See Neoh, 'The Rhetoric of Precedent and Fulfillment in the Sermon on the Mount and the Common Law', 419.

which the theological could be tied to the political. They could have a shared *systematic structure*, or a shared *historical development*, or both.[42] Understanding their shared systematic structure requires the drawing of analogy between the theological and the political, while understanding their historical development requires the tracing of genealogy from the theological to the political. Analogy and genealogy are the twin methods in linking the theological with the political. The prior narrative from monasticism to constitutionalism is primarily an account of their historical development, and their relationship is more genealogical than analogical. In contrast, the counter narrative of antinomianism and anarchism is primarily an account of their systematic structure, and their relationship is more analogical than genealogical. Their analogy consists in their shared valuation of law as resistance, love as attention, and freedom as independence. On the basis of these values, the following counter narrative will draw a systematic structural analogy between antinomianism and anarchism, with the Reformation as the bridge between the two.

In addition to what I have written in the preceding chapter about the changes brought by the Reformation, I will highlight several other crucial changes in this chapter. The Reformation intensified both the world within and the world without: it changed the inner world of the person and the outer world of the people. In the inner world, it lifted the Christian sense of interiorization to new heights, or rather, pushed it to new depths. It intensified the interiorization and pushed it deeper into the head, the heart and the gut. In the outer world, the Reformation made the state omnipotent and omnipresent. It removed all intermediaries between God and the person, and later, between the people and the state. It intensified the immediacy of these relationships in the religious and political realms. The combined effect of these developments was that the human subject became increasingly hemmed in. Contrary to the ancient Israelite wisdom that no one could see the face of God and live, the Reformation allowed the human subject to see God and meet the state directly. However, like staring at the sun, one cannot sustain it for too long. When things became too intense and too much to bear, the resulting reaction was anarchism, which was where the antinomian ideal reared its head. This plot is, in gist, the story that I will tell in this section.

---

[42] Schmitt, *Political Theology*, 36.

The Inner World: Radical Interiorization

The Protestants take all matters to heart, with an ever-increasing range of human affairs being made matters of conscience. Max Stirner characterizes (or caricatures) Protestantism with the following imagery: 'Protestantism has actually put a man in the position of a country governed by secret police. The spy and eavesdropper, "conscience" watches over every motion of the mind, and all thought and action is for it a "matter of conscience", that is, police business. This tearing apart of man into "natural impulse" and "conscience" (inner populace and inner police) is what constitutes the Protestant'.[43] This conscience-governed country exists, not on the face of the earth, but deep in the heart of humans. When one is pricked by conscience, the good old Catholics have a convenient way of getting rid of the irritant through the sacrament of confession and, if need be, the purchase of indulgences. Traditional Catholic canon law divided the enforcement of moral discipline into two categories: the 'internal forum' whose jurisdiction belongs to the priest in the confessional and the 'external forum' whose jurisdiction belongs to the judge in court.[44] For matters that fall within the internal forum – so long as the penitent confesses his or her sins to the confessor, and the confessor absolves the sins using the stipulated formula, and the penitent subsequently performs the prescribed penance – the guilt is gone and life moves on. At one stroke, the penitent is simultaneously released from the fires of hell, the pain of purgatory and the agony of conscience. By contrast, the Protestant is permitted no such luxury. There is no easy way out (or a get out of jail free card) for 'the strictly moral, dark, fanatical, repentant, contrite, praying Protestants'.[45] The Protestants have freed themselves from the dominion of the Church, only to be repossessed, but this time by the dominion of conscience that is seven times more powerful than the Church.

In taking all matters to heart and making an ever-increasing range of human affairs matters of conscience, Protestants sacralize the mundane, which is markedly different from how Catholics sacramentalize the mundane. Let's take marriage as an example. For Catholics, marriage, in and of itself, is mundane. However, if the marriage receives the blessing of the Church in the person of the priest, it is sacramentalized: marriage becomes matrimony, that is, it becomes a sacrament. The sacrament is withheld from those who have been called to a higher form of life, particularly monks and nuns. They live a consecrated life, which excludes the marital life. They live a better and

---

[43] Stirner, *Ego and Its Own*, 81.
[44] Berman, *Law and Revolution II*, 188.
[45] Stirner, *Ego and Its Own*, 82.

higher life, for as Paul says, 'he who marries his betrothed does well, and he who refrains from marriage will do better'.[46] In contrast to the Catholics, the Protestants view marriage as sacred in and of itself. That which is sacred needs no further sacramentalization by a priest. Given that marriage is sacred – inherently, intrinsically – there is no reason to bar the Protestant minister from marrying. At the hands of the Reformers, the mundane, too, could be sacred, the result of which is that one can run, but one cannot hide from the sacred. There is nowhere to hide. 'Catholicism ... lets the profane world stand, yes, and relishes its pleasures, while the rational, consistent Protestant sets about annihilating the mundane altogether, simply by hallowing it'.[47] The Protestants hallow the world, and thereby, hollow the self of mundane pleasures. Henceforth, one should not only do sacred things, but also think sacred thoughts.

The Outer World: Omnipotence of the State

In the Catholic Middle Ages, one's access to the heavenly God or the earthly Lord was mediated through a thick and tight network of hierarchical relationships, whether of the natural or supernatural kind. To get to the heavenly King, one required the mediation of the Church, with its own hierarchy of priests, bishops, archbishops, cardinals, and finally, the Pope as the Vicar of Christ. To get to the earthly King, one's access to the King was similarly mediated by a host of feudal lords, guilds, universities, monasteries, municipalities, cities and communes. The relationship of the individual to the King was distant in one sense, yet personal in another. It was distant because it was separated by a host of intermediaries, yet it was personal because every link in the chain of intermediaries was constituted by interpersonal relationships. This model of continuously hierarchical relationships reflects the Great Chain of Being, 'in which the cosmos is well ordered in a series of steps, from God's authority over angels through a king's authority over his subjects down to a patriarchal husband's authority over his wife and children'.[48]

This chain of intermediaries between the subject and the monarch was an integral part of what came to be called ancient constitutionalism (ancient as in the *ancien regime*, not ancient as in classical antiquity). The intermediaries were 'self-created, self-governing, intergenerational corporate bodies', which constituted a landscape of social and legal pluralism that kept the monarch in

---

[46] 1 Corinthians 7:38.
[47] Stirner, *Ego and Its Own*, 83.
[48] Levy, *Rationalism, Pluralism and Freedom*, 285.

check.[49] Royal coronation oaths are good examples of how these intermediate institutions kept the monarchy in check. In France, for example, a new king was received formally into the cities in a ceremony of entrée, in which the king made a commitment to respect ancient customs, privileges and liberties held by certain specified institutions; and the pledge of allegiance to the king was conditioned on the king's fulfilling his commitment.[50] This ancient reciprocal pledge affirms the principle of subsidiarity, which makes it illegitimate for a higher authority, such as the monarch or the state, to usurp the self-governing authority that lower intermediate institutions rightly have over their own members.[51]

One of the earliest instances of an intermediate institution was the monastery, which became an established part of the feudal world in the Middle Ages, with guarantees of independence from the local lord and the diocesan bishop.[52] The monastery was regulated by its own internal monastic laws and custom. The medieval monastery, like the medieval city, was walled and set apart from the feudal order, which protected its dwellers against 'both disorganized violence and organized feudal domination'.[53] Universities would later mimic monasteries, and scholars would mimic monks. Universities and monasteries were regulated by their own internal laws and custom. Scholars and monks wore distinctive robes partly to signal their distinguished status. Cities, universities and monasteries were intermediate institutions, which were self-organized and self-governing. As the power of the state grew, the right of these intermediate institutions to govern themselves was in due course 'interpreted as an anomalous privilege, one that eventually gave way to state rationalization'.[54] The Reformation was a pivotal event in accelerating the growth of state power and the concomitant process of state rationalization, which stripped these intermediate institutions of their powers and privileges. Without their powers and privileges, these intermediate institutions would no longer be able to act as bulwarks between the people and the state.

The Reformation introduced the idea of a believer's direct access to God in the theological sphere, and the idea of a citizen's direct access to the state in the political sphere. After the Reformation demolished the intermediaries in the religious domain, it was just a matter of time before the analogous intermediaries in the political domain were similarly thrown out the window. The Reformation

---

[49] Levy, *Rationalism, Pluralism and Freedom*, 4, 91.
[50] Levy, *Rationalism, Pluralism and Freedom*, 119.
[51] Finnis, 'Subsidiarity's Roots and History', 133.
[52] Levy, *Rationalism, Pluralism and Freedom*, 90.
[53] Levy, *Rationalism, Pluralism and Freedom*, 96.
[54] Levy, *Rationalism, Pluralism and Freedom*, 100.

gave rise to the modern direct-access society, first in the religious sphere, and then in the political sphere. With the Reformation, there was a shift from intermediacy to immediacy: from the 'hierarchical order of personalized links to an impersonal egalitarian one', and from the 'vertical world of mediated access to horizontal, direct-access societies'.[55] Accompanying the shift from intermediacy to immediacy was the shift from heterogeneity to homogeneity. In the previous order, there were diverse sets of relationships arranged hierarchically. In the religious domain, the laity stood in a different relation to the divine from that of the priest, which was different from that of the monk, which was different from that of the saint. With the Reformation, the diversity was replaced with uniformity: all are to be Christians, pure and simple. In the political domain, there could no longer be differentiations among estates, or among serfs, peasants, artisans, barons and lords. All are to be Citizens, pure and simple. The modern notion of citizenship is built on this notion of homogeneity and directness of access: 'I stand, alongside all my fellow citizens, in direct relationship to the state which is the object of our common allegiance'.[56] In place of an interlocking set of personal political relationships, the newly minted citizen is only allowed one kind of relationship to the impersonal political entity of the state. Instead of a relational identity, the citizen's identity is categorical.[57] It was the Reformation which first introduced this way of thinking. It started with the reformed Christians believing that they have direct access to God, and it ended with the reformed Citizens believing that they have direct access to the State. It was a reformation, first of the religious order, then of the political one.

The immediacy of access cuts both ways. With the removal of intermediaries, the stare of the state can now glare directly at the citizen. It reduces 'to impotence, and then to nullity, all that intervenes between Man and the State'.[58] 'The [old] monarch in the person of the "royal master" had been a paltry monarch compared with this new monarch, the "sovereign nation"', which is 'a thousand times severer, stricter, and more consistent'.[59] 'The political order of the Middle Ages had been organic in form, a balance of church and king, of baronies and free cities, whose haphazard nature was illustrated most vividly by the fact that the kings had no permanent capitals, but travelled from royal castle to royal castle followed by vast trains of wagons'.[60] In contrast to the old 'sovereign monarch' whose potency was

[55] Taylor, *A Secular Age*, 209.
[56] Taylor, *A Secular Age*, 210.
[57] Taylor, *A Secular Age*, 211.
[58] Maitland, *Collected Papers*, 3:303.
[59] Stirner, *Ego and Its Own*, 92.
[60] Woodcock, 'Anarchism: A Historical Introduction', 32.

'limited by a thousand little lords',[61] the new 'sovereign nation' is omnipotent. The English Reformation replaced the Roman Church with the Anglican Church, and replaced the Roman Pontiff with the English King as the head of the Church. The 'sovereign nation' assumed direct control over the Church, and intermediate institutions such as the monasteries were dissolved. On the continent, the Peace of Augsburg in 1555 adopted the principle of *cuius regio, eius religio* (whose realm, his religion), which allowed each local lord to define the locally established religion, thus 'strengthening local rulers and providing a critical step in the process of imperial disintegration and domestic state consolidation'.[62] The concept of national sovereignty was paired with the concept of territorial integrity. The Reformation, and the resultant fracturing of Christendom, 'crystallized a new concept of territory in the geographical sense', with the concomitant concept of territorial sovereignty: each national territory was supreme in its legislative authority, which it could exercise with no imperial or feudal limitation.[63] With this transformation, the essential contours of the modern nation-state had been drawn. The 'medieval patchwork of jurisdictions' gave way to a modern and 'monopolistic system of authority'.[64]

The Outer World: Omnipresence of the State

Prior to the Protestant Reformation, the Papal Revolution in the eleventh century had centralized the power of the Catholic Church in the Roman Pontiff and established an elaborate ecclesiastical governmental apparatus to support the centralization of power. The Papal Revolution established papal control over the Church and its independence from secular domination.[65] It entrenched the practice of papal election by cardinals alone, with the Emperor having no say in the process.[66] The formalization of canon law gave expression to the status of the 'Church of Rome as an independent, corporate, political and legal entity, under the papacy'.[67] Gratian's *Decretum*, which was originally called the *Concordia Discordantium Canonum*, purported to be a comprehensive reconciliation of discordant canons, in which 'thousands of distinct legal rules and judgments were

---

[61] Stirner, *Ego and Its Own*, 92.
[62] Levy, *Rationalism, Pluralism and Freedom*, 123.
[63] Berman, *Law and Revolution II*, 66.
[64] Levy, *Rationalism, Pluralism and Freedom*, 135.
[65] Berman, *Law and Revolution*, 23.
[66] Levy, *Rationalism, Pluralism and Freedom*, 92.
[67] Berman, *Law and Revolution*, 520.

brought together, contradictions laid out and, in principle, resolved'.[68] It systematized canon law, and integrated the entire hierarchy of the Church under the papacy. Pope Gregory VII claimed for himself the authority to legislate and adjudicate, to collect taxes in the form of tithes, to confer church citizenship by baptism and strip it by excommunication. The doctrine of the two swords was introduced to demarcate 'the relation between the ecclesiastical and lay authorities'.[69] The state had a sword, and so did the church. The doctrine of the two swords created a structure of legal, including jurisdictional, pluralism between secular and church authorities. It created a kind of division of power between church and state. The church limited the power of the state, and reciprocally, the state limited the power of the church.

The Reformation abolished this division of power when it rejected the authority of the Roman Pontiff. The Protestant states abolished the Catholic ecclesiastical governmental apparatus, and with it, canon law. Canon law texts were burned and canon law courts were shut down. At first glance, one might perceive what happened as a demolition of legal structures. However, if one were to look closely, what actually happened was not so much the demolition of legal structures as the substitution of one set of legal structures for another. The Reformers might have been able to sweep canon law away in one stroke, but the huge array of matters that were hitherto governed by canon law could not be so easily swept under the carpet. These matters still needed to be settled, if not by canon law, then by law of some other sort. Consequently, the 'deconstruction of the canon law [of the church] gave way to reconstruction of the civil law [of the state]'.[70] The state took over the jurisdiction of the church. With the transferral of jurisdiction from the church to the state, the jurisdiction of the state expanded exponentially. The state could now reach into every nook and cranny of one's life.

The theological device that was used to accomplish this transferral of jurisdiction from church to state was Luther's variation of the two-sword doctrine, which was rebranded as the two-kingdom framework. There are two kingdoms: earthly and heavenly. A Christian belongs to both. As a heavenly citizen, the Christian is free from law; but as an earthly citizen, the Christian remains bound by law. Following the two-kingdom framework, the church, as the heavenly kingdom, is governed by the Gospel; while the state, as the earthly kingdom, is governed by Law. In the earthly kingdom, the Christian is called to obey the law issued by the state. The state is 'the powers

---

[68] Levy, *Rationalism, Pluralism and Freedom*, 93.
[69] Berman, *Law and Revolution*, 521.
[70] Witte, *Law and Protestantism*, 3.

that be', which Paul says is 'ordained by God'.[71] The state, in turn, is called 'to protect peace, to punish crimes, to promote the common good'.[72] On earth, the church has nothing to do with the law. The church is the fellowship of the faithful; it is neither a law-making nor a law-enforcing institution. Legal authority rests solely in the hands of the state magistrate, not the church cleric. The power of the sword belongs to the state alone. The magistrate is charged to enact laws as the 'father of the community': in addition to keeping the peace, he is to safeguard public morality, nurture his subjects and educate them.[73] Following the Reformation, the state became the keeper of the peace and the guardian of morality, the purveyor of welfare and the provider of education. The state began to make laws to regulate marriage and divorce, and punish licentiousness and sumptuousness; it took over the responsibility for the relief of the poor from the religious orders; and it set up public schools to replace parochial schools.

Compared to the Lutheran Reformation, the English Reformation was even more explicit in its intention to replace the transnational papal authority in Rome with the national monarchical authority in England. In England, the King replaced the Pope as the supreme head of the Church of England. Here, the struggle was primarily political, not theological. At least in the first phase of the English Reformation, the Church of England kept most of the theological beliefs and liturgical practices of the Church of Rome. Prior to the English Reformation, the English people were Roman Catholic. What the English Reformation wanted to achieve was to keep the English people Catholic, but not Roman. The English Reformation resulted in the 'Anglicization of Catholicism' and the creation of a state church, the Church of England, 'to which all English subjects were required by law to belong'.[74] Consequently, the English Crown assumed direct control of both church and state, that is, of both spiritual and secular matters. These powers were subsequently transferred from the monarch to parliament. In addition to introducing laws to regulate the public life of the church, laws were also introduced to regulate the moral life of the people, including laws criminalizing heresy and blasphemy, sodomy and buggery.

'Protestantism transferred spiritual authority and spiritual responsibilities to the secular lawmakers of the various principalities and nation-states, whose supreme authorities now embraced all the jurisdictions that had previously

---

[71] Letter to the Romans 13:1.
[72] Witte, *Law and Protestantism*, 5–7.
[73] Witte, *Law and Protestantism*, 8–9.
[74] Berman, *Law and Revolution II*, 208, 349.

been autonomous'.[75] As a result, secular state law came to absorb matters hitherto within the jurisdiction of religious canon law. The consequence was an expansion of the jurisdiction of the state. The jurisdiction of the state became all-encompassing. Protestantism set the mold for the 'pouring into secular political and social movements the religious psychology as well as many of the religious ideas that had previously been expressed in various forms of [Christianity]'.[76] Like God, the state became both omnipotent and omnipresent. In response to the newfound omnipotence and omnipresence of the state, there arose the most extreme reaction: anarchism. Anarchism developed during the period of the Reformation, which was also 'the period when the modern nation state, to which anarchism is the extreme antithesis, began to take shape'.[77] Like the Gnostics before them who were denounced by the church authorities as wild heretics, the anarchists were denounced by the state authorities as loony extremists.

ANARCHISM

Just as Gnosticism could exist in two forms – ascetic or antinomian – so anarchism too could assume two forms: collectivist or individualist.

- In the *collectivist* form, anarchism seeks to move away from the state to the collective, where everything is shared. This form of anarchism is sometimes associated with communism.
- In the *individualist* form, anarchism seeks to move away from the state to the individual, where nothing is shared. This form of anarchism is sometimes associated with egoism.

In either form, anarchism could exist on two planes: political or philosophical.

- On the *political* plane, anarchism seeks to make an actual difference to the governing political structure. There are two ways to make this difference: fight or flight. Anarchists could either fight the state or take flight from the state. The former would become rebels, while the latter would become runaways.[78]

---

[75] Berman, *Law and Revolution II*, x.
[76] Witte, *Law and Protestantism*, 31.
[77] Woodcock, 'Anarchism: A Historical Introduction', 24.
[78] Those who ran away from the state often settled in the forest or the hills; they are sometimes called the forest peoples or the hill tribes. From the perspective of the state, they are the barbarian tribes. However, what if their move to the forest or the hills was the result of an astute political calculation? If their move was a conscious choice at state evasion, they were not

- On the *philosophical* plane, anarchism seeks to make a difference, not politically, but attitudinally. It seeks to change one's attitude toward the state, while living within it.

This section will focus on anarchism in its *individualist* form on the *philosophical* plane.

While the political anarchist strives for nothing less than the actual destruction of the state, the philosophical anarchist strives for the destruction of the moral authority of the state even if the state itself remains intact. Just as Gnostic antinomianism is primarily spiritual, not material, so philosophical anarchism is primarily moral, not political. In the same way that, for the antinomian Gnostics, material compliance with the law is compatible with spiritual freedom, for the philosophical anarchists, political compliance is compatible with moral freedom. Like the antinomian Gnostics, the philosophical anarchists may choose to obey the law – out of prudence, for example – but they will not be under a moral obligation to do so.[79] Anarchists are antinomian insofar as they treat the law as adiaphorous. They may be obliged, but they are never under a moral obligation, to obey the law.[80]

Philosophical anarchists attack the moral legitimacy of the state. As Nozick explains, 'the fundamental problem of political philosophy, one that precedes questions about how the state should be organized, is whether there should be any state at all'.[81] The anarchic answer to this question is no, at least not in its post-Reformation form. Their philosophical attack on the state often proceeds via a two-prong argumentative strategy: negative and positive. The negative argument seeks to undermine the authority of statehood and the positive argument seeks to promote the value of selfhood. Taken together, the negative and positive arguments pit statehood against selfhood. This section will address these two sets of arguments sequentially, with the help of Max Stirner. Stirner is 'widely regarded as a patriarchal figure' among those 'who set out to narrate the development of anarchist ideas'.[82] Although his work might not have been the most influential ideologically, it is 'arguably the most philosophically intriguing work of anarchism'.[83]

---

barbaric, but shrewd. They voted with their feet to stay away from the state. See Scott, *The Art of Not Being Governed*, 6–7.

[79] McLaughlin, *Anarchism and Authority*, 97.
[80] For the distinction between obliged and obligation, see Hart, *The Concept of Law*, 6–7.
[81] Nozick, *Anarchy, State, and Utopia*, 4.
[82] Paterson, *The Nihilistic Egoist Max Stirner*, 127.
[83] McLaughlin, *Anarchism and Authority*, 139.

Negative Argument: Statehood

The negative argument seeks to undermine the authority of the state. 'Authority is the right to command, and correlatively, the right to be obeyed', which 'must be distinguished from power, which is the ability to compel compliance, whether through the use or the threat of force'.[84] A band of robbers has power, but no authority over me. As Augustine famously asks, 'Without justice, what are kingdoms but great bands of robbers?' If the state merely has power, but no authority over me, then the state is no better than a band of robbers. The anarchist removes Augustine's caveat altogether and argues that the state can never ever satisfy the moral requirements that are needed for it to have the kind of authority that it claims to have. The kind of authority that the state claims – 'territorially supreme, pervasive, permanent, and involuntary' – is the direct result of the Reformation, which entrenched 'the supremacy of the modern State as an autonomous, self-validating institution'.[85] In response, anarchism presents a skeptical argument: it is skeptical that the state can ever gain the moral legitimacy for the kind of authority that it claims.

Wolff relies on Kant to make this argument. Wolff begins his argument with the morally autonomous person. The morally autonomous person gives laws to himself. She decides for herself what is right. If the defining mark of statehood is authority (the right to rule) and the primary obligation of selfhood is autonomy (the refusal to be ruled), then 'anarchism is the only political doctrine consistent with the virtue of autonomy'.[86] Hence, an autonomous person, *who gives laws to himself*, is also an anarchic person, *who is a law unto herself*. Either you pursue selfhood or statehood. You cannot have your cake and eat it too, for statehood rests on the denial of selfhood: 'what generates and sustains the state is the willingness of individuals to subordinate their own will to the will of their own creation [the state]'.[87] The state's good hap is my mishap.[88]

'I am free in no state'.[89] A state may shift from personal to popular sovereignty, but that is merely a change of master from the prince to the people: 'We are accustomed to classify states according to the different ways in which "the supreme might" is distributed. If an individual has it – monarchy; if all

---

[84] Wolff, *In Defense of Anarchism*, 4.
[85] McLaughlin, *Anarchism and Authority*, 82, 103.
[86] Wolff, *In Defense of Anarchism*, 18.
[87] Leopold, 'Introduction', in Stirner, *Ego and Its Own*, xxvi.
[88] Stirner, *Ego and Its Own*, 207.
[89] Stirner, *Ego and Its Own*, 201.

have it – democracy. Supreme might then! Might against whom? Against the individual and his "self-will"'.[90] In a system of popular sovereignty, it is the people who are sovereign, not I. In a majoritarian democracy, it is the majority who are sovereign, not I. Even in a system of popular sovereignty, the popular sovereign is reduced to a sleeping sovereign, like a *deus otiosus* (an idle god) or a *deus absconditus* (a hidden god). Given the huge mass of citizens involved in a modern democracy, *sovereignty* has to be separated from *government* for the system to be workable. The popular sovereign reveals itself in rare moments, akin to theophany, to create the government, and then it withdraws, like a *deus otiosus* or a *deus absconditus* who creates the world and then retires from its governance. It is the government that runs the shop and rules the people, from day to day. The popular sovereign has the sole role of authorizing laws, without authoring them.[91] The sovereignty of the state, whether it rests in the people or the prince, whether popular or personal, is equally detrimental to the freedom of the self.

Freedom lies in the assertion of selfhood against statehood. Indeed, the only way to destroy statehood is through the assertion of selfhood. The assertion is to be found, not in revolution, which merely effectuates a change of master, but in insurrection, 'which represents the opposition of individuals to any order'.[92] Insurrection consists in disobedience against the state: not civil disobedience, but outright disobedience. Stirner contrasts Socrates with Alcibiades: the former's disobedience is civil, while the latter's disobedience is outright and hence, the latter is the better of the two. Socrates, who voluntarily drank the hemlock, 'was a fool to concede to the Athenians the right to condemn him; his failure to escape was a weakness, a product of his delusion that he was a member of a community rather than an individual'. In contrast, Alcibiades, who fled Athens to avoid trial, 'is praised as an intriguer of genius, an egoist who undermined the state'.[93]

According to Stirner, the state is a spook; and we are possessed by it. 'A good patriot brings his sacrifice to the altar of the fatherland; but it cannot be disputed that the fatherland is an idea, since for beasts incapable of mind, or children as yet without mind, there is no fatherland and no patriotism'.[94] The 'I of the people' – this 'moral, mystical, political person' – is nothing but a spook.[95] I, the real I, must exorcise the spook and free myself of it.

[90] Stirner, *Ego and Its Own*, 176.
[91] Tuck, *The Sleeping Sovereign*, 249.
[92] Leopold, 'Introduction', in Stirner, *Ego and Its Own*, xxviii.
[93] Leopold, 'Introduction', in Stirner, *Ego and Its Own*, xxviii.
[94] Stirner, *Ego and Its Own*, 32.
[95] Stirner, *Ego and Its Own*, 199.

The problem, however, is that, after we exorcise one evil spirit, we conjure up seven other spirits to repossess us with greater ferocity. After being freed of one fetter, 'people think up new ties again and again, and think that they have arrived at the right one if one puts upon them the tie of a so-called free constitution, a beautiful, constitutional tie'.[96] So, they tie themselves with one constitution after another, each longer than the previous one.

Luther has to bear part of the blame. The combination of the Lutheran notion of a calling in the world with the idea of the state is the source of much confusion and deception: people begin to think that they are called to be loyal and productive citizens, and thereby, realize the idea of the state in the world. One is called to sacrifice selfhood to statehood: to love the state in times of peace and to defend it in times of war. The omnipotent and omnipresent God is transformed and transfigured into the omnipotent and omnipresent State. One is called to serve the state: 'to serve the state or the nation became the highest ideal, the state's interest the highest interest'.[97] To this notion of a calling, Stirner retorts: 'A man is "called" to nothing, and has no "calling", no "destiny", as little as a plant or a beast has a "calling" . . . The bird lives up to no calling, but it uses its forces as much as is practicable; it catches beetles and sings to its heart's delight'.[98] The anarchic move is to abandon the state and return to the self. It is movement from solicitude to solitude.

Positive Argument: Selfhood

The existence of the self precedes any essence that society or the state may ascribe to it. Being true to the self, on Stirner's view, is to be true to one's existence, not one's supposed essence. Let no one kid you about how the spirit of Humanity, or the spirit of Christ, or the spirit of the People (Volksgeist) dwells in you. This obsession with spiritualizing and essentializing the things of this world is attributable to Luther, who 'tries to bring the spirit into all things', to hallow, and thereby hollow, everything worldly.[99] Stirner thinks that this spiritual obsession is ridiculous. You and I are not the dwelling place for any spirit. Only the possessed has spirit in them. The free, on the other hand, are free of spirit possession. The free are not possessed, but *self*-possessed. Freed of all spirits, 'I am the creative nothing, the nothing out of which I myself as creator create everything'.[100] Freed of all presuppositions, 'I am

[96] Stirner, Ego and Its Own, 192.
[97] Stirner, Ego and Its Own, 91.
[98] Stirner, Ego and Its Own, 288.
[99] Stirner, Ego and Its Own, 84–5.
[100] Stirner, Ego and Its Own, 7.

every moment just positing or creating myself'.[101] I create myself: 'I am creator and creature in one'.[102] Stirner's 'flamboyant individualism' calls for 'a celebration of abandoned self-enjoyment and an exultation in the originality of the unique subject'.[103] 'No concept expresses me, nothing that is designated as my essence exhausts me', for I am the 'transitory, mortal creator, who consumes [my] self from moment to moment in the act of self-creation.[104] The question, 'what is man?' or 'what is an Englishman?', does not concern me at all. 'These states and nations with their ideals ... what are they to me?'[105] I am only concerned with the question of who I am, or rather, who I want to be from one moment to the next.

'Let every man take his own, and go his own way, regardless of system and state': 'he must single himself out'.[106] On the spiritualization of the self, Stirner and the Gnostics could not be further apart, but on the singularity of the self, Stirner and the Gnostics are on the same page. The Gnostics are all spirit, while Stirner hates this whole spirit talk. However, despite Stirner's dislike for the things of the spirit – which he likens to spirit possession – he shares with the Gnostics the same elitist and exceptionalist attitude and aspiration. Like Gnostic antinomianism, Stirner's anarchism is a radical philosophy that consciously sets itself apart from the hoi polloi. They define themselves in opposition to the masses. In the early Christian period, as the Church grew more powerful, antinomianism became more appealing to a select few. Analogously, in the post-Reformation period, as the state grew more powerful, anarchism became more appealing to a select few. Both the Gnostics and anarchists want to be exceptional – they want to be different from and better than the masses. Through circumcision, the Jews set themselves in opposition to Gentile society. Through the rejection of circumcision, the Christians set themselves in opposition to Jewish society. Through the rejection of the very terms of this debate, the Gnostics went a step further and set themselves in opposition to mass society altogether. Just as monasticism and constitutionalism brought the logic of union to its apotheosis, so Gnosticism and anarchism brought the logic of differentiation to its apotheosis.

Stirnerian selfhood invokes a radical sense of autonomy. I do not give myself over to anything: neither to God and his words, nor to the State and its laws.

---

[101] Stirner, *Ego and Its Own*, 135.
[102] Stirner, *Ego and Its Own*, 135.
[103] Paterson, *The Nihilistic Egoist Max Stirner*, 130.
[104] Stirner, *Ego and Its Own*, 324.
[105] Lawrence, *Study of Thomas Hardy*, 39. For a study of the elements of anarchism in the work of D. H. Lawrence, see Casey, *Naked Liberty and the World of Desire*.
[106] Lawrence, *Study of Thomas Hardy*, 38–9.

As D. H. Lawrence says, 'There is no need to break laws. The only need is to be a law unto oneself'.[107] In addition to exercising autonomy over external entities outside the self, the autonomous person also exercises autonomy over internal elements within the self. The autonomous person is a master of himself or herself: he or she maintains continuous control – that is, self-mastery – over the ideas of the mind and the appetites of the flesh. 'If any idea or desire plants itself firmly in me, and becomes indissoluble, then I have become a prisoner and servant, a possessed man'.[108] To quote D. H. Lawrence again, 'If I say to myself: I am this, I am that! – then, if I stick to it, I turn into a stupid fixed thing like a lamp-post'.[109] Externally, to the extent that I am not independent of the state, I am, pro tanto, not the master of myself, but a mere servant of the state. Internally, to the extent that I am not independent of my ideas and desires, I am, pro tanto, not the master of myself, but a mere slave to my passions. When that happens, it signals the end of autonomy, and of selfhood.

ANARCHISM: LAW, LOVE AND FREEDOM

Law as Resistance

The end of anarchism is the end of law. The moment the end of law is achieved, the political anarchist would thereby cease to be an anarchist. However, the end of law is not simply the change of law. Insofar as a revolution merely substitutes one legal order for another legal order, revolution is merely a cosmetic change. What the anarchist wants is not revolution, but insurrection: 'What constitution was to be chosen, this question busied the revolutionary heads ... The insurgent strives to become constitution-less'.[110] Nor will reform suffice. All that a reform movement can do is to petition the state to come to its senses and change the law: 'it presupposes the state as the giver, and can hope only for a present, a permission, a chartering'.[111] The insurgent does not petition for the permission of the state; the insurgent demands to be free of the state. No, not reform or revolution, but insurrection.

For Stirner, Jesus was neither a reformer nor a revolutionary, but an insurgent. Jesus could not care less for the petty politics of the Jews and the Romans. He could not be bothered if the ruling government was Jewish or Roman, 'because he expected no salvation from a change of conditions, and

---

[107] Lawrence, *Study of Thomas Hardy*, 38.
[108] Leopold, 'Introduction', in Stirner, *Ego and Its Own*, xxiii.
[109] Lawrence, *Study of Thomas Hardy*, 19.
[110] Stirner, *Ego and Its Own*, 279–80.
[111] Stirner, *Ego and Its Own*, 249.

this whole business was indifferent to him', 'for he was not carrying on any liberal or political fight against the established authorities, but wanted to walk his own way, untroubled about, and undisturbed by, these authorities'.[112] He was 'wise as serpents', yet 'innocent as doves'.[113] Until his arrest at the Garden of Gethsemane, Jesus would simply, and literally, walk away – his own way – when confronted with the authorities. He has no time for the nicety of legality. Jesus is happy to live outside the law when it is necessary, yet he is also happy to bring himself within the law when the situation calls for it.[114]

Jesus was eventually executed, leaving the early Christians in a quandary. The anarchist confronts the same dilemma as the early Christians: how to approach the law in the time gap between the 'now' and the 'not yet'. Christians look forward to the end of the world. Anarchists look forward to the end of the state. But they are not there yet. Until they get there, they have to learn to live with the law. Anarchists, like the Gnostics before them, ascribe a kind of strategic value to the law. In response to the dilemma as to whether the anarchist should accept legal concessions from the state, Stirner says: 'Certainly, with joy; for their permission would be to me a proof that I had fooled them and started them on the road to ruin'.[115] Stirner sees 'no reason to injure himself by a public crusade against authority when his ends can be just as well achieved by *cheating* the state'.[116] The anarchist will use the law strategically, by pitting the law against itself. At the hands of the anarchist, the law will be the instrument for resisting the state: 'I sue for [my legal right] in order to make [the state] bleed to death by it'.[117] When the law is beneficial to me, I will use it; but when the law stands in my way, I will simply avoid it. 'I get around a rock that stands in my way, until I have powder enough to blast it; I get around the laws of a people, until I have gathered strength to overthrow them'.[118] The folly of Socrates was that, instead of getting around the rock, he knocked his head against it – voluntarily!

Michael Tigar calls this approach to law the jurisprudence of insurgency. This approach taps into the value of law as resistance and incorporates multiple strategies to use law to resist those in power. For example, if there is a rule that 'no three or more persons shall conduct a political meeting', the rule will be treated in practice to mean that 'no three or more persons shall conduct

[112] Stirner, *Ego and Its Own*, 280.
[113] Gospel of Matthew 10:16.
[114] Bankowski, 'Law, Love and Legality', 210.
[115] Stirner, *Ego and Its Own*, 252.
[116] Paterson, *The Nihilistic Egoist Max Stirner*, 137.
[117] Stirner, *Ego and Its Own*, 252.
[118] Stirner, *Ego and Its Own*, 150.

a political meeting so that the authorities will be able to prove, by the accepted means of proof and a sufficient quantum of evidence, that the meeting took place and who was present'.[119] If caught and charged, the insurgent will use the law to argue that they should not be convicted, due to the lack of evidence based on the criminal law of the state, or due to the invalidity of the rule based on the constitutional law of the state. The insurgent cites the provisions of the dominant legal ideology to resist the power of the state, and to demand that the state acts in accordance with its own pronounced and professed legal ideology. The law forms the basis for the insurgent's demand that the state acts in a certain way.

Love as Attention

The anarchist conception of love is particularistic: love is always directed to the unique individual. Universal love, such as the love of humanity, or collective love, such as the love of nation, is illusory. Those who think they love humanity universally merely love some abstract essence of humanity. They love, not actual human persons, but the spirit of humanity – a spook. They proceed by stripping humans of all particular characteristics; they 'cut away attribute after attribute from the conception of the moral persona' to find that one universal quality that is deserving of universal love.[120] The Benthamite capacity for pleasure and pain, the Kantian capacity for reason, and the Rawlsian capacity for choice among the conceptions of the good: 'all of these and more have been tried and found wanting'.[121] 'At this point one begins to lose one's grip on what a person might be: separated from every describable feature, the person has become a geometrical point with neither form nor substance'.[122] When confronted with a human person, instead of loving the unique person before one's eyes, the lover of humanity loves the spirit of humanity who, so happens, dwells in the person. Instead of loving the real you, I love the spirit in you. I love a spook. The same applies, *mutatis mutandis*, to the love of nation, the love of my country and the love of my people. All these pious feelings are ghostly love: the love of an illusion.

True love involves an accurate perception of oneself and the other. I give to my beloved an amount of attention that I do not give to any Tom, Dick and Harry. But for my love for her, I would have been indifferent to her; she would

---

[119] Tigar, *Law and the Rise of Capitalism*, 315.
[120] Simmonds, 'Judgment and Mercy', 66.
[121] Simmonds, 'Judgment and Mercy', 66.
[122] Simmonds, 'Judgment and Mercy', 67.

not have got the attention that I have given her. My love trains my attention on her and picks her out from the mass of humanity. Without love, there is no attention, and reciprocally, without attention, there is no love. It is not that love comes first and then attention comes later, as if attention is *consequent on* love, but rather, love and attention come together, such that love *consists in* attention. From an accurate perception of the beloved, 'I can with joy sacrifice to [her] numberless enjoyments, I can deny myself numberless things for the enhancement of [her] pleasure', but 'I do not on that account go so far as to sacrifice myself, nor sacrifice anything of that whereby I truly am myself'.[123] In short, I do not sacrifice my autonomy. 'If I see the loved one suffer, I suffer with him, and I know no rest until I have tried everything to comfort and cheer him; if I see him glad, I too become glad over his joy. From this it does not follow that suffering or joy is caused in me by the same thing that brings out this effect in him, as is sufficiently proved by every bodily pain which I do not feel as he does; his tooth pains him, but his pain pains me'.[124] I preserve the distinctness of myself, from whose distinctive vantage point I can perceive my beloved accurately. When one truly understands what love is, in the poetic words of D. H. Lawrence, 'the great movement of centralizing into oneness will stop, and there will be a vivid recoil into separateness . . . like a kaleidoscope, all colours and all the differences given free expression'.[125] The false illusion of oneness is nothing but 'the dream helplessness of the mass-psyche':[126] this illusion is not love, but the pathology of love. The ideal of love is not oneness, but separateness. In contrast to the view of love as union that makes the dissolution of selfhood the ideal of love, on this view of love as attention, the dissolution of selfhood marks the extinction, not the realization, of love.

Freedom as Independence

Recall that under the previous view of freedom as identification, there could be freedom in obedience. For the anarchist, nothing could be further from the truth: 'The obedient servant is the free man! What glaring nonsense!'[127] Anarchic freedom is freedom as independence. It consists in getting rid of 'everything that is not you': 'get yourselves rid, relieve yourselves, of everything burdensome'.[128] Freedom as independence lies in self-liberation, not

---

[123] Stirner, *Ego and Its Own*, 257–8.
[124] Stirner, *Ego and Its Own*, 258–9.
[125] Lawrence, *The Complete Poems of D. H. Lawrence*, 611.
[126] Lawrence, *Aaron's Rod*, 145.
[127] Stirner, *Ego and Its Own*, 95.
[128] Stirner, *Ego and Its Own*, 148.

emancipation or manumission. The man who is set free (emancipated, manumitted) is simply a freed man, but not yet a free man.[129] Freedom is not a gift from others, but a self-assertion of independence. After getting rid of all the knick-knackery that is thrust on me by others, I may not have much left in myself, but 'this little is everything, and is better than what I allow to be made out of me by the might of others'.[130]

What I have to be independent from is both internal and external to me. Externally, I have to be independent of the state, or of anyone else for that matter. Internally, I have to be independent of the ideas and desires that are swirling inside me. If I am free only as the 'rational I', then it is rationality that is free; I am not. 'I want to be full of thoughts, but at the same time I want to be thoughtless'.[131] I am free of my thoughts if I can change my thoughts at will, that is, at my pleasure. The free person relieves the robust, lively particular self from the generality of ideas.[132] This sense of freedom is part of what George Woodcock, the anarchist historian, calls the anarchist's cult of the natural and spontaneous individual who sets himself or herself apart from the organized structure of society.[133] Only those who are free, internally and externally, can be part of the association of the free. Stirner gives the paradigm example of the father-son relationship before and after the son reaches the age of majority. As a minor, the son is not independent of the father. The son is bound to the father. He is tied to him. As an adult, the son becomes independent of the father. The son becomes free of the father. As an adult, the son may choose to associate with the father, but this time, it will be on a free basis. They will 'come together independently': 'sonship and fatherhood remain, but son and father no longer pin themselves down to these'.[134]

Perpetual peace can only be attained in the association of the free, when we are all independent of one another. Stirner rejects the liberal strategy of trying to dissolve social division by creating an enlarged entity that will unite the division, such as trying to dissolve the division between hostile social factions by subsuming the division under an enlarged entity called Humanity. The problem, Stirner says, is not that there are social divisions; on the contrary, the problem is that the existing social divisions do not cut deep enough. The social divisions have to cut deeper and there have to be more of them, until 'everybody asserts himself from top to toe as unique'.[135] Like the

[129] Stirner, *Ego and Its Own*, 151–2.
[130] Stirner, *Ego and Its Own*, 163.
[131] Stirner, *Ego and Its Own*, 305.
[132] Stirner, *Ego and Its Own*, 205.
[133] Woodcock, *Anarchism: A History of Libertarian Ideas and Movements*, 26.
[134] Stirner, *Ego and Its Own*, 122.
[135] Stirner, *Ego and Its Own*, 185.

Gnostics, Stirner too has no qualms about drawing sharp divisions between persons. According to Stirner, the solution does not lie in generalization, but in individualization; not in a flight to abstraction, but in a return to the concrete self; not in enlarging the collective entity, but in emphasizing the uniqueness of the individual self. As a unique individual, I have nothing in common with you or anyone else, and therefore nothing hostile either; the previous opposition between hostile social factions vanishes, not in unity, but in complete severance or singleness.[136] Everyone is independent of everyone else. Parity is achieved through the most radical kind of individual disparity: we will be on a par of disparity.[137]

LAW, LOVE AND FREEDOM FROM ANTINOMIANISM TO ANARCHISM

The antinomian and anarchic ideal unites *law as resistance* with *love as attention* and *freedom as independence*. It brings together the second half of the bipolarity of law, love and freedom that was laid out in Chapter 2. From this configuration of values, we can make three claims about the linkages of these values. Recall that in the previous chapter (Chapter 4), I argued that (i) law constitutes freedom, (ii) love is impossible without law, and (iii) love sets us free. In this chapter, I will make a similar set of claims about the relationship between law, love and freedom. On the surface, the three claims that I will make about antinomianism in this chapter are the same as the three claims that I made about nomianism in the previous chapter. However, once we scratch beneath the surface, we will find that the three claims in this chapter encode a different configuration of values from the three claims in the previous chapter. Antinomianism and anarchism, properly understood, do not mean the absence of law. Antinomianism literally means anti-law, but it does not mean no-law. Although the end of anarchism is the end of law, anarchism itself is not the end of law, for there is a gap between the 'now' and the 'not yet'. Seen in its proper light, the contrast between nomianism and antinomianism, and between constitutionalism and anarchism, is not actually the contrast between lawful and lawless, but rather, it is the contrast between law as authority and law as resistance. It stems from the ascription of different values to law.

First, law constitutes freedom. Law as resistance constitutes freedom as independence. For the antinomian Gnostics, reliance on the law is a means

---

[136] Stirner, *Ego and Its Own*, 186.
[137] Stirner, *Ego and Its Own*, 186.

of support for the weak, while resistance against the law is a means of freedom for the strong. The law is the ladder that one can kick away once one has reached the top. Hence, according to the Gnostics, the faithless should be lawful, while the faithful could be lawless. As the faithful, the Gnostics could express their transcendence of the law by transgressing it, just as a son at the cusp of majority and maturity might transgress his limits in a strategic and calculated way as an expression of his newfound freedom as independence. The ecstatic existential feeling of freedom in pushing one's boundaries could only be felt insofar as there are boundaries to be pushed. Law provides those initial boundaries. The complex interplay between compliance and transgression leads to transcendence. For the Gnostics, being freed from the world means being independent of it, which in turn means being indifferent to it and being able to deal with it *ad libitum*, like Jesus who is happy to live both within and without the law.

Anarchists, like the Gnostics before them, ascribe a kind of strategic value to the law. At the hands of the anarchist, the law will be the instrument for resisting the state. Anarchists use the law strategically, by pitting the law against itself. This approach taps into the value of law as resistance and incorporates multiple strategies to use law to resist those in power. The insurgent cites the provisions of the dominant legal ideology to resist the power of the state, and to demand that the state acts in accordance with its own stated legal ideology. Law provides the terms for the powerless to talk back to power: 'recourse to law forces the powerful to talk in terms in which the powerless can also participate and can also make claims'.[138] Law allows its subjects to resist authority, thus allowing its subjects to assert their freedom as independent agents.

Second, love is impossible without law. The value of law as resistance preserves the independence and individuality of the self, which enables the attainment of love as attention. Antinomianism advocates, not for the negation of law per se, but its transcendence. Law is transcended in love, just as the common law is transcended in equity and the criminal law in mercy, both of which are expressions of love as attention to the particular. Law is a step on the way to love, for it teaches us certain valuable lessons about love. The practice of law teaches us that, although the law may attempt to impose a common plan on everyone, each person has an individual plan for his or her own life. As an autonomous agent, the legal subject is capable of interacting with the law to further his or her individual plan. If the law supports one's individual plan, one could use it. If the law obstructs one's individual plan, the nature of

[138] Balkin, 'Critical Legal Theory Today', 67.

law is such that one will have the option of resisting it. The practice of law teaches us that any common plan will have to accommodate individual plans. Having appreciated the individuality of selves, and how they escape the imposition of uniformity, one begins to see the distinctness of persons. One senses the futility of any effort at the erasure of difference. One then learns not to erase, but to embrace difference. One has to, in the words of Paul, 'become all things to all men',[139] and apply different strokes for different folks. With this move, one comes close to love as attention to the particular.

Law as resistance preserves individuality, and by preserving individuality, it enables love as attention. Without individuality, there is no love as attention. There can be no love without you and me as distinct individuals, and law keeps you from trampling over me. The anarchic conception of love is ineluctably particular: love is always directed to the unique individual. Universal love, such as the love of humanity, or collective love, such as the love of nation, is illusory. True love fixes one's gaze on the beloved as an individual in his or her full individuality. The beloved captures one's attention, just as the wounded Jew captures the attention of the Good Samaritan. The love that is evoked in the encounter is particularistic. Tribal and national generalities dissolve in that encounter. True love is always directed to the individual, not to a collectivity or some generic and general abstraction. The former is real, while the latter is illusory. True love involves an accurate perception of oneself and the other. It requires an appreciation of the other as an independent agent in the world. Separateness is not to be eliminated, but appreciated. The individual 'will' is central to both law as resistance and love as attention.

Third, love sets us free. Love as attention sets both the lover and the beloved free to be independent agents in the world. For this primal lesson, let's return to the primordial story of the Fall in Chapter 1. With the Fall, Adam and Eve become aware, not only of their nakedness, but also of their separateness: the man and the woman begin to see that they are separate and different from each other and from God. They proceed to clothe themselves with fig leaves.[140] The newfound sense of individuality makes possible a new plethora of experiences that require some kind of distinctness and distance between persons. One such experience is the experience of loving in the sense of paying attention to the other as the other, that is, as a separate and distinct being. It makes possible freedom as independence. This sense of freedom is part of

---

[139] 1 Corinthians 9:19–22.
[140] Book of Genesis 3:7.

the anarchist's cult of the natural and spontaneous individual.[141] Freedom is a spontaneous self-assertion of independence, as illustrated by King David when he strips off his clothes and dances naked before the ark of the Lord.[142]

It is important that I preserve the distinctness of myself, from whose distinctive vantage point I can perceive the other accurately. Attaining an accurate perception of the other may entail drawing sharp divisions between oneself and the other, like the Gnostics who draw sharp divisions between the spiritually strong and the spiritually weak. Having accurately perceived the predicament of the spiritually weak, the spiritually strong can then attend to the weak out of love. This kind of love is the result of attention. Love as attention is not the thrusting forward of oneself toward a fusion of will, but a stepping back. On this view, love is not blind. On the contrary, there is nothing as clear-sighted as love. The lover sees the beloved as a separate individual and desires that the beloved flourishes, for the beloved's own good. Love as attention leaves the lover and the beloved free to be independent selves, in an association of the free. Hence, love sets you free.

---

[141] Woodcock, *Anarchism: A History of Libertarian Ideas and Movements*, 26.
[142] 2 Samuel 6:14–22.

6

Value Pluralism and the Search for Coherence

In the beginning, I said that there would be a theoretical payoff at the end. Now is the time to cash the check. I have not begun the book with a theoretical framework. My reason for postponing the theory till the final chapter is to allow the theory to emerge over time, or more specifically, over the course of the preceding five chapters. The preceding chapters describe and analyze the practices that have shaped our thinking about law, love and freedom. 'We are all of us agents before we are theorists', and it is the task of theory to 'enable rational agents to learn what they need to learn from the social and cultural tradition that they inherit'.[1] This final chapter will take up the task of theory. The book will end on the high note of value pluralism. This chapter will conclude with an endorsement of value pluralism, but with a twist. Although values are plural, my life is singular. There are many values, but there is only one life. Hence, there is a search for coherence amid a pluralism of values. The coherence of values is to be found within a form of life.

We began in Chapter 1 by considering two views of human nature. We did that through an extended meditation on the creation myth in the Book of Genesis. The two views of human nature emerge chronologically in the myth, before and after the Fall: prelapsarian and fallen. We then mapped those two views of human nature onto the two dominant accounts of the state of nature provided by Rousseau and Hobbes, respectively. Paul struggled to mediate these two opposing views of human nature in his letters, particularly in his Letter to the Romans. Paul see-sawed between these two views. The see-saw is most evident in his equivocal treatment of the values of law, love and freedom. Chapter 2 presents a sustained analysis of three concepts of law, love and freedom. It unpacks the three concepts. It shows that law, love and freedom are bipolar concepts, each of which is structured by two opposing values. Law is

[1] MacIntyre, *Ethics in the Conflicts of Modernity*, 72, 76.

polarized between authority and resistance. Love is polarized between union and attention. Freedom is polarized between identification and independence. How do we make sense of this multipolar world?

Chapter 3 argues that the way to proceed is not through further abstract conceptual analysis, but through a historical and narrative turn. Chapter 3 proposes a methodological turn to historical narrative. It suggests that what legal philosophy needs is 'not only more arguments, but also more narratives'.[2] The subsequent two chapters, Chapters 4 and 5, present two historical narratives that help to make sense of the three bipolar concepts of law, love and freedom. Chapter 4 sets forth the prior narrative that charts the history of ideas from monasticism to constitutionalism. Chapter 5 sets forth the counter narrative that charts the history of ideas from antinomianism to anarchism. The prior narrative brings together the values of law as authority, love as union and freedom as identification. The counter narrative brings together the values of law as resistance, love as attention and freedom as independence. In both narratives, Paul is where the story begins, and the Reformation is where the story turns.

Having identified the competing values in law, love and freedom in Chapter 2, Chapters 4 and 5 show how different groups of people in different times and places have 'succeeded to greater or lesser degree in integrating the pursuit of those goods into a life which was and perhaps is their best attempt so far to flourish as a human being'.[3] One could think of the presentation of the argument in this book as having a parabolic structure. A parabolic structure presents the parable first, and explicates the lesson later. One could treat the prior and counter narratives as an extended parable, and this chapter as the explication of the lesson. The lesson is a philosophical one. Philosophical lessons are learned, 'not from abstract theorizing, but in key part from the stories of those who, in various very different [pre and post] modern social contexts, have discovered what had to be done, if essential human goods were to be achieved'.[4] I have postponed any explicit philosophical theorizing till the last chapter because the philosophical theses of this chapter cannot be 'adequately spelled out and understood independently of and prior to telling those stories that provide examples of how and why those theses find application in our practical lives': both stories and theses 'have to be understood together or not at all'.[5]

---

[2] MacIntyre, *Ethics in the Conflicts of Modernity*, 242.
[3] MacIntyre, *Ethics in the Conflicts of Modernity*, 74.
[4] MacIntyre, *Ethics in the Conflicts of Modernity*, 238.
[5] MacIntyre, *Ethics in the Conflicts of Modernity*, 236.

WHY PHILOSOPHIZE

Let's begin by reflecting on what philosophy is and why philosophize. To start off, there is the deflationary sense of philosophy as a professional discipline that is preoccupied with conceptual clarification, but there is also the inflationary sense of philosophy as a panoramic worldview that paints a sweeping map of reality.[6] Philosophy, in the grand tradition, is inflationary. Philosophers, in the grand tradition, give themselves 'the function of articulating certain very general pictures of the real', the goal of which is to produce a picture 'capable of satisfying not only the emotions but the intellect as well, the latter by virtue of logical coherence, the former by virtue of being an embodiment of an attractive metaphysic'.[7] In this task, the aim is not completeness, but insight; and the yardstick is not the provision of indubitable proof, but the presentation of a panoramic worldview. The worldview could be bright or bleak, optimistic or pessimistic, uplifting or downcast. The purpose of the worldview is not to settle disagreements, but to inspire them, by clarifying what lies behind our disagreements.

Philosophy, we are told, begins with wonder about the world, 'for it is owing to their wonder that men [and women] both now begin and at first began to philosophize'.[8] It begins with the attempt to paint a picture of the world, of what the world is like. Insofar as it deals with the human world, it must include a picture of human nature, of what we are like. Hobbes and Rousseau, as philosophers in the grand tradition, produce two very different, but equally panoramic, views of human nature, which generate divergent political philosophies. Their theories begin with human nature and end with the state. The first chapter of this book, Chapter 1, follows in this grand tradition by opening with a panoramic picture of human nature. Chapter 1 starts from the very beginning, with the creation myth in Genesis. Chapter 1 argues that the prototypes of Rousseau's noble savage and Hobbes's nasty brute are found in the Garden of Eden: the former before the Fall and the latter after the Fall. The Edenic myth contains within itself the two views of human nature – prelapsarian and fallen – that Hobbes and Rousseau subsequently elaborate in their accounts of the state of nature.

If philosophy is the painting of a picture of the world, then moral philosophy is the painting of a picture of the moral world. The moral world consists of norms and values. Norms operate according to what Fuller calls the morality

---

[6] Craig, *The Mind of God and the Works of Man*, 1.
[7] Craig, *The Mind of God and the Works of Man*, 2.
[8] Aristotle, *Metaphysics*, Bk 1, §982b, [12].

of duty, whereas values operate according to the morality of aspiration. The morality of duty starts at the bottom by laying down the baseline of acceptable conduct, whereas the morality of aspiration starts at the top by articulating the aim of the good life.[9] Moral values are aspirational: they are the 'values whose realization would make lives good'.[10] For these values to be realized, they have to be both 'objectively justified' and 'subjectively accepted'.[11] Taylor calls these values 'life goods': they are the 'actions, modes of being, virtues [that] define a good life for us'.[12] These life goods have to find their place within 'a certain kind of picture of the universe, our capacities, and the possible stances toward this universe they make possible for us'.[13] On this conception, law, love and freedom are values, or what Taylor calls 'life goods'. Chapter 2 shows what they are good for. What they are good for has to be understood within 'a certain kind of picture of the universe', which Chapter 1 articulates in mythological terms. In the domain of values, what matters is not simply the facts of human life, but the significance of the facts. Its central concerns are 'not how the world is, but the significance that we attribute to how the world is'.[14]

There are 'irreducibly different ways of understanding the significance of facts' because there is a plurality of conflicting values.[15] Hence, 'living a good life requires the achievement of a coherent ordering of plural and conflicting values'.[16] The coherence of values is achieved within a form of life. Chapters 4 and 5 show that there are different ways of ordering plural and conflicting values. Since there are different ways of ordering them, there are different forms of life. Consequently, there is a 'repertoire of conceptions of life that we may recognize as good'.[17] The plurality of good lives is a plurality twice over: 'on account of the values it embodies and on account of the ways in which coherence among the values is achieved'.[18] Following this line of thought, one could revise the initial proposition to say that moral philosophy is the painting of a picture of the way values interact to make up good lives. The picture that this chapter wants to paint is one of objective value pluralism, coupled with

---

[9] Fuller, *Morality of Law*, 5.
[10] Kekes, *Morality of Pluralism*, 9.
[11] Kekes, *Morality of Pluralism*, 14.
[12] Taylor, 'Leading a Life', 173.
[13] Taylor, 'Leading a Life', 173.
[14] Kekes, *Pluralism in Philosophy*, 5.
[15] Kekes, *Pluralism in Philosophy*, 72.
[16] Kekes, *Morality of Pluralism*, 11.
[17] Kekes, *Morality of Pluralism*, 12.
[18] Kekes, *Morality of Pluralism*, 11.

a subjective search for coherence, both of which are equally central to understanding our moral world.

OBJECTIVE VALUE PLURALISM

There are two views of values that one could take: a view from nowhere or a view from somewhere. The former is objective, while the latter is subjective. The former sees the world as God sees it, from nowhere in particular. The latter sees the world from a particular time and place in the world, from somewhere particular. Although a human person is always situated in a particular time and place, the person also has 'the impulse and the capacity to transcend its particular point of view and to conceive of the world as a whole'.[19] A person is capable of moving from somewhere to nowhere, from the subjective to the objective: 'a view or form of thought is more objective than another if it relies less on the specifics of the individual's makeup and position in the world'.[20] To attain a more objective view of the world, one needs to step back from the specific contingencies of one's personal and particular point of view to 'develop an expanded consciousness that takes in the world more fully', and thereby acquire 'an impersonal conception of the world'.[21] Adopting a view from nowhere, what one sees is objective value pluralism. However, adopting a view from somewhere, what one sees is a subjective search for coherence. This section will examine the objective point of view, while the next section will examine the subjective counterpoint.

Chapter 1 opens with the observation that, in the moral domain, the challenge is not scarcity but surplus. The source of embarrassment is not the scarcity but the superabundance of values – more than could be realized in a single life. There is pluralism, not only among values, but also within values. Chapter 1 tells the story of the fracturing of values in the cosmological beginning and the attempt by Paul to restore the fractured values in his vision of the eschatological end. The story of Eden and the paradox of Paul show the complexity of the values of law, love and freedom in this fallen world. Chapter 2 illustrates their bipolar structure analytically. Law is polarized between the values of authority and resistance. Love is polarized between the values of union and attention. Freedom is polarized between the values of identification and independence. These plural and conflicting values 'pick

---

[19] Nagel, *View from Nowhere*, 3.
[20] Nagel, *View from Nowhere*, 5.
[21] Nagel, *View from Nowhere*, 5, 9.

out as virtues very different dispositions or traits of character, which will be elements in very different forms of life'.[22]

The pluralism of values means that some values are incompatible and incommensurable. Incompatible values cannot be realized in equal measure jointly. The realization of one value excludes the realization of another, either wholly or proportionally. The incompatible values are, in their own ways, desirable, but they cannot be aggregated without loss. The value of authority is incompatible with the value of resistance. The value of union is incompatible with the value of attention. The value of identification is incompatible with the value of independence. The challenge of the incompatibility of values is exacerbated by their incommensurability. Incommensurable values cannot be ranked, for they are incomparable. There is neither an Archimedean point nor a *summum bonum* from whose vantage point one could compare and rank these values. As a result, in law, 'we find ourselves painfully suspended somewhere in the middle' between authority and resistance.[23] The same, *mutatis mutandis*, goes for love and freedom. Incompatible values are also often incommensurable. Some of the values that we want to realize jointly, but cannot, are also often values that cannot be ranked. The nature of these values is such that they can neither be ranked nor aggregated.

The coincidence of the incommensurability and incompatibility of some values is an unavoidable feature of our ethical life.[24] It is a fact of life, just as death is a fact of life. For many, this unavoidable feature of our ethical life is deeply unsettling. Just as accepting the inevitability of death does not make living any less agonizing, so accepting the objective truth of value pluralism does not make ethical life any less agonizing. On the contrary, it makes it more agonizing. Value pluralism saddles one with the burden of choice. In order to create for oneself a conception of the good life, one needs to construct coherence out of an array of values, some of which are incommensurable and incompatible. It is the ontological fact of objective value pluralism that triggers, as an ethical response, the subjective search for coherence, to which we will now turn.

SUBJECTIVE SEARCH FOR COHERENCE

We are not God. We cannot maintain an objective, God's eye view of the world indefinitely. We cannot see the world permanently as God sees it, from

---

[22] Gray, *Isaiah Berlin*, 81.
[23] Griffin, 'Incommensurability: What's the Problem?', 51.
[24] Kekes, *Morality of Pluralism*, 57.

nowhere in particular. The objective viewpoint is created by leaving the subjective behind, but we cannot ignore our subjectivity forever. The subjective search for coherence arises in response to objective value pluralism. The objective view takes us up and away from our particular and peculiar situation, but eventually, whatever goes up has to come down. At some point, we have to return to somewhere particular. We have individual lives to lead – this particular life, at this particular time and place. Going up into the clouds, we might gain a transfigured view of the objective moral world, but we cannot stay up in the clouds forever. We have to return from nowhere to live somewhere in the world. We live in the world as individuals with our specific constitution and situation. Hence, 'it is necessary to combine the recognition of our contingency, our finitude, and our containment in the world with an ambition of transcendence'.[25]

The objective plurality of values may leave one in a state of moral paralysis. The view of objective value pluralism is the viewpoint of a passive observer. From the outside, all options appear equally open, and any choice seems fatuous. It just depends on what one chooses, and there is no right choice. Choice does not seem to matter, and one might as well adopt an attitude of indifference. In the contemplative mode, one becomes detached and disengaged. However, life does not just consist of these theoretical moments. It has practical moments too. In the active mode, one plunges into the thick of battle and confronts the chaos of values. One moves from being a passive observer to being an active participant in the grind of everyday life. Confronted with the chaos of values, one is driven to construct coherence out of the chaos. One needs to choose one's values and make them coherent. From the inside, coherence and choice matter terribly. The choice makes all the difference. Instead of being detached, one is deeply attached to this life and this choice. One is 'subjectively committed to a personal life in all its rich detail', for 'the attitude toward one's own life is inevitably dominated by the fact that it, unlike all those others, is one's own'.[26] In a form of life, the universal meets the parochial, whereby the universal plurality of values has to coexist with the contingent choice of values. Objective value pluralism exists alongside the subjective search for coherence.

Hence, the challenge of moral reasoning is to reconcile the one and the many: the one life and the many moral goods. Moral reasoning is the process of coming to grips with how moral goods fit together in a whole and wholesome life. The 'diversity of goods' need to be fitted within the 'unity of life'.[27]

---

[25] Nagel, *View from Nowhere*, 9.
[26] Nagel, *View from Nowhere*, 210, 221.
[27] Taylor, 'Leading a Life', 183.

'Every person has a life of his own, his one and only life, and that life he leads'.[28] The question that has preoccupied us thus far is how one could lead a life of law, love and freedom. Note the word *lead*: a life well lived is a life well led. Ordinary language is especially illuminating here. One does not just live a life. One leads a life. The former could be done willy-nilly, while the latter requires a conscious effort. Leading a life requires giving it a certain direction and not just drifting hither and thither where the wind blows in the sea of values. The process of leading a life aims to achieve an internal concord within one's life, to make one's life of a piece by giving it a pattern and a sense of overallness,[29] and to make it a 'unity instead of a plurality',[30] so that one has, not only a life span, but also a life course. To be sure, one may choose to lead a life that embraces the vagaries of fate, along the path of what Nietzsche calls amor fati, but even then, it is a choice. When Nietzsche posits amor fati as the 'formula for greatness in a human being',[31] he is presenting it as a conscious and considered choice. It is a choice to lead one's life in a particular way. Leading a life is simply the ordinary-language way of expressing the Socratic insight that an unexamined life is not worth living.

Berlin calls Tolstoy a fox who wants to be a hedgehog: Tolstoy is 'a fox bitterly intent upon seeing in the manner of a hedgehog'.[32] The hedgehog rolls into one: it fits everything into a single system. The fox, on the other hand, runs after scattered things: the fox pursues many ends rather than one, entertains ideas that are centrifugal rather than centripetal, and thinks in ways that are diffused rather than unified. Translating the metaphor into jargon, the hedgehog is a value monist, while the fox is a value pluralist. Tolstoy is a pluralist who is bitterly intent upon seeing in the manner of a monist. Tolstoy responds to the objective fact of value pluralism with a subjective search for coherence. To be clear, the relationship between the objective and the subjective is *not* a relationship between the noumenal and the phenomenal or between reality and illusion. Rather, the relationship is one of objective fact and subjective response. It is a subjective response to an objective fact, like fear is a subjective response to the objective fact of danger, or awe is a subjective response to the objective fact of greatness. Fear and awe are no less real than danger and greatness. Life without fear and awe is possible only in a world without danger and greatness. Likewise, the search for coherence is a subjective response to the objective fact of value pluralism. That which is true of Tolstoy is true of

---

[28] Wolheim, 'On Persons and Their Lives', 299.
[29] Wolheim, 'On Persons and Their Lives', 299.
[30] Plato, *Republic*, 443d–e.
[31] Nietzsche, 'Why I Am So Clever', §10.
[32] Berlin, 'The Hedgehog and the Fox', 493.

most, if not all, of us. In response to the pluralism of values, there is a constant search for coherence in values, like 'a fox bitterly intent upon seeing in the manner of a hedgehog'.[33]

The search for coherence in the domain of values is carried out through our capacity for moral imagination. Moral imagination is the philosophical and psychological process involved in the mental exploration of what it would be like to realize particular values in one's life.[34] Objective value pluralism means that there is a breadth of values that are up for grabs. One cannot have them all, not least because of the incompatibility and incommensurability of certain values. Consequently, one has to focus on a subset of values and fit them coherently into one's life. The subjective search for coherence gives these values a certain depth in one's life. The moral imagination allows one to envision, in the mind's eye, the various ways that the values of law, love and freedom could be made coherent and given depth in one's life. For example, one could imagine what it would be like to live a life structured by authority, union and identification, by imagining how a monk or a Puritan would have lived. The monastic life adds depth to these values by showing how they could be rendered concrete and coherent as a form of life. One could be attracted to the monastic ideal without being a monk. Although the ideal arises in the context of a particular form of life, once it has arisen, it could be manifested in countless variations through other forms of life, for that is what an ideal is. You do not have to be a monk to follow the ideal. As Chapter 4 has shown, the Puritans were not monks, but they nonetheless absorbed the monastic ideal. It is the task of the moral imagination to reveal the multiple possibilities for one's life. Through moral imagination, one could be inspired by a form of life, without necessarily imitating it.

Humans are not like beasts or gods, who do not have to 'concern themselves with what they are becoming', their qualities being fixed and immutable.[35] We, humans, need to care about who we are and what we are becoming. We need to *lead* a life. Values being what they are and we being who we are, what am I to do? The values in each pair – authority and resistance, union and attention, identification and independence – are incompatible and incommensurable. Consequently, if we want to lead a life of law, love and freedom, we need to choose, and bring what we have chosen into a complementary configuration of values. 'We have to design a life in which they can be somehow integrated, in some proportions, since my life is finite and cannot admit of

---

[33] Berlin, 'The Hedgehog and the Fox', 493.
[34] Kekes, *Morality of Pluralism*, 99, 101.
[35] Taylor, 'Leading a Life', 181.

unlimited pursuit of all goods'.[36] Some values are wholly or proportionally incompatible and incommensurable, while others are perfectly compatible and commensurable. The subjective search for coherence attempts to integrate as many values as possible in order to create as rich a life as possible. It connects diverse values to construct a life that is rich in terms of values. Its goal is to make one value reinforce another within an integrated whole. Law, love and freedom constitute an integrated whole when we arrive at a coherent conception in which (i) law constitutes freedom, (ii) love is impossible without law, and (iii) love sets us free.

Chapter 3 argues that the coherence of values is to be found within a form of life. A form of life 'belongs to the world of common practices', which can be inherited and subsequently transmitted.[37] An individual life is always embedded within a social form of life. A social form of life is sustained by socially meaningful occasions (holy days and holidays), spaces (churches and courts), officials (priests and judges), performances (masses and trials), texts (bibles and constitutions) and beliefs (dogmas and doctrines).[38] An individual does not 'first arrive at a set of theoretical conclusions and then put them into practice', but rather, an individual is first 'educated into and in the various practices' that constitute the social form of life.[39] A social form of life, although sustained by humans, is independent of any individual person. It has an independent existence vis-à-vis any individual human person. It is like language, which is sustained by speakers of that language, but is independent of any individual speaker.

'We are engaged in self-creation through choice-making, but never ex nihilo, for the self that transforms itself through the choices it makes is itself unchosen, since it is always a deposit of the choices made by others'.[40] The subjective search for the coherence of values in life is the result of individual choice, but always with collective choices in the background, as embodied in the established forms of life. The prior narrative and the counter narrative in Chapters 4 and 5 illustrate this point with reference to law, love and freedom. Different forms of life integrate the values of law, love and freedom in different ways. Chapter 4 argues that monasticism and constitutionalism combine law as authority, love as union and freedom as identification. Chapter 5 argues that antinomianism and anarchism combine law as resistance, love as attention and freedom as independence. They find their

---

[36] Taylor, 'Leading a Life', 183.
[37] Gray, *Isaiah Berlin*, 107.
[38] Walzer, 'Objectivity and Social Meanings', 168.
[39] MacIntyre, *Ethics in the Conflicts of Modernity*, 63.
[40] Gray, *Isaiah Berlin*, 108.

coherence in a particular configuration of values within a social form of life. Abstract values have to be concretized in actual forms of life, so that what is disconnected in the abstract is connected in the concrete. In this process, one moves from objective value pluralism, without a form of life, to a subjective search for coherence, within a form of life.

There are many different values and different ways of combining them; hence, there are many different forms of life. In this sense, forms of life are open-ended. However, to participate in a form of life, one has to conform to the requirements internal to that form. In this sense, each form of life is closed-in. Each form of life brings together its own configuration of values. Within a form of life, any value conflicts could, in principle, be settled by assigning priorities to the conflicting values based on the commitments internal to that form of life.[41] Each form of life has its own internal coherence and speaks in its own idiom. The truly intractable conflict of values often exists, not within a form of life, but between forms of life that incorporate competing values. The task of historians and anthropologists is to describe and analyze forms of life in different times and places, which appear alien to us, but which seem to make sense on their own terms. Historians and anthropologists endeavour to uncover this inner logic. Anthropologists do that for forms of life in a foreign land, while historians do that for forms of life in the past, for the past is like a foreign land. We routinely do the same when we remark that 'I do not agree with them, but I can see where they are coming from'.

Monks and Gnostics, constitutionalists and anarchists, all seek to 'live life by their own lights': to comprehend their commitments requires a kind of epistemological humanism that seeks 'a rich understanding of particular, historically situated human beings based on empathetic insight'.[42] The presence of these different forms of life, each of which has its own 'mode of imagining' and speaks 'in its own idiom', constitutes what Oakeshott calls the 'conversation of mankind', in which no voice is without an idiom of its own: 'the voices are not divergences from some ideal non-idiomatic manner of speaking, they diverge only from one another'.[43] They are a repository of 'the ideals of good lives that stood the test of time'.[44] By examining how different people in different historical periods have conceived and combined the values of law, love and freedom, I hope to have shown that we are always faced with 'choices between ends equally ultimate,

---

[41] Kekes, *Moral Tradition*, 149.
[42] Cherniss, *A Mind and Its Time*, 222.
[43] Oakeshott, *The Voice of Poetry in the Conversation of Mankind*, 19, 55.
[44] Kekes, *Moral Tradition and Individuality*, 5.

and claims equally absolute, the realisation of some of which must inevitably involve the sacrifice of others'.[45] So, pick we must. However, I also hope to have shown that, when we construct a form of life out of a diverse range of values, we are, in effect, constructing coherence in our lives, specifically a coherence of values. Without the coherence of values within a form of life, we will be pulled hither and thither and consigned to drifting where the wind blows in the sea of values.

This talk of social forms of life is an endorsement of value pluralism, not cultural relativism. Values are universally plural and they are universally in conflict. Universal values produce universal dilemmas, dilemmas that cut across time and space. Freedom is a universal value, and it is universally polarized between independence and identification. The same, *mutatis mutandis*, goes for law and love. These values and the conflicts within them are 'rooted in enduring features of human beings'; hence, 'the universality of certain recurring moral dilemmas'.[46] However, to emphasize the universality of values is not to deny that the social forms, in which those values manifest themselves and are realized in the world, are culturally specific. Monasticism and constitutionalism, Gnosticism and anarchism, are culturally and historically specific. There is a universality of values in a vast diversity of realizations.[47]

Recall the thick and thin distinction in Chapter 3. 'Moral terms have minimal and maximal meanings; we can give thin and thick accounts of them'.[48] The thin account floats up to universality, while the thick account sinks down to particularity. The conceptual analysis in Chapter 2 provides a thin account of the values of law, love and freedom. Chapters 4 and 5 thicken the account by embedding those values within particular historical narratives. The thin account gives you the bare bones, while the thick account puts flesh to the bones. The thicker it gets, the more complex, but also the more complete, it becomes. The thin universal values acquire their depth when they are particularized, that is, when they are realized in a particular cultural context. The values of law, love and freedom are realized, now and then, here and there: they are embodied in different histories and expressed in different idioms. Any value that is realized in a 'human society' is simultaneously universal and particular: 'universal because it is human, particular because it is a society'.[49] Its universality is natural, while its particularity is cultural.

[45] Berlin, 'Two Concepts of Liberty', 168.
[46] Gray, *Isaiah Berlin*, 17–18.
[47] Finnis, *Natural Law and Natural Rights*, 84.
[48] Walzer, *Thick and Thin*, 2.
[49] Walzer, *Thick and Thin*, 8.

Hence, any social form that embodies moral values is ineluctably universal and particular, natural and cultural, objective and subjective.

Each social form has its own subjective ordering of objective values. By tracing the roots and routes of monasticism and constitutionalism alongside antinomianism and anarchism, one could see that the crystallization of social forms is agonistic. It occurs in the context of intense rivalry between competing values. Choosing one entails giving up another, either wholly or proportionally. Viewing the glass as half empty, one could lament the loss of value. Viewing the glass as half full, one could celebrate the diversity of the forms of the good. There is the famous aphorism from Berlin that what is good for the wolves may bring death to the lambs,[50] which is a variation of the old adage that one person's meat is another person's poison. The takeaway point here is not relativism, but the recognition of the fact that there are different and competing values out there, and different and competing forms of life, which requires that, in the political sphere, we need to strike a balance and find a compromise in order to live together. We need to learn to live and let live. Complementary to Berlin's aphorism is Arendt's maxim that 'men, not Man, live on the earth'.[51]

As extensive as they are, the range of realizable values is not unlimited. They are limited by human nature, that is, they are limited by what is realizable by beings like us. They are limited by 'culturally invariant and historically constant' characteristics of human beings.[52] There are many values and many ways of combining them, and hence, there are many forms of life to choose from, but not infinitely many, for 'they must be within the human horizon'.[53] Values, in the sense that we have been using them here, are rightly and outrightly anthropocentric. Values are good, insofar as their realization makes lives good, insofar as they make *our* lives good. The values of law, love and freedom may not be good in all possible worlds, but they are good in our world, which is all that matters, isn't it?

BURDEN OF CHOICE

Commitment connects the universality of values with the historicity of choice. Commitment is key to a life of integrity. Integrity has two dimensions: synchronic and diachronic. In its synchronic dimension, it requires acting

---

[50] Berlin, 'Pursuit of the Ideal', 10. I have modified the saying slightly. Berlin said: 'total liberty for wolves is death to the lambs'.
[51] Arendt, *The Human Condition*, 7.
[52] Kekes, *Morality of Pluralism*, 39.
[53] Berlin, 'The Pursuit of the Ideal', 10.

in accordance with one's commitment at any given point in time. In its diachronic dimension, it involves developing commitments that endure through time. We are not born with commitments. We develop our commitments as we live, just as we live by our commitments. Having surveyed the range of values on offer, one commits oneself to realize some values and not others. Of those values to which one is committed, one is committed to them with varying levels of intensity. What would emerge at the end, if one were to reflect deeply enough, is 'a well-ordered hierarchy of commitments', which constitutes one's conception of the good life.[54] The hierarchy of commitments could include incompatible values, provided that those values are proportionally incompatible, but not wholly incompatible. Wholly incompatible values exclude one another totally. In contrast, proportionally incompatible just means that the increase of one value leads to the decrease of another. Hence, 'choices among proportionally incompatible values often involve balancing [and] aiming at a life that embodies a mixture of them'.[55] In this case, some prioritizing of values may be required in the hierarchy of commitments. Insofar as one could prioritize incommensurable values in one's life, the priority is not due to any intrinsic ranking of those values, but due to one's commitment to them. While the cause of the conflict of values lies in the nature of those values, the means for resolving the conflict lies, not in the values themselves, but in one's attitude toward those values. I have my commitments; you have yours. Monks have their commitments, and the Gnostics have theirs. Constitutionalists have their commitments, and the anarchists have theirs.

There are many good things in life. But life is short. Values are in abundance, but our time on earth is scarce. Within a single short life, a cenobitic monk cannot be an antinomian gnostic, just as a constitutionalist cannot be an anarchist. These different forms of life pick out and combine 'very different dispositions or traits of character'; consequently, it will not usually be possible 'to combine these forms of life within the compass of a single biography'.[56] Berlin calls this necessity of choice the 'Question of Machiavelli', for Machiavelli posed the stark choice between two incompatible and incommensurable systems of value, structures of thought and ways of life; in his case, Christian versus Roman.[57] One chooses, that is, one commits oneself to a certain configuration of values. In exercising that choice, one considers

---

[54] Kekes, *Morality of Pluralism*, 194.
[55] Kekes, *Morality of Pluralism*, 79.
[56] Gray, *Isaiah Berlin*, 81, 90.
[57] Berlin, 'The Question of Machiavelli'.

a range of factors, including one's character and circumstances, and one's inclinations and aspirations. Having considered these factors, one makes a choice, which is ultimately an exercise of will. It is an exercise of will 'in the self-creation of an individual' and 'the collective creation of a form of life'.[58] Although never on a clean slate, we are nonetheless part authors of our lives. Although never *ex nihilo*, we are nonetheless participants in the creation of the world in the act of 'self-creation through choice-making'.[59]

One way to think about the exercise of choice is in terms of the interaction between reason and will. Reason renders options eligible; the will picks one of them out. Once reason has run its course, it is often the case that more than one option remains open. At that point, one simply picks, for no further reason. The will leads one to pick this rather than that. The final choice is underdetermined by reasons. Reason does not determine conclusively what is to be done; rather, 'it sets a range of eligible options before agents, who choose among them'.[60] Reason will demarcate a range of values, the realization of which will produce a good life. Within that range, 'much remains to be settled by individual and group commitment',[61] that is, by choice through an exercise of will. Choice presupposes options. Moral choice presupposes value-laden options. In being constrained by reason, the choice is rational. In being underdetermined by reason, the choice is radical. The possibility of choice is that which allows for what Mill calls the 'experiments in living'. Consider the diverse cast of characters that we have encountered in this book: from Paul to Luther; from martyrs, hermits and monks to the Puritans and constitutionalists; from Gnostics to anarchists. Their choices – that is, their 'experiments in living' – have produced different ways of selecting and combining the values of authority and resistance, union and attention, identification and independence.

The good life is not 'some gigantic synthesis of all the instantiations of [values] in a vast state of affairs';[62] instead, the good life is a matter of picking and choosing among values, and doing so wisely. Owing to the pluralism of values, there are bound to be hard choices, of the kind that exist among law, love and freedom. Each of these values is 'internally complex and inherently pluralistic'.[63] They can be fitted together only by prioritizing one aspect of law over another, one aspect of love over another, and one aspect of freedom over

[58] Gray, *Isaiah Berlin*, 59.
[59] Gray, *Isaiah Berlin*, 108.
[60] Raz, 'Incommensurability and Agency', 127.
[61] Finnis, 'Commensuration and Public Reason', 233.
[62] Finnis, 'Commensuration and Public Reason', 224.
[63] Gray, *Isaiah Berlin*, 79.

another. They cannot all be combined without loss. Like a jigsaw puzzle with surplus pieces, one picks a piece of law, a piece of love and a piece of freedom, and one pieces them together in one's life. There will be other pieces that are left out, but that is the fate of life in the face of objective value pluralism. In choosing to commit oneself to a configuration of values within a form of life, one constructs a subjective coherence amid the objective pluralism of values. Inside this configuration of values, 'collisions, even if they cannot be avoided, can be softened'.[64] The form of life, which houses this configuration of values, is 'something invented, and perpetually reinvented through choice'.[65] The maintenance of the form of life – as with the maintenance of any human invention – will be in need of constant renovation and repair.[66] The coherence may turn out to be a temporary and transient one, as forms of life appear and disappear. The subjective search for coherence can resolve the challenge of objective value pluralism, but it cannot dissolve it. If a problem is dissolved, it disappears; if it is only resolved, it is defused, but it does not disappear.[67] The value pluralism is real and objective, and hence, it will not go away. The subjective search for coherence can resolve, but not dissolve, the fact of objective value pluralism. The coherence will hold for a while, but the context will change, the conflict will recur, and the search for coherence will have to be renewed.[68]

The burden of choice and the weight of judgment is the price that we have to pay for the knowledge of good and evil. If ignorance is bliss, then Adam and Eve lost their eternal bliss when they consumed the knowledge of good and evil. The innocence of ignorance is gone forever. The childlike innocence of naïve ignorance is incompatible with the knowledge that the world contains evil as much as good. Henceforth, they have to discern, not only between good and evil, but also between the various forms of the good. They have to construct a good life for themselves through the repeated search for coherence amid the pluralism of values. Moral life would be anything but simple: a brave new moral world lay before them, to make or break. The task requires continuous reflection and constant choice. 'The point of reflection is, first, to step back from how we live, understand it, evaluate it, and then question, criticize, or justify it'.[69] Although our first nature might have been innocent, it has become our second nature to be reflective.

[64] Berlin, 'Pursuit of the Ideal', 14.
[65] Gray, *Isaiah Berlin*, 59.
[66] Berlin, 'The Apotheosis of the Romantic Will', 578.
[67] Kekes, *Pluralism in Philosophy*, 78.
[68] Kekes, *Pluralism in Philosophy*, 78.
[69] Kekes, *Human Predicaments*, 222.

Conclusion

Prior to Paul's conversion, Saul the Pharisaic Jew led a nomian life. After his conversion, Paul the Apostle preached a Christian gospel that sometimes verged on antinomianism. After Paul left the scene, monasticism rehabilitated the nomian life and reintroduced it into Catholic Christianity.

Prior to Luther's rebellion, Luther the Augustinian monk led a nomian life. After his rebellion, Luther the Protestant preached a Reformed gospel that sometimes verged on antinomianism. After Luther left the scene, Puritanism rehabilitated the nomian life and reintroduced it into Reformed Christianity.

Paul and Luther moved back and forth between nomianism and antinomianism, without resolving this age-old dispute that stretched all the way back to the Garden of Eden. Neither can I resolve this dispute. Having analyzed the bipolar structure of the values of law, love and freedom, and having examined the prior and counter narratives of these values in the previous chapters, one way to bring this book to a close would have been to tell you the reader, in a climactic conclusion, which of the two configurations of values is to be preferred. The other way to bring this book to a close would have been to collapse the dichotomy that I have so painstakingly built by synthesizing it or subsuming it within a larger unitary framework. Either way would have ended the book with a bang. The former would end on the right note, by telling the reader what the right choice is. The latter would pull the rug from under the reader's feet, by telling the reader that the dichotomy is, ultimately, a false one. I am afraid I could do neither.

This concluding chapter will zero in on the dilemma. 'A dilemma may sometimes be more significant than the solution, serving to remind us that our own thought is a historical project: poised, conditional, and perpetually incomplete'.[1] What this chapter will present is not an ethical system, but an

---

[1] Simmonds, 'Judgement and Mercy', 54.

ethical outlook, which does not claim to have a solution to every dilemma that occurs within it.[2] Life, including ethical life, is messy. Sometimes, to let a dilemma stand is more honest than to resolve it in a systemic way, for as Nietzsche says, 'the will to a system is a lack of integrity'.[3] Letting a dilemma stand avoids abandoning 'the polymorphic and polyvalent richness and diversity of real life for the grey uniformity of a [systemic] theory'.[4] Having been expelled from paradise, Adam and Eve and their descendants have to confront both the physical and moral challenges of the world. With the knowledge of good and evil comes the responsibility for deciding between good and evil, with no guarantee that the decision will be correct. The simplicity of innocence has been replaced with the complexity of judgment. In heaven, there might be the perfect harmony of values, while in hell, there might be the complete absence of values, but as we are neither in heaven nor in hell, we have to continue to struggle with the plurality of values within the liminal space of the present.

This book has presented two configurations of values. On the one hand, there is the nomian life with the monastic ideal at its core. The Reformation links the story of monasticism with constitutionalism. The monastic ideal brings together law as authority, love as union, and freedom as identification. On the other hand, there is the antinomian life with the antinomian ideal at its core. The Reformation links the story of antinomianism with anarchism. The antinomian ideal brings together law as resistance, love as attention, and freedom as independence. Antinomianism here does not mean the absence of law. The contrast between nomian and antinomian is not the contrast between lawful and lawless; rather, the contrast stems from the bipolar structure of the values of law, love and freedom, as discussed in Chapter 2. An ethical outlook that is true to the dilemma in question is one that keeps this duality of values in focus. This concluding chapter will argue that the ethical outlook that befits this duality is analogous to the ethical outlook that Nietzsche proposes in *The Birth of Tragedy* when he contrasts the two divinely inspired drives of Apollo and Dionysus. That which is analogous is not identical, so one must not push the analogy too far and give it more weight than it can bear, but with this caution and caveat, this chapter will show that the analogy is, nonetheless, fit for purpose. Through this analogy, this chapter will argue that the duality requires mutuality.

---

[2] Chappell, *Ethics and Experience*, 201.
[3] Nietzsche, *Twilight of the Idols*, 25.
[4] Chappell, *Ethics and Experience*, 188.

What I have been calling the 'configurations of values' is analogous to what Nietzsche calls 'drives'. Both the 'configurations of values' and 'drives' are metaphysical entities that are realized in cultural forms. Their 'metaphysics becomes manifest' in and through history.[5] Nietzsche examines the manifestation of the drives in the history of Greek theater in order to illuminate the aesthetic experience, while this book examines the manifestation of the configurations of values in the history of Christianity in order to illuminate the constitutional experience. This book turns to Christian theology for its inspiration, while Nietzsche turns to the Greek gods. Nietzsche opens his essay *The Dionysian Vision of the World* with the grand claim that 'the Greeks, who in their gods at once declare and conceal the secret doctrine of their vision of the world, established two deities as the twinned source of all their art: Apollo and Dionysus'.[6] Apollo is the god of light and dream, while Dionysus is the god of intoxication: 'Apollo is associated with visible form, rational knowledge, and moderation; Dionysus with formless flux, mysticism, and excess'.[7] The distinction between the Apollonian and Dionysian drives 'echoes the eighteenth century distinction between the beautiful and the sublime': 'in opposition to the finite and symmetrical nature of the beautiful, whose experience elicits pleasure in the viewer, the sublime induces fear through its lack of limits and recognizable form'.[8] The Apollonian and Dionysian, like the nomian and antinomian, 'represent opposing styles; nearly always entangled and entering into struggle with one another'.[9]

'Apollo demands measure from all who belong to him'.[10] He demands 'the drawing and respecting of boundaries and limits' and he teaches 'an ethic of moderation and self-control'.[11] The Apollonian emphasis on boundaries and limits, moderation and self-control, is analogous to the monastic idealization of normative order. The history of Christianity, from Paul to Luther and from Luther to Calvin, was 'a long, ascending series of attempts to establish a Christian order': 'the attempt was always to make people over as more perfect practicing Christians, through articulating codes and inculcating disciplines, until the Christian life became more and more identified with these codes and disciplines'.[12] Whereas monasticism only attempted to turn a select few into

---

[5] Burnham and Jesinghausen, *Nietzsche's The Birth of Tragedy*, 45.
[6] Nietzsche, *The Dionysian Vision of the World*, 29.
[7] Smith, 'Introduction', in Nietzsche, *The Birth of Tragedy*, xvi.
[8] Smith, 'Introduction', in Nietzsche, *The Birth of Tragedy*, x.
[9] Nietzsche, *The Dionysian Vision of the World*, 29.
[10] Nietzsche, *The Birth of Tragedy*, 27.
[11] Geuss, 'Nietzsche: The Birth of Tragedy', 48.
[12] Taylor, 'Perils of Moralism', 351.

more perfect Christians, the Reformation attempted to make over entire peoples, which required the transformation of whole societies and the establishment of a new form of moral order. While monasticism attempted to show this world what the other world would look like, Puritanism attempted to remake this world itself. It tied the requirements of Christianity to the establishment of a particular form of social order in this world, in the here and now. The quickest way of accomplishing this transformative feat was through the imposition of a code of conduct on everyone.

Within this code-bound nomian worldview, duties are paramount, and rules define those duties. Moral righteousness consists in performing one's duties, which in turn requires following rules. It requires an Apollonian respect of 'boundaries and limits' and an Apollonian ethic of 'moderation and self-control'. What this nomian worldview ended up creating was a moral order of dutiful individuals, who led 'disciplined forms of life', which enabled the smooth operation of 'the market economy, the public sphere and the sovereign people'.[13] As Weber has argued, 'the predisposition to discover, construct and follow rules' is the hallmark of 'judicial institutions, capitalist economics, rational social ethics, and Puritanism'.[14] Or more accurately, the predisposition was first popularized by Puritanism, and it subsequently permeated the domains of judicial institutions, capitalist economics and rational social ethics. Just as the apotheosis of the Apollonian drive was the Roman imperium,[15] so the apotheosis of the nomian life is the modern legal order. The historical narrative of the nomian life starts with the monasteries and ends with the courts. The end product is the disciplined self who proves to be a worthy subject of the modern legal order.

The Dionysian drive turns the Apollonian world upside down, just as antinomianism turns nomianism on its head. Dionysus turns speech into song and walking into dancing. One who is seized by the Dionysian drive forgets 'how to walk and talk and is on the brink of flying and dancing, up and away into the air above'.[16] Whereas Apollo demands 'the drawing and respecting of boundaries and limits', Dionysus calls for 'the transgression of limits [and] the dissolution of boundaries'.[17] Dionysus storms into the dammed-up world of Apollo with ecstatic and orgiastic song and dance. Under the spell of Dionysus, every civil bond and social restraint is broken and torn asunder in the unbridled desire for 'universal release and redemption'.[18] The Dionysian drive unleashes the primitive anarchic

[13] Taylor, 'Perils of Moralism', 352.
[14] Shklar, *Legalism*, 21.
[15] Nietzsche, *Birth of Tragedy*, 99.
[16] Nietzsche, *Birth of Tragedy*, 18.
[17] Geuss, 'Nietzsche: The Birth of Tragedy', 48.
[18] Nietzsche, *Birth of Tragedy*, 20.

force, which 'stirs powerfully in momentous times'.[19] Nietzsche identifies the early stages of the Reformation as one of those momentous times: 'The German Reformation grew up out of the depths of this abyss', when Luther responded to the 'enticing call of the Dionysiac'.[20] However, the Reformation lost its Dionysian edge when it turned Puritanical. When the Reformation turned Puritanical, Pietism arose in response to Puritanism. In contrast to the Puritan emphasis on order and orderliness, Pietism 'took ecstatic, often spectacular forms, deeply disturbing to those who feared above all "enthusiasm"'.[21] From yesterday's Pietism to today's Pentecostalism, the recurring gripe is that true Christianity 'has to engage the whole heart': it has to be authentic and spontaneous.[22] In short, it has to be Dionysian.

The Apollonian exists alongside the Dionysian, just as the nomian exists alongside the antinomian. An ethical outlook that is true to this duality should see the 'opposites connected without fusing them'.[23] As the historical narratives of this book have shown with regard to the nomian–antinomian duality, and as Nietzsche's analysis of Greek theater has shown with regard to the Apollonian–Dionysian duality, historical development is built upon a 'seesawing conflict' between the two halves of the duality.[24] The duality of the drives is exemplified by the child on a beach 'who builds up piles of sand only to knock them down again'.[25] The duality here requires mutuality. The child requires the rigor of Apollo to build up the sandcastles and the vigour of Dionysus to knock them down again. The world of sandcastles that the child creates is 'nothing but a momentary configuration of shapes in the sand'.[26] Although the Apollonian and the Dionysian are separate drives, each require the other to propel itself forward.

Nietzsche illustrates the interdependence of Apollo and Dionysus through a study of Greek tragedy. Attic tragedy is born when the 'singing and dancing of a chorus is joined with the more restrained and ordered speech and action of individual players on a stage'.[27] The former is Dionysian, while the latter is Apollonian. Tragedy 'absorbs the supreme, orgiastic qualities of music', but then 'allies it with the tragic myth and the tragic hero'.[28] Dionysian music

[19] Geuss, 'Nietzsche: The Birth of Tragedy', 66; Nietzsche, *The Birth of Tragedy*, 109.
[20] Nietzsche, *Birth of Tragedy*, 109.
[21] Taylor, 'Perils of Moralism', 354.
[22] Taylor, 'Perils of Moralism', 354.
[23] Ulfers, 'Introduction', in Nietzsche, *The Dionysian Vision of the World*, 8.
[24] Burnham and Jesinghausen, *Nietzsche's The Birth of Tragedy*, 58.
[25] Nietzsche, *Birth of Tragedy*, 114.
[26] Geuss, 'Nietzsche: The Birth of Tragedy', 61.
[27] Geuss, 'Nietzsche: The Birth of Tragedy', 48.
[28] Nietzsche, *Birth of Tragedy*, 99.

elevates Apollonian speech, which 'soars upward, as it were, borne on the wings of music'.[29] In return, Apollonian speech makes Dionysian music bearable. Nietzsche claims, hyperbolically, that anyone who listens to pure Dionysian music, without the accompaniment of Apollonian speech, would 'suffocate as their soul attempted, convulsively, to spread its wings'.[30] Apollonian speech enables the spectator to survive the Dionysian ordeal. It allows the spectator to listen to Dionysian music and live. The result of the duality of drives in tragedy is the duality of experience in the spectator. The spectator sees 'the tragic hero with all the clarity and beauty of the epic [the Apollonian drive], and yet he takes delight in his destruction [the Dionysian drive]'.[31] However, despite the coexistence and interdependence of the two drives, they remain distinct drives. They can come together momentarily in Greek tragedy, but they also can, just as quickly, fall apart. Just as the birth of 'Greek tragedy has given us some sense of their mutual interaction and intensification', so the demise of Greek tragedy should also give us some sense of the 'tearing-apart of these two primal artistic drives'.[32]

Just as the Apollonian and the Dionysian can come together momentarily and then fall apart, so can nomianism and antinomianism. When they fall apart, each will attempt to deny the other, while still requiring the other. Radical antinomians may try to banish the value of nomianism from their lives, but they will not be able to banish it from the world. The former is a matter of a subjective search for coherence in one's life, while the latter is a matter of objective value pluralism in the world, as this book explains in Chapter 6. In fact, the antinomian needs to have nomianism in the world in order for his or her antinomianism to be meaningful. One can commit oneself subjectively to antinomianism in one's life, while recognizing the value of nomianism in the world, and indeed, the necessity of having nomianism in the world in order for one's antinomianism to make sense. The same is true of the radical nomian. Radical nomians may try to banish the value of antinomianism from their lives, but they will not be able to banish it from the world. The one whose life is subjectively committed to nomianism still requires antinomianism in the world in order for one's nomianism to make sense. The radical antinomian who fails to recognize the value of nomianism is like Kant's dove, while the radical nomian who fails to recognize the value of antinomianism is like Wolf's saint. They are mirror images of each other.

[29] Nietzsche, *Birth of Tragedy*, 112.
[30] Nietzsche, *Birth of Tragedy*, 100.
[31] Nietzsche, *Birth of Tragedy*, 104.
[32] Nietzsche, *Birth of Tragedy*, 110.

On the one hand, the radical antinomian who fails to recognize the value of nomianism is like Kant's dove that, feeling the resistance of the air on its wings, thinks that its flight would be still easier in empty space, when in fact it is the air that makes its flight possible.[33] The dove dreams that it would be so much nicer to soar through the sky without the resistance of the air to hold it back, but it does not reflect on the fact that, if it were not for the resistance of the air, it would not be able to fly at all.[34] Just as the dove fails to notice that it is the friction with the air that provides the support upon which the dove could fly, so the radical antinomian fails to notice that it is the friction with nomianism that provides the support upon which the person could take an antinomian stand. On the other hand, the radical nomian who fails to recognize the value of antinomianism is like Wolf's rational moral saint, who always acts scrupulously 'out of reverence for the moral law as such', and who only 'values his activities and character traits insofar as they were manifestations of respect for the moral law'.[35] The radical nomian and the moral saint treat the law as 'a universal medium into which all other values must be translated'.[36] Wolf's moral saint aims to have no idiosyncrasies or eccentricities, or 'an identifiable, personal self'.[37] Idiosyncrasies and eccentricities give color and character to the self. What Wolf's moral saint fails to realize is that sainthood is built on selfhood. It does not exist in lieu of it. The moral saint's obsession with the moral law blinds the saint to the reality of the self. Just as the moral saint needs a healthy dose of idiosyncrasies or eccentricities in order to sustain the pursuit of sainthood, so the radical nomian too needs to confront the occasional outbursts of antinomianism in order to affirm the pursuit of nomianism. It takes the exception to affirm the norm.

The two sides of the antinomy – nomianism and antinomianism, Apollonian and Dionysian – require each other and gain their respective identities only in virtue of the relationship. We are stuck with the clashing values, not only because we are attracted by both of them and cannot choose, but also because we cannot have either of them *in our lives* without the other *in the world*. The value pluralism here is an entangled value pluralism, in which the opposing values are inextricably intertwined with each other. Paul and Luther oscillated between nomianism and antinomianism in their lifetimes. Christianity moved back and forth between the monastic ideal and the antinomian ideal with movements and countermovements across multiple

---

[33] Kant, *Critique of Pure Reason*, §A5-B9.
[34] Mason, *Philosophical Rhetoric*, 137.
[35] Wolf, 'Moral Saints', 430–1.
[36] Wolf, 'Moral Saints', 428.
[37] Wolf, 'Moral Saints', 424.

Conclusion

lifetimes. Although constitutional orders are now the order of the day in the West, anarchism, in theory if not in practice, continues to lurk in the shadow of constitutionalism. Constitutionalism attempts to fend off totalitarianism, on the one side, and anarchism, on the other. To see the oscillation in operation, we have to turn to history. To get to its source, we have to turn to myth.

The equivocation between nomianism and antinomianism is mythic in origin. The source of it lies in the myth of origin. For that reason, Chapter 1 began with an exploration of the Edenic myth to examine where and when the values of law, love and freedom arise in the myth. The bifurcation of the values of law, love and freedom – which results in the two configurations of values clustered around the monastic ideal and the antinomian ideal – has its genesis in the mythic division of human nature into prelapsarian and fallen. In the fallen world, humans experience imperfection, yet dream of perfection. Hence, Hobbes and Rousseau could generate the images of the nasty brute and the noble savage, respectively, in the state of nature. Both images are plausible because humans are caught between the nightmare and the noble dream. The Edenic myth brings together the nightmare and the noble dream within its mythic frame, and thereby provides us with a 'contracted image of the world'.[38]

This book has appealed to theory and theology, history and myth, to illuminate the values of law, love and freedom in the construction of the nomian life and the antinomian alternative. Theology casts a shadow over theory, and myth over history. History gazes into the past, while myth gazes into infinity. History is time-bound, but when combined with myth, it can tell us something timeless. Myth 'shows us this life' in order to 'transfigure it before our eyes'.[39] In the Socratic dialogues, often, 'when the Socrates character's dialectical reasoning leads to a dead end, a mythical story is told'.[40] If one feels that the dialectic between nomianism and antinomianism has reached a dead end, I can only refer back to the mythical story that was told at the beginning. At the end, we need to go back to the beginning.

---

[38] Nietzsche, *Birth of Tragedy*, 108.
[39] Nietzsche, *Birth of Tragedy*, 113.
[40] Burnham and Jesinghausen, *Nietzsche's The Birth of Tragedy*, 104.

Bibliography

Abbruzzese, Salvatore, 'Monastic Asceticism and Everyday Life', in Isabelle Jonveaux, Enzo Pace and Stefania Palmisano (eds), *Sociology and Monasticism: Between Innovation and Tradition* (Leiden: Brill, 2014), 3–20

Adams, Gretchen, *The Specter of Salem* (Chicago: University of Chicago Press, 2008)

Agamben, Giorgio, *The Time that Remains: A Commentary on the Letter to the Romans*, trans Patricia Dailey (Stanford, CA: Stanford University Press, 2005)

Agamben, Giorgio, *The Highest Poverty: Monastic Rules and Form-of-Life*, trans Adam Kotsko (Stanford, CA: Stanford University Press, 2013)

Anscombe, Elizabeth, *Intention* (Cambridge, MA: Harvard University Press, 2000)

Aquinas, Thomas, *Summa Theologica*, trans Fathers of the English Dominican Province (London: Burns Oates and Washbourne, 1920)

Aquinas, Thomas, *Commentary on Saint Paul's Epistle to the Galatians*, trans F. R. Larcher (Albany, NY: Magi Books, 1966)

Aquinas, Thomas, *On Love and Charity: Readings from the Commentary on the Sentences of Peter Lombard*, trans Peter Kwasniewski, Thomas Bolin and Joseph Bolin (Washington, DC: Catholic University of America Press, 2008) ('Commentary on the Sentences of Peter Lombard')

Arendt, Hannah, *The Human Condition* (Chicago: Chicago University Press, 1958)

Arendt, Hannah, 'What Is Freedom?', in *Between Past and Future* (New York: Viking Press, 1968), 143–71

Arendt, Hannah, *Love and Saint Augustine*, ed Joanna Scott and Judith Stark (Chicago: University of Chicago Press, 1996)

Atkinson, James, *Martin Luther and the Birth of Protestantism* (London: Penguin Books, 1968)

Augustine, 'Homilies on the First Epistle of John', trans H. Browne, in Philip Schaff (ed), *From Nicene and Post-Nicene Fathers*, vol 7 (Buffalo, NY: Christian Literature Publishing, 1887), available at: www.newadvent.org/fathers/1702.htm

Augustine, 'On Christian Doctrine', trans James Shaw, in Philip Schaff (ed), *From Nicene and Post-Nicene Fathers*, vol 2 (Buffalo, NY: Christian Literature Publishing, 1887), available at: www.newadvent.org/fathers/1202.htm

Augustine, *Select Letters*, trans James Baxter (Cambridge, MA: Harvard University Press, 1930)

Augustine, *City of God*, trans George McCracken (Cambridge, MA: Harvard University Press, 1957)
Augustine, 'Praeceptum', trans George Lawless, in George Lawless, *Augustine of Hippo and His Monastic Rule* (Oxford: Oxford University Press, 1990), 110–23
Augustine, 'The Work of Monks', trans Mary Muldowney, in *Treatises on Various Subjects*, ed Roy Deferrari (Washington, DC: Catholic University of America Press, 2014), 321–94
Austin, John, *Lectures on Jurisprudence or the Philosophy of Positive Law* (London: John Murray, 1885)
Badiou, Alan, *Saint Paul: The Foundation of Universalism*, trans Ray Brassier (Stanford, CA: Stanford University Press, 2003)
Baker, Emerson, *A Storm of Witchcraft: The Salem Trials and the American Experience* (Oxford: Oxford University Press, 2015)
Balkin, Jack, 'Critical Legal Theory Today', in Francis Mootz III (ed), *On Philosophy in American Law* (Cambridge: Cambridge University Press, 2008), 64–72
Balkin, Jack, *Constitutional Redemption: Political Faith in an Unjust World* (Cambridge, MA: Harvard University Press, 2011)
Bankowski, Zenon, 'Law, Love and Legality' (2001) 14 *International Journal for the Semiotics of Law* 199–213
Bellah, Robert, *The Broken Covenant* (Chicago: University of Chicago Press, 1992)
Bergmann, Frithjof, *On Being Free* (Notre Dame, IN: University of Notre Dame Press, 1977)
Berlin, Isaiah, 'Two Concepts of Liberty', in *Four Essays on Liberty* (Oxford: Oxford University Press, 1969), 118–72
Berlin, Isaiah, 'The Question of Machiavelli', *The New York Review of Books*, November 4, 1971
Berlin, Isaiah, 'Two Concepts of Freedom: Romantic and Liberal', in *Political Ideas in the Romantic Age*, ed Henry Hardy (London: Chatto & Windus, 2006), 195–260
Berlin, Isaiah, 'Does Political Theory Still Exist?', in *The Proper Study of Mankind*, ed Henry Hardy and Roger Hausheer (London: Vintage Books, 2013), 59–90
Berlin, Isaiah, 'The Apotheosis of the Romantic Will', in *The Proper Study of Mankind*, ed Henry Hardy and Roger Hausheer (London: Vintage Books, 2013), 553–80
Berlin, Isaiah, 'The Hedgehog and the Fox', *in The Proper Study of Mankind*, ed Henry Hardy and Roger Hausheer (London: Vintage Books, 2013), 436–98
Berlin, Isaiah, 'The Pursuit of the Ideal', in *The Proper Study of Mankind*, ed Henry Hardy and Roger Hausheer (London: Vintage Books, 2013), 1–16
Berman, Harold, *Law and Revolution: The Formation of the Western Legal Tradition* (Cambridge, MA: Harvard University Press, 1983)
Berman, Harold, *Law and Revolution II: The Impact of the Protestant Reformations on the Western Legal Tradition* (Cambridge, MA: Harvard University Press, 2006)
Bernstein, J. M., 'Love and Law: Hegel's Critique of Morality' (2003) 70 *Social Research* 393–431
Bird-Pollan, Stefan, 'Hegel's Grounding of Intersubjectivity in the Master–Slave Dialectic' (2012) 38 *Philosophy and Social Criticism* 237–56
Bosman, Philip, 'Selling Cynicism: The Pragmatics of Diogenes' Comic Performances' (2006) 56 *Classical Quarterly* 93–104

Boyarin, Daniel, *A Radical Jew: Paul and the Politics of Identity* (Berkeley: University of California Press, 1994)
Brett, Annabel, *Changes of State: Nature and the Limits of the City in Early Modern Natural Law* (Princeton, NJ: Princeton University Press, 2011)
Brett, Mark, *Genesis: Procreation and the Politics of Identity* (London: Routledge, 2000)
Bronstein, Daniel, 'The Principle of Polarity in Cohen's Philosophy', in S. W. Baron, E. Nagel, and K. S. Pinson (eds), *Freedom and Reason* (Glencoe, IL: The Free Press, 1951), 44–58
Bultmann, Rudolf, 'The Problem of Ethics in the Writings of Paul', in *The Old and the New Man*, trans Keith Crim (Richmond: John Knox Press, 1967), 7–32
Burnham, Douglas, and Martin Jesinghausen, *Nietzsche's The Birth of Tragedy* (London: Continuum, 2010)
Burt, Robert, *In the Whirlwind: God and Humanity in Conflict* (Cambridge, MA: Harvard University Press, 2012)
Caputo, John, 'Postcards from Paul: Subtraction versus Grafting', in John Caputo and Linda Alcoff (eds), *Saint Paul among the Philosophers* (Bloomington: Indiana University Press, 2009), 1–23
Carr, David, *Erotic Word: Sexuality, Spirituality and the Bible* (Oxford: Oxford University Press, 2005)
Casey, Simon, *Naked Liberty and the World of Desire* (New York: Routledge, 2003)
Chappell, Timothy, *Ethics and Experience* (London: Routledge, 2009)
Cherniss, Joshua, 'Isaiah Berlin's Political Ideas: From the Twentieth Century to the Romantic Age', in Isaiah Berlin, *Political Ideas in the Romantic Age*, ed Henry Hardy (London: Chatto & Windus, 2006), xliii–xcii
Cherniss, Joshua, *A Mind and Its Time: The Development of Isaiah Berlin's Political Thought* (Oxford: Oxford University Press, 2013)
Cohen, Morris, 'Concepts and Twilight Zones' (1927) 24 *Journal of Philosophy* 673–83
Cohen, Morris, *Reason and Nature* (New York: Harcourt, Brace and Co, 1931)
Cohen, Morris, *A Preface to Logic* (New York: Routledge, 1946)
Cohen, Morris, *A Dreamer's Journey* (Glencoe, IL: The Free Press, 1949)
Cohen, Morris, *Studies in Philosophy and Science* (New York: H Holt, 1949)
Collingwood, R. G., *The Idea of History* (Oxford: Clarendon Press, 1961)
Collins, Randall, *Weberian Sociological Theory* (Cambridge: Cambridge University Press, 1986)
Collinson, Diane, 'Ethics and Aesthetics Are One' (1985) 25 *British Journal of Aesthetics* 266–72
Constant, Benjamin, 'The Liberty of the Ancients Compared with that of the Moderns', in *Political Writings*, ed and trans Biancamaria Fontana (Cambridge: Cambridge University Press, 1988), 308–28
Coughlin, John, *Canon Law: A Comparative Study with Anglo-American Legal Theory* (Oxford: Oxford University Press, 2010)
Cousins, Ewert, 'The Fourfold Sense of Scripture in Christian Mysticism', in Steven Katz (ed), *Mysticism and Sacred Scripture* (Oxford: Oxford University Press, 2000), 118–37
Craig, Edward, *The Mind of God and the Works of Man* (Oxford: Oxford University Press, 1996)

Cunningham, Adrian, 'Type and Archetype in the Eden Story', in Paul Morris and Deborah Sawyer (eds), *A Walk in the Garden: Biblical, Iconographical, and Literary Images of Eden* (Sheffield: Sheffield Academic Press, 1992), 290–309

Davies, W. D., 'Paul and the Law: Reflections on Pitfalls in Interpretation' (1978) 29 *Hastings Law Journal* 1459–504

Davies, W. D., 'From Schweitzer to Scholem', in Marc Saperstein (ed), *Essential Papers on Messianic Moments and Personalities in Jewish History* (New York: New York University Press, 1992), 529–58

Derrida, Jacques, 'Signature, Event, Context' (1977) 1 *Glyph* 172–97

Derrida, Jacques, *Positions*, trans Alan Bass (Chicago: University of Chicago Press, 1981)

Derrida, Jacques, 'Force of Law: The Mystical Foundation of Authority', trans Mary Quaintance (1990) 11 *Cardozo Law Review* 920–1045

Dershowitz, Alan, *The Genesis of Justice* (New York: Warner Books, 2000)

Dunn, James, 'Reconstructions of Corinthian Christianity and the Interpretation of 1 Corinthians', in Edward Adams and David Horrell (eds), *Christianity at Corinth: The Quest for the Pauline Church* (London: Westminster John Knox Press, 2004), 295–310

Dunn, James, 'The New Perspective on Paul: Whence, What, Whither?', in *The New Perspective on Paul: Collected Essays* (Tubingen: Mohr Siebeck, 2005), 1–88

Dunn, James, 'The New Perspective on Paul (1983)', in *The New Perspective on Paul: Collected Essays* (Tubingen: Mohr Siebeck, 2005), 89–110

Dunn, Marilyn, *The Emergence of Monasticism: From the Desert Fathers to the Early Middle Ages* (Oxford: Blackwell, 2000)

Dworkin, Ronald, 'Law as Interpretation' (1982) 9 *Critical Inquiry* 179–200

Dworkin, Ronald, *Law's Empire* (Cambridge, MA: Harvard University Press, 1986)

Dworkin, Ronald, 'Hart's Postscript and the Character of Political Philosophy' (2004) 24 *Oxford Journal of Legal Studies* 1–37

Dyzenhaus, David, 'Hobbes and the Legitimacy of Law' (2001) 20 *Law and Philosophy* 461–98

Dyzenhaus, David, 'Hobbes's Constitutional Theory', in Ian Shapiro (ed), *Hobbes: Leviathan* (New Haven, CT: Yale University Press, 2010), 453–80

Finnis, John, *Natural Law and Natural Rights* (Oxford: Oxford University Press, 1980)

Finnis, John, 'Commensuration and Public Reason', in Ruth Chang (ed), *Incommensurability, Incomparability, and Practical Reason* (Cambridge, MA: Harvard University Press, 1998), 215–33

Finnis, John, 'What Is the Philosophy of Law?' (2014) 59 *American Journal of Jurisprudence* 133–42

Finnis, John, 'Subsidiarity's Roots and History: Some Observations' (2016) 61 *American Journal of Jurisprudence* 133–41

Fletcher, George, 'Thinking about Eden' (2003) 22 *Quinnipiac Law Review* 1–21

Flikschuh, Katrin, *Freedom: Contemporary Liberal Perspectives* (Cambridge: Polity Press, 2007)

Fox, Richard, 'Sentencing in the Garden of Eden' (2006) 32 *Monash University Law Review* 4–27

Frankfurt, Harry, *The Reasons of Love* (Princeton, NJ: Princeton University Press, 2004)

Freud, Sigmund, *Civilisation and Its Discontent*, trans James Strachey (London: WW Norton, 1962)
Frye, Northrop, *The Great Code: The Bible and Literature* (New York: Harcourt Brace Jovanovich, 1982)
Fuller, Lon, 'Reason and Fiat in Case Law' (1946) 59 *Harvard Law Review* 376–95
Fuller, Lon, *The Problems of Jurisprudence* (New York: Foundation Press, 1949)
Fuller, Lon, *The Morality of Law* (New Haven, CT: Yale University Press, 1964)
Fuller, Lon, 'Two Principles of Human Association', in *The Principles of Social Order: Selected Essays of Lon Fuller*, ed Kenneth Winston (Durham, NC: Duke University Press, 1981), 67–85
Gager, John, *Reinventing Paul* (Oxford: Oxford University Press, 2000)
Gans, Eric, *The Scenic Imagination* (Stanford, CA: Stanford University Press, 2008)
Geertz, Clifford, 'Religion as a Cultural System', in *The Interpretation of Cultures* (New York: Basic Books, 1973), 87–125
Geertz, Clifford, 'Thick Description: Toward an Interpretive Theory of Culture', in *The Interpretation of Cultures* (New York: Basic Books, 1973), 3–30
Geertz, Clifford, 'Found in Translation: On the Social History of the Moral Imagination' (1977) 31 *The Georgia Review* 788–810
Geertz, Clifford, *Available Light: Anthropological Reflections on Philosophical Topics* (Princeton, NJ: Princeton University Press, 2012)
Geuss, Raymond, *Public Goods, Private Goods* (Princeton, NJ: Princeton University Press, 2001)
Geuss, Raymond, 'Nietzsche: The Birth of Tragedy', in Robert Pippin (ed), *Introductions to Nietzsche* (Cambridge: Cambridge University Press, 2012), 44–66
Gilmore, Grant, *The Ages of American Law* (New Haven, CT: Yale University Press, 1977)
Ginzberg, Louis, *The Legends of the Jews*, trans Henrietta Szold (Philadelphia: Jewish Publication Society, 1910)
Girard, Rene, *Deceit, Desire, and the Novel* (Baltimore, MD: Johns Hopkins University Press, 1976)
Golding, William, *Lord of the Flies* (London: Faber and Faber, 1954)
Gray, John, 'On Negative and Positive Liberty' (1980) 28 *Political Studies* 507–26
Gray, John, *Isaiah Berlin: An Interpretation of His Thought* (Princeton, NJ: Princeton University Press, 2013)
Griffin, James, 'Incommensurability: What's the Problem?', in Ruth Chang (ed), *Incommensurability, Incomparability, and Practical Reason* (Cambridge, MA: Harvard University Press, 1998), 35–51
Hart, H. L. A., 'American Jurisprudence through English Eyes: The Nightmare and the Noble Dream' (1977) 11 *Georgia Law Review* 969–89
Hart, H. L. A., *The Concept of Law*, 2nd ed, ed Joseph Raz and Penelope Bullock (Oxford: Clarendon Press, 1994).
Hausheer, Roger, 'Introduction', in Isaiah Berlin, *Against the Current: Essays in the History of Ideas*, ed Henry Hardy (Princeton, NJ: Princeton University Press, 2013), xxxi–lxxxiv
Hegel, G. W. F., *Phenomenology of Spirit*, trans A. V. Miller (Oxford: Oxford University Press, 1977)

Hill, Craig, 'Romans', in John Muddiman and John Barton (eds), *The Oxford Bible Commentary* (Oxford: Oxford University Press, 2007), 1083–108

Hobbes, Thomas, *Leviathan with Selected Variants from the Latin Edition of 1668*, ed Edwin Curley (Indianapolis, IN: Hackett Publishing, 1994)

Hobbes, Thomas, *Leviathan, or the Matter, Form, and Power of a Commonwealth, Ecclesiastical and Civil* (Adelaide: University of Adelaide Library, 2014)

Holmes, Oliver Wendell, 'The Path of the Law' (1897) 10 *Harvard Law Review* 457–78

Horrell, David, and Edward Adams, 'The Scholarly Quest for Paul's Church at Corinth: A Critical Survey', in Edward Adams and David Horrell (eds), *Christianity at Corinth: The Quest for the Pauline Church* (London: Westminster John Knox Press, 2004), 1–43

Houlgate, Stephen, *An Introduction to Hegel: Freedom, Truth and History* (Oxford: Blackwell, 2005)

Jollimore, Troy, *Love's Vision* (Princeton, NJ: Princeton University Press, 2011)

Jonveaux, Isabelle, 'Redefinition of the Role of Monks in Modern Society: Economy as Monastic Opportunity', in Isabelle Jonveaux, Enzo Pace and Stefania Palmisano (eds), *Sociology and Monasticism: Between Innovation and Tradition* (Leiden: Brill, 2014), 71–86

Jung, Carl, *Answer to Job*, trans R. F. C. Hull (Princeton, NJ: Princeton University Press, 2012)

Kahn, Paul, *Legitimacy and History* (New Haven, CT: Yale University Press, 1992)

Kahn, Paul, *Law and Love: The Trials of King Lear* (New Haven, CT: Yale University Press, 2000)

Kahn, Paul, *Putting Liberalism in Its Place* (Princeton, NJ: Princeton University Press, 2008)

Kant, Immanuel, *Critique of Pure Reason*, trans Norman Kemp Smith (London: Macmillan, 1929)

Kant, Immanuel, 'Idea for a Universal History from a Cosmopolitan Point of View', in *On History*, trans Lewis Beck (Indianapolis, IN: Bobbs-Merrill, 1963), 11–26

Kaplan, Mordecai, *Judaism as a Civilization* (Philadelphia: Jewish Publication Society, 2010)

Keck, Leander, *Paul and His Letters* (Philadelphia: Fortress Press, 1979)

Kekes, John, *Moral Tradition and Individuality* (Princeton, NJ: Princeton University Press, 1989)

Kekes, John, *The Morality of Pluralism* (Princeton, NJ: Princeton University Press, 1996)

Kekes, John, *Pluralism in Philosophy* (Ithaca, NY: Cornell University Press, 2000)

Kekes, John, *Human Predicaments* (Chicago: University of Chicago Press, 2016)

Krasnoff, Larry, *Hegel's Phenomenology of Spirit* (Cambridge: Cambridge University Press, 2008)

Laidlaw, James, *The Subject of Virtue: An Anthropology of Ethics and Freedom* (Cambridge: Cambridge University Press, 2013)

Larsen, Robert, 'Morris Cohen's Principle of Polarity' (1959) 20 *Journal of the History of Ideas* 587–95

Lawless, George, *Augustine of Hippo and His Monastic Rule* (Oxford: Oxford University Press, 1990)

Lawrence, D. H., *The Complete Poems of D. H. Lawrence*, ed Vivian de Sola Pinto and Warren Roberts (London: Heineman, 1964)

Lawrence, D. H., *Study of Thomas Hardy and Other Essays*, ed Bruce Steele (Cambridge: Cambridge University Press, 1985)

Lawrence, D. H., *Aaron's Rod*, ed Mara Kalnins (Cambridge: Cambridge University Press, 1988)

Lear, Jonathan, *Love and Its Place in Nature* (New Haven, CT: Yale University Press, 1999)

Lee, Philip, *Against the Protestant Gnostics* (Oxford: Oxford University Press, 1987)

Leibowitz, Yeshayahu, 'Religious Praxis: The Meaning of Halakhah', in *Judaism, Human Values, and the Jewish State*, ed Eliezer Goldman (Cambridge, MA: Harvard University Press, 1995), 3–29

Leopold, David, 'Introduction', in Max Stirner, *Ego and Its Own*, trans Steven Byington, ed David Leopold (Cambridge: Cambridge University Press, 1995), xi–xxxii

Levy, Jacob, *Rationalism, Pluralism and Freedom* (Oxford: Oxford University Press, 2015)

Locke, John, *Second Treatise of Civil Government* (Adelaide: University of Adelaide Library, 2014)

Lytton, Timothy, 'Due Process and Legal Authority in the Garden of Eden: Jurisprudence in Aggadic Midrash' (2006) 16 *Jewish Law Annual* 185–201

MacIntyre, Alasdair, 'Plain Persons and Moral Philosophy' (1992) 66 *American Catholic Philosophical Quarterly* 3–19

MacIntyre, Alasdair, *After Virtue* (London: Bloomsbury Publishing, 2013)

MacIntyre, Alasdair, *Ethics in the Conflicts of Modernity* (Cambridge: Cambridge University Press, 2016)

Magonet, Jonathan, 'The Themes of Genesis 2–3', in Paul Morris and Deborah Sawyer (eds), *A Walk in the Garden: Biblical, Iconographical, and Literary Images of Eden* (Sheffield: Sheffield Academic Press, 1992), 39–46

Maitland, F. W., *Collected Papers* (Cambridge: Cambridge University Press, 1911)

Mali, Joseph, 'Berlin, Vico and the Principles of Humanity', in Joseph Mali and Robert Wokler (eds), *Isaiah Berlin's Counter-Enlightenment* (Philadelphia: The American Philosophical Society, 2003), 51–72

Markus, R. A., *The End of Ancient Christianity* (Cambridge: Cambridge University Press, 1990)

Mason, Jeff, *Philosophical Rhetoric: The Function of Indirection in Philosophical Writing* (London: Routledge, 1989)

May, Larry, *Limiting Leviathan: Hobbes on Law and International Affairs* (Oxford: Oxford University Press, 2013)

May, Simon, *Love: A History* (New Haven, CT: Yale University Press, 2011)

McCabe, Herbert, *God Matters* (New York: Continuum, 1987)

McLaughlin, Paul, *Anarchism and Authority* (Aldershot: Ashgate, 2007)

McNulty, Tracy, 'The Event of the Letter: Two Approaches to the Law and Its Real' (2008) 29 *Cardozo Law Review* 2209–238

Mendus, Susan, 'The Importance of Love in Rawls's Theory of Justice' (1999) 29 *British Journal of Political Science* 57–75

Miller, Char, 'Time of the Antichrist: Paul's Subversion of Empire' (2009) 37 *Political Theory* 562–70
Morris, Paul, 'A Walk in the Garden: Images of Eden', in Paul Morris and Deborah Sawyer (eds), *A Walk in the Garden: Biblical, Iconographical, and Literary Images of Eden* (Sheffield: Sheffield Academic Press, 1992), 21–38
Murdoch, Iris, *The Sovereignty of the Good* (London: Routledge, 1970)
Nagel, Thomas, *View from Nowhere* (Oxford: Oxford University Press, 1986)
Neoh, Joshua, 'Text, Doctrine and Tradition in Law and Religion' (2013) 2 *Oxford Journal of Law and Religion* 175–99
Neoh, Joshua, 'Just Jurisprudence: Review of Philip Pettit's Just Freedom' (2015) 40 *Australian Journal of Legal Philosophy* 237–40
Neoh, Joshua, 'Law and Love in Abraham's Binding of Isaac' (2015) 9 *Law and Humanities* 237–61
Neoh, Joshua, 'The Rhetoric of Precedent and Fulfilment in the Sermon on the Mount and the Common Law' (2016) 12 *Law, Culture and the Humanities* 419–47
Neoh, Joshua, 'Law Imprisons, Love Liberates' (2018) 30 *Law and Literature* 221–44
Neoh, Joshua, 'Political Theology and Legal Theory', in *The Research Handbook on Interdisciplinary Approaches to Law and Religion* (Edward Elgar, forthcoming)
Nietzsche, Friedrich, *Twilight of the Idols*, trans R. J. Hollingdale (Harmondsworth: Penguin, 1968)
Nietzsche, Friedrich, *The Gay Science*, trans Walter Kaufmann (New York: Vintage Books, 1974)
Nietzsche, Friedrich, *Beyond Good and Evil*, trans Walter Kaufmann (New York: Vintage Books, 1989)
Nietzsche, Friedrich, *On the Genealogy of Morals*, trans Walter Kaufmann and R. J. Hollingdale (New York: Vintage Books, 1989)
Nietzsche, Friedrich, *The Birth of Tragedy*, trans Ronald Speirs (Cambridge: Cambridge University Press, 1999)
Nietzsche, Friedrich, 'Why I Am So Clever', in *Ecce Homo*, trans Anthony Ludovici (New York: Dover Publications, 2004)
Nietzsche, Friedrich, *The Dionysian Vision of the World*, trans Ira Allen (Minneapolis: University of Minnesota Press, 2013)
Norman, Richard, *Hegel's Phenomenology: A Philosophical Introduction* (Sussex: Sussex University Press, 1976)
Nozick, Robert, *Anarchy, State and Utopia* (New York: Basic Books, 1974)
Nozick, Robert, 'Love's Bond', in Robert Solomon and Kathleen Higgins (eds), *The Philosophy of (Erotic) Love* (Lawrence: University Press of Kansas, 1991), 417–32
Oakeshott, Michael, *The Voice of Poetry in the Conversation of Mankind* (London: Bowes & Bowes, 1959)
Oakeshott, Michael, 'Rationalism in Politics', in *Rationalism in Politics and Other Essays* (Indianapolis, IN: Liberty Fund, 1991), 6–42
O'Daly, Gerard, *Augustine's City of God: A Reader's Guide* (Oxford: Oxford University Press, 1999)
O'Donovan, Oliver, *Common Objects of Love: Moral Reflection and the Shaping of Community* (Grand Rapids, MI: William B. Eerdmans, 2002)

Pace, Enzo, 'Seguy and the Monastic Utopia', in Isabelle Jonveaux, Enzo Pace and Stefania Palmisano (eds), *Sociology and Monasticism: Between Innovation and Tradition* (Leiden: Brill, 2014), 277–83

Pagels, Elaine, *The Gnostic Paul: Gnostic Exegesis of the Pauline Letters* (Philadelphia: Fortress Press, 1975)

Pagels, Elaine, *Adam, Eve and the Serpent* (New York: Random House, 1988)

Pagels, Elaine, and Karen King, *Reading Judas: The Gospel of Judas and the Shaping of Christianity* (London: Viking, 2007)

Parker, Kim, 'Mirror, Mirror on the Wall, Must We Leave Eden, Once and for All? A Lacanian Pleasure Trip through the Garden' (1999) 24 *Journal for the Study of the Old Testament* 19–29

Paterson, R. W. K., *The Nihilistic Egoist Max Stirner* (Oxford: Oxford University Press, 1971)

Pettit, Philip, *Republicanism: A Theory of Freedom and Government* (Oxford: Oxford University Press, 1997)

Plato, *Plato's Symposium: Collected Works of Plato*, trans Benjamin Jowett (Oxford: Oxford University Press, 1953)

Plato, *Republic*, trans Robin Waterfield (Oxford: Oxford University Press, 1993)

Postema, Gerald, *Bentham and the Common Law Tradition* (Oxford: Clarendon Press, 1986)

Raisanen, Heikki, 'Paul's Conversion and the Development of His View of the Law' (1987) 33 *New Testament Studies* 404–19

Rawls, John, 'Outline of a Decision Procedure for Ethics' (1951) 60 *Philosophical Review* 177–97

Rawls, John, *A Theory of Justice* (Oxford: Oxford University Press, 1972)

Rawls, John, *Lectures on the History of Political Philosophy*, ed Samuel Freeman (Cambridge, MA: Harvard University Press, 2009)

Raz, Joseph, *The Authority of Law* (Oxford: Oxford University Press, 1979)

Raz, Joseph, *Morality of Freedom* (Oxford: Oxford University Press, 1988)

Raz, Joseph, 'Incommensurability and Agency', in Ruth Chang (ed), *Incommensurability, Incomparability, and Practical Reason* (Cambridge, MA: Harvard University Press, 1998), 110–28

Raz, Joseph, *Practical Reason and Norms* (Oxford: Oxford University Press, 1999)

Raz, Joseph, *The Practice of Value* (Oxford: Oxford University Press, 2003)

Raz, Joseph, 'On the Guise of the Good', in Sergio Tenenbaum (ed), *Desire, Practical Reason and the Good* (Oxford: Oxford University Press, 2010), 111–37

Ricoeur, Paul, 'Life in Quest of Narrative', in David Wood (ed), *On Paul Ricoeur: Narrative and Interpretation* (New York: Routledge, 1991), 20–34

Ricoeur, Paul, 'Narrative Identity', in David Wood (ed), *On Paul Ricoeur: Narrative and Interpretation* (New York: Routledge, 1991), 188–99

Ricoeur, Paul, *Oneself as Another*, trans Kathleen Blamey (Chicago: University of Chicago Press, 1992)

Rousseau, Jean-Jacques, *The Social Contract* (Adelaide: The University of Adelaide Library, 2008)

Rousseau, Jean-Jacques, *Discourse on the Origin and the Foundations of Inequality among Men*, trans Ian Johnston (Adelaide: University of Adelaide Library, 2009)

Rundle, Kristen, *Forms Liberate: Reclaiming the Jurisprudence of Lon L Fuller* (Oxford: Hart, 2012)

Ryan, Alan, *The Making of Modern Liberalism* (Princeton, NJ: Princeton University Press, 2012)

Sanders, E. P., *Paul and Palestinian Judaism* (Philadelphia: Fortress Press, 1977)

Sanders, E. P., *Paul, the Law and the Jewish People* (Philadelphia: Fortress Press, 1983)

Sawyer, Deborah, 'The New Adam in the Theology of Saint Paul' in Paul Morris and Deborah Sawyer (eds), *A Walk in the Garden: Biblical, Iconographical, and Literary Images of Eden* (Sheffield: Sheffield Academic Press, 1992), 105–16

Schmidtz, David, *Elements of Justice* (Cambridge: Cambridge University Press, 2006)

Schmitt, Carl, *Political Theology: Four Chapters on the Concept of Sovereignty*, trans George Schwab (Cambridge, MA: MIT Press, 1985)

Scott, James, *The Art of Not Being Governed* (New Haven, CT: Yale University Press, 2009)

Scottow, J., 'Narrative of the Planning of Massachusetts' (1694), in *Collections of the Massachusetts Historical Society* (4th ser.) (1871) 4:279

Seguy, Jean, 'A Sociology of Imagined Societies: Monasticism and Utopia', in Isabelle Jonveaux, Enzo Pace and Stefania Palmisano (eds), *Sociology and Monasticism: Between Innovation and Tradition* (Leiden: Brill, 2014), 71–86

Shakespeare, William, *As You Like It* (Oxford: Clarendon Press, 1993)

Shapiro, Scott, 'Authority', in Jules Coleman and Scott Shapiro (eds), *The Oxford Handbook of Jurisprudence and Philosophy of Law* (Oxford: Oxford University Press, 2002), 382–439

Shapiro, Scott, *Legality* (Cambridge, MA: Harvard University Press, 2013)

Sherwin, Michael, *By Knowledge and By Love: Charity and Knowledge in the Moral Theology of Saint Thomas Aquinas* (Washington, DC: Catholic University of America Press, 2005)

Shklar, Judith, *Legalism: Law, Morals and Political Trials* (Cambridge, MA: Harvard University Press, 1964)

Shklar, Judith, 'The Liberalism of Fear', in Nancy Rosenblum (ed), *Liberalism and the Moral Life* (Cambridge, MA: Harvard University Press, 1989), 21–38

Siedentop, Larry, *Inventing the Individual: The Origins of Western Liberalism* (Cambridge, MA: Harvard University Press, 2014)

Silber, Ilana, 'Monasticism and the Protestant Ethic' (1993) 44 *British Journal of Sociology* 103–23

Simmonds, Nigel, 'Judgment and Mercy' (1993) 13 *Oxford Journal of Legal Studies* 52–68

Simmonds, Nigel, 'Jurisprudence as a Moral and Historical Inquiry' (2005) 18 *Canadian Journal of Law and Jurisprudence* 249–76

Simmonds, Nigel, *Law as a Moral Idea* (Oxford: Oxford University Press, 2007)

Simmonds, Nigel, 'Reflexivity and the Idea of Law' (2010) 1 *Jurisprudence* 1–23

Simmonds, Nigel, 'The Bondwoman's Son and the Beautiful Soul' (2013) 58 *American Journal of Jurisprudence* 111–13

Smedley, Francis, *Frank Fairleigh* (London: W Scott, 1850)

Smith, Douglas, 'Introduction', in Friedrich Nietzsche, *The Birth of Tragedy*, trans Douglas Smith (Oxford: Oxford University Press, 2000), vii–xxxvi

Spinoza, Baruch, *Theologico-Political Treatise*, in *The Chief Works*, trans R. H. M. Elwes (New York: Dover, 1951), 1–266
Stirner, Max, *Ego and Its Own*, trans Steven Byington, ed David Leopold (Cambridge: Cambridge University Press, 1995)
Taylor, Charles, 'Kant's Theory of Freedom', in *Philosophical Papers*, vol 2 (Cambridge: Cambridge University Press, 1985), 318–38
Taylor, Charles, 'What's Wrong with Negative Liberty', in *Philosophical Papers*, vol 2 (Cambridge: Cambridge University Press, 1985), 211–29
Taylor, Charles, 'Cross-Purposes: The Liberal-Communitarian Debate', in Nancy Rosenblum (ed), *Liberalism and the Moral Life* (Cambridge, MA: Harvard University Press, 1989), 159–82
Taylor, Charles, *Sources of the Self* (Cambridge: Cambridge University Press, 1989)
Taylor, Charles, 'Leading a Life', in Ruth Chang (ed), *Incommensurability, Incomparability and Practical Reasoning* (Cambridge, MA: Harvard University Press, 1997), 170–83
Taylor, Charles, 'Modern Social Imaginaries' (2002) 14 *Public Culture* 91–124
Taylor, Charles, *A Secular Age* (Cambridge, MA: Harvard University Press, 2007)
Taylor, Charles, 'Perils of Moralism', in *Dilemmas and Connections: Selected Essays* (Cambridge, MA: Harvard University Press, 2011), 347–66
Teachout, Peter, 'The Soul of the Fugue: An Essay on Reading Fuller' (1985) 70 *Minnesota Law Review* 1073–148
Third Plenary Council of Baltimore, *A Catechism of Christian Doctrine, Prepared and Enjoined by Order of the Third Plenary Council of Baltimore* (New York: Benziger, 1885)
Thomson, E. P., *Witness against the Beast: William Blake and the Moral Law* (Cambridge: Cambridge University Press, 1993)
Thornton, Helen, *State of Nature or Eden?* (Rochester, NY: University of Rochester Press, 2005)
Tigar, Michael, *Law and the Rise of Capitalism* (New York: Monthly Review Press, 1977)
Tillich, Paul, 'Being and Love' (1954) 5 *Pastoral Psychology* 43–8
Tillich, Paul, *Love, Power and Justice* (Oxford: Oxford University Press, 1954)
Tuck, Richard, *The Sleeping Sovereign: The Invention of Modern Democracy* (Cambridge: Cambridge University Press, 2015)
Ulfers, Friedrich, 'Introduction', in Friedrich Nietzsche, *The Dionysian Vision of the World*, trans Ira Allen (Minneapolis: University of Minnesota Press, 2013), 1–28
Waldron, Jeremy, 'Kant's Legal Positivism' (1996) 109 *Harvard Law Review* 1535–66
Waldron, Jeremy, *Law and Disagreement* (Oxford: Oxford University Press, 1999)
Waldron, Jeremy, 'Normative (or Ethical) Positivism', in Jules Coleman (ed), *Hart's Postscript: Essays on the Postscript to 'The Concept of Law'* (Oxford: Oxford University Press, 2001), 410–33
Waldron, Jeremy, 'Dead to the Law: Paul's Antinomianism' (2006) 28 *Cardozo Law Review* 301–32
Walzer, Michael, *The Revolution of the Saints: A Study in the Origins of Radical Politics* (Cambridge, MA: Harvard University Press, 1982)
Walzer, Michael, *Exodus and Revolution* (New York: Basic Books, 1985)
Walzer, Michael, *The Company of Critics* (London: Peter Halban, 1989)

Walzer, Michael, 'The Legal Codes of Ancient Israel' (1992) 4 *Yale Journal of Law and the Humanities* 335–50
Walzer, Michael, *Interpretation and Social Criticism* (Cambridge, MA: Harvard University Press, 1993)
Walzer, Michael, 'Objectivity and Social Meanings', in Martha Nussbaum and Amartya Sen (eds), *The Quality of Life* (Oxford: Oxford University Press, 1993), 165–77
Walzer, Michael, *Thick and Thin: Moral Argument at Home and Abroad* (Notre Dame, IN: University of Notre Dame Press, 1994)
Walzer, Michael et al. (eds), *The Jewish Political Tradition*, vol 1 (New Haven, CT: Yale University Press, 2000)
Weber, Max, *The Sociology of Religion* (London: Methuen, 1965)
Weber, Max, *The Protestant Ethic and the Spirit of Capitalism*, trans Talcott Parsons (London: Routledge, 2001)
White, James, *When Words Lose Their Meaning: Constitutions and Reconstitutions of Language, Character and Community* (Chicago: University of Chicago Press, 1984)
Williams, Bernard, 'Ethical Consistency', in *Problems of the Self* (Cambridge: Cambridge University Press, 1973), 166–86
Williams, Bernard, *Moral Luck* (Cambridge: Cambridge University Press, 1981)
Williams, Bernard, 'Reply to Simon Blackburn' (1986) 27 *Philosophical Books* 203–8
Williams, Bernard, *Ethics and the Limits of Philosophy* (London: Routledge Classics, 2011)
Williams, Garrath, 'Normatively Demanding Creatures' (2000) 6 *Res Publica* 301–19
Wilson, A. N., *Paul: The Mind of the Apostle* (New York: WW Norton, 1997)
Wilson, R. M., 'How Gnostic Were the Corinthians?' (1972) 19 *New Testament Studies* 65–74
Winston, Kenneth, 'The Ideal Element in a Definition of Law' (1986) 5 *Law and Philosophy* 89–111
Winthrop, John, 'A Model of Christian Charity' (1630), in Edmund Morgan (ed), *Puritan Political Ideas* (Indianapolis, IN: Bobbs-Merrill, 1965), 75–93
Witte, John, *Law and Protestantism* (Cambridge: Cambridge University Press, 2002)
Witte, John, *God's Joust, God's Justice* (Grand Rapids, MI: Williams B Eerdmans, 2006)
Witte, John, *The Reformation of Rights* (Cambridge: Cambridge University Press, 2007)
Wittgenstein, Ludwig, *Tractatus Logico-Philosophicus*, trans C. K. Ogden (London: Kegan Paul, 1922)
Wittgenstein, Ludwig, *Philosophical Investigations*, trans G. E. M. Anscombe (Oxford: Basil Blackwell, 1953)
Wittgenstein, Ludwig, *Notebooks 1914–1916*, trans G. E. M. Anscombe (Oxford: Basil Blackwell, 1969)
Wolf, Susan, 'Moral Saints' (1982) 79 *Journal of Philosophy* 419–39
Wolf, Susan, *The Variety of Values: Essays on Morality, Meaning, and Love* (Oxford: Oxford University Press, 2014)
Wolff, R. P., *In Defense of Anarchism* (Berkeley: University of California Press, 1998)
Wolfson, Elliot, *Venturing Beyond: Law and Morality in Kabbalistic Mysticism* (Oxford: Oxford University Press, 2006)

Wollheim, Richard, 'On Persons and Their Lives', in Amelie Rorty (ed), *Explaining Emotions* (Berkeley: University of California Press, 1980), 299–321

Wollheim, Richard, *The Thread of Life* (Cambridge, MA: Harvard University Press, 1984)

Woodcock, George, *Anarchism: A History of Libertarian Ideas and Movements* (New York: Meridian, 1962)

Woodcock, George, 'Anarchism: A Historical Introduction', in George Woodcock (ed), *The Anarchist Reader* (Glasgow: Fontana Press, 1977), 11–56

Wright, N. T., *What Saint Paul Really Said* (Grand Rapids, MI: William B Eerdmans Publishing Company, 1997)

Wright, N. T., 'New Perspectives on Paul', Presented at the 10th Edinburgh Dogmatics Conference, Rutherford House, Edinburgh, 25–28 August 2003

Yamauchi, Edwin, *Gnostic Ethics and Mandaean Origins* (Cambridge, MA: Harvard University Press, 1970)

Zornberg, Avivah, *Genesis: The Beginning of Desire* (Philadelphia: Jewish Publication Society, 1995)

Index

abbot, 103–106, 128
Abraham, 34, 38–39, 57–58, 62, 129
Adam and Eve, 13–15, 16–17, 20, 21, 31–32, 59, 64, 69, 117, 164, 181
aesthetics, 7, 58
Agamben, Giorgio, 27, 34, 105–106
agape, 61
agent, agency, 20, 56, 64, 163–164, 180
America, 119–126
amor fati, 9, 173
analogy, 143, 183
analytic philosophy, 45, 84
anarchism, 151–159, 161, 162–165
ancients, 72, 74
antinomianism, 5, 35, 96–97, 133–143, 162–163, 182, 183, 187–189
Apollo, 184–187
Aquinas, Thomas, 42, 61, 87
archetype, 43–44, 55
Arendt, Hannah, 60, 67, 71, 73–74, 85, 178
asceticism, 101–102, 105–106, 113–114, 135
association, 76, 86, 110, 132, 161
attention. *See* love
Augustine, Saint, 60, 63, 103–104, 106, 131, 153
authority. *See* law
  generally, 153
autonomy, 17, 31, 60, 153, 156, 160

Bellah, Robert, 119–120
Benedict, Saint, 104, 107
Berlin, Isaiah, 67–69, 72, 74–76, 91, 128, 173, 178–180
Berman, Harold, 91, 98, 144, 148–149, 150, 151
Bible, 1, 13, 17, 19, 29
bipolarity, 43–47
Birth of Tragedy, 183–187, 189

bishop, 104, 139, 146
Book of Exodus, 1–2, 29, 32, 90
Book of Genesis, 12–22, 27, 31, 59–60, 69
Burt, Robert, 14, 15–16

calling, 112–114, 155
Calvinism, 37, 115, 118, 139, 184
canon law, 3, 139, 144, 148–149, 151
caritas, 60–61, 63
Catholicism, 112–115, 144–145, 148–149, 150
cenoby, cenobitism, 102–103, 106, 107, 109, 120, 122, 179
chastity, celibacy, 103, 112–113
choice, 9, 77, 111, 135, 159, 172–173, 175, 178–181
Christianity, 36, 99–101, 112, 114, 135, 140
Church, 100, 102–103, 109, 136, 139, 144, 148–151
circumcision, 3, 33, 35, 38, 135, 156
clergy, cleric, 104, 112, 139, 150
code, 1, 29, 105–106, 107–109, 184–185
coherence, 6, 98, 171–177, 181, 187
collective, 19, 56, 72–73, 86, 89, 90, 117–118, 120, 127, 130, 151, 162, 175
command, commandment, 12–18, 19, 20, 29, 33, 63, 116, 118, 153
commonwealth, 117, 121, 126
community, communitarianism, 3, 26, 28, 33, 36, 38, 40, 48, 79, 90, 99, 103, 109, 117–118, 122–123, 125, 126–127, 129–132
confession, 115, 144
conflict, 4, 9, 77, 169, 176–177, 179, 181
conscience, 87, 110, 118, 144
consciousness, conscious, 9, 14, 18–19, 38, 58, 75, 79, 170, 173
Constant, Benjamin, 67–68, 72, 127
Constitution, constitutionalism, 3, 5, 89, 96, 119–131, 145, 155, 157, 189

cosmology, 12–26, 32
covenant, covenantalism, 2–3, 29, 35, 36, 39, 115, 117–118, 119–121, 122–123, 129
creation, 10–12, 16–18, 19, 21, 23, 27, 32, 39, 53–54, 59–60, 175, 180
critical legal theory, 54–55

deconstructionism, 44–45
description, 80–82, 89, 94
desire, 16–17, 18–19, 30–31, 59, 60–63, 66, 69–70, 74, 79, 108, 116–117, 128, 129–130, 131–132, 157, 161, 185
dietary laws, 33, 38, 137, 138
differentiation, 17, 20, 64, 86, 99, 141, 147, 156
dilemma, 37, 41, 58, 99, 158, 177, 182–183
Dionysus, 183–184, 185–187
direct access, 146–147
disagreement, 50, 52, 55, 85–86, 89, 95, 124, 130, 168
discipline, 43, 114, 116–118, 123, 126, 128, 136, 144, 168, 184–185
disorder, 17, 44, 116, 121
distance, 20, 62, 64, 145, 164
distinction, distinctness, 20, 45, 47–48, 59, 64–65, 78, 140, 160, 164–165
diversity, 9, 92, 147, 172, 177, 178, 183
divine, 14, 17–18, 19, 22, 25, 31–32, 43, 61, 106, 111, 116, 117, 122–123, 129, 136, 147
Dworkin, Ronald, 48, 50–51, 81

ecclesia, 40, 99, 111, 115, 133, 139, 148–149
Eden, 10–22, 24–26, 29, 30–32, 38–39, 40–41, 59, 63, 69, 119
equality, 61, 123
eschaton, eschatology, 26, 35, 41, 99
ethic, ethics, 4, 7, 45, 58, 70, 83, 94, 113–114, 171, 182–186
ethnographic stance, 94
evaluation, 79–82, 89, 90, 114
evil, 13–14, 34, 55–56, 85–87, 91, 107, 117, 155, 181, 183
existentialism, 62, 70–71, 88, 131–132, 142, 163

faith, 33, 34–35, 42, 60, 113–115, 118–119, 138–142, 163
Fall, fallen state, 5, 11, 20–26, 39–41, 63–64, 105, 117, 126, 128, 164
feudalism, 145–146, 148
Finnis, John, 43, 48, 50, 51–52, 80–81, 87, 126, 146, 177, 180
flesh, 16, 41, 59, 135–136, 137, 157

focal meaning, 43–44
forbidden fruit, 17, 19–21, 29, 30–31, 64, 69, 117
form of life, 1, 4, 6, 35, 83, 84, 91, 94, 97, 98, 105–108, 111, 117, 120, 127, 133, 144, 166, 172, 174–177, 181
freedom
  as identification, 6, 20, 67, 72–77, 97, 108–109, 125, 126–128, 131–132
  as independence, 6, 20–21, 67–71, 97, 140, 160–165
  generally, 67–68
Freud, Sigmund, 62, 69
friar, 113
frugality, 113–114
Fuller, Lon, 44, 45–46, 53–56, 141, 168

genealogy, 143
General Will, 26, 75–76, 132
Gnosticism, 134–142, 156, 162–163
good, goods, goodness, 9–10, 12–14, 16, 34, 49, 52, 58, 80–81, 86–87, 110–111, 112, 114, 126, 129, 167, 169, 171, 172, 175, 178–181, 183
grace, 34, 122
Great Chain of Being, 145

Hart, H. L. A., 51–52
hedgehog and fox, 173–174
Hegel, G. W. F., 18, 59, 84, 130
hermeneutics, 37, 42–43
hermit, hermitage, 101–103, 107–108, 109, 115, 120, 122
heteronomy, 31
hierarchy, 17–18, 44–45, 124, 139, 145, 147, 149, 179
history, historicity, historian
  historical development, 143, 186
  historical narrative, 5, 78–79, 82, 87–95, 119
  history of ideas, 91–93
Hobbes, Thomas, 5, 11, 15, 22–26, 30, 40–41, 49–50, 53, 128, 168
homogeneity, 147
human beings, 12, 15, 167, 173, 176–177, 178
human nature, 10, 15, 27, 40, 59, 168, 178

identification. *See* freedom
imaginative empathy, 93–95
incommensurability, 171, 174–175, 179
incompatibility, 171, 174–175, 179
independence. *See* freedom
individualism, individuality, individuation, 19–21, 102, 151–152, 156, 162, 163–165

Index

inequality, 62
insurgency, 157–159, 163
integrity, 81, 105, 148, 178, 183
interiorization, 143–145
intermediary, 143, 145–148
interpretation, 4, 11, 37–39, 48, 50, 81, 95, 138
Israel, Israelite, 1–3, 29, 32, 38–39, 90, 115, 117, 120, 125

Jesus Christ, 3, 27, 28, 32, 34, 63, 100–101, 129, 133, 136, 142, 157–158, 163
Judaism, 3, 26–27, 36, 38–39, 99–100, 109, 135
judgment, 13, 36, 51, 79–81, 82, 86, 100, 130, 148, 181, 183
Jung, Carl, 16, 18
jurisdictional pluralism, 149
jurisprudence, 28, 47–48, 51, 79, 116–117, 158
justice, 22, 36, 39, 44, 49, 52, 54, 57, 153
justification, 36, 39, 88, 113

Kant, Immanuel, 52, 70, 71, 75, 159, 187–188
knowledge, 13–14, 30, 61, 65, 181

labor, 108, 110–113, 114
laity, 112, 114–115, 147
Last Judgment, 36
law
    as authority, 6, 48–52, 97, 115–117, 126–130
    as resistance, 6, 53–58, 97, 141–142, 157–159, 162–164
    generally, 23–25, 28–41, 47–48
lawlessness, 24, 37, 40–41
legal positivism, 52
legalism, 23, 37, 49, 118, 122, 140
Leviathan, 22–24, 25–26, 49–50, 53, 128
libertine pneumatics, 134, 135, 138
liberty, 2, 44, 55, 72, 74, 76, 138
logic, 13, 17–18, 19, 29, 34, 40, 45, 115, 122, 129, 156, 176
love
    as attention, 6, 20, 63–67, 97, 140–141, 159–160, 163–165
    as union, 6, 16–17, 19–20, 59–63, 97, 106, 125, 128–132
    generally, 58–59
Luther, Martin, 3, 112, 115, 118, 149, 155, 182, 184, 186, 188
Lutheranism, 37, 118, 150, 155

MacIntyre, Alasdair, 82, 88, 106, 167
martyr, martyrdom, 101–102, 105, 109, 114
materiality, 135, 137
Messiah, 3, 27, 35, 99
messianic age, 27, 32
messianic community, 35–36, 99
metaphysics, 68, 184
method, methodology, 42–43, 45, 78–97, 143
Middle Ages, 109, 145–147
mimesis, 30
monarch, monarchy, 53, 124, 145–150, 153
monasticism, monastery, monk, 1, 5, 98, 102–111, 114, 126–132, 182
moral, morality, 9, 13, 42–44, 47, 50–56, 80, 83–86, 90, 106–108, 119, 121, 141, 150, 152–153, 168–170, 172, 174, 185, 188
moral saint, 188
Moses, 33, 34, 57, 125, 127, 142
mysticism, mystic, 108, 125, 154, 184
myth, 5, 10–11, 21, 59, 95, 99, 119, 189

Nagel, Thomas, 170, 172
narrative, 87–91, *See* historical narrative
nasty brute, 15, 22–26, 189
nation, 3, 119, 121, 123, 130–132, 147–148, 150–151, 155, 159, 164
natural law, 23, 50–52, 116, 122
Nietzsche, Friedrich, 9, 34, 58, 92, 136, 173, 183–187
noble savage, 15–22, 24–25, 70, 102, 189
nomianism, 109, 122, 134, 182–189
norm, 20, 34, 50, 52, 55, 69, 103, 139, 142, 168, 188
normativity, 46, 49, 51–52, 79–80, 184
now and not yet, 36, 158, 162
Nozick, Robert, 60, 68, 130, 152

obedience, 2, 15–16, 23, 29, 31, 37–38, 62, 76, 103–109, 115–118, 128, 129, 131, 154, 160
objective, 9, 85, 170–178, 181, 187
obligation, 23, 28, 47, 90, 122, 152–153
omnipotence, 23, 143, 148, 151, 155
omnipresence, 143, 151, 155
order, 17, 24–25, 40, 44, 78, 97, 107, 109, 114, 115–117, 126, 147, 185, 186, 189

paradise, 15, 21, 26–27, 40–41, 119–120
particular, 28, 82, 170, 172
passion, 10, 22, 30, 69–71, 75, 87, 137, 157
Paul, Saint, 2–4, 26–41, 59, 96–97, 99–101, 109, 133–140, 166–167, 182

Paul's letters
  to the Corinthians, 32–33, 134–137
  to the Ephesians, 107
  to the Galatians, 28, 33, 137, 141
  to the Romans, 28, 29–30, 32, 41, 133, 166
penance, 144
perfection, 10, 36, 70, 83, 99, 100, 106, 189
Pharisee, 3, 26, 115, 118, 127
philosophy, 4, 28, 43, 44, 88, 90, 91, 152, 168–170
polarity, 4, 44–46
political theology, 122, 142
politics, polis, 3–5, 54, 73, 101, 121–122, 123–124, 142–143, 146–147, 151–152
Pope, 3, 125, 145, 149, 150
positive law, 29, 52, 116, 122
poverty, 103, 104, 110, 113–114
power, 14, 17, 21, 22–23, 53–54, 62–63, 102–104, 146, 148–150, 153, 158–159, 163
practical reason, 80–81, 86–87
practice, 43, 48, 82–87, 90–91, 92–94, 101–103, 110
prelapsarian state, 5, 11, 13, 15–22, 34, 39, 40, 59, 105, 189
prohibition, 12–13, 15–18, 29–32, 33, 69
prophecy, prophet, 27, 29, 90, 91
Protestantism, 112–116, 144–145, 150–151
psychoanalysis, 16, 18, 21, 89, 92
psychology, 29–31, 60, 72, 115, 151, 174
punishment, 2, 12–13, 29, 36, 38, 57, 101, 104, 105, 135, 150
Puritanism, 2, 113, 115–118, 120–131, 182, 185–186

rationalism, rationality, rationalization, 69–71, 75, 107–108, 111, 146, 161
Rawls, John, 23, 24, 59, 68, 130, 159
Raz, Joseph, 50–51, 62, 84, 117
reason, reasoning, 9, 13, 45–46, 66, 70–71, 75, 80–81, 86–87, 172, 180, 189
recognition, 18–19, 92, 172, 178
reflection, 18, 43, 48, 77, 80, 85, 87, 93, 181
Reformation, 3, 5, 96–97, 111–118, 142–151, 183, 186
regularity, 105, 108, 109, 117, 121
religion. *See* theology
resistance. *See* law
revolution, revolutionary, 109, 119–121, 123–124, 148, 154, 157
righteousness, 29, 34, 37, 57, 185
Romanticism, 70, 75
Rome, 35, 99–101, 107, 115, 148, 150

Rousseau, Jean-Jacques, 5, 10–11, 15–22, 26, 30, 70, 75–76, 102, 117, 132
rules, regulations, 29, 48, 51, 52, 103–109, 123, 141–142, 185

sacrament, sacramentalization, 112, 115, 144–145
sacred, 1, 7, 106, 111, 145
sacrifice, 62, 111, 129, 131–132, 154–155, 160, 177
scene, scenic imagination, skene, 10–11
Schmitt, Carl, 41, 49, 97, 142
secularism, 1, 7, 27, 41, 75, 97, 106, 126, 148–149, 150–151
self, selfhood, 64–66, 71–76, 127, 130–132, 152–157, 188
separation, separateness, 14, 20, 21, 59–61, 64, 66, 84, 130, 140, 160, 164–165
Simmonds, Nigel, 44, 55–56, 84
social form, 83, 85–86, 91, 175–178
social imaginary, 90–91
sovereign, sovereignty, 17, 23–24, 49–50, 53–54, 72, 121, 125, 148, 153–154
spirituality, spiritualization, 42–43, 113–114, 135–137, 140–141, 150, 155–156
state, statehood, 55, 101–102, 130, 132, 143, 145–155, 156–159, 163, 168
state of nature, 15–26, 40–41, 49–50, 52–53, 128–129
Stirner, Max, 144, 152–162
story
  generally. *See* myth, narrative, historical narrative
  storytelling, 88–95
subjective, 171–178, 181, 187
submission, 2, 62, 106, 125, 129–130
subsidiarity, 146
surveillance, 103, 118
systematic structure, 143

Taylor, Charles, 10, 70, 74–75, 90–91, 111–112, 124, 169
temptation, 17, 101, 105
Ten Commandments, 29, 33, 116–117
text, 42–43, 124–125
theology, 6, 114, 122, 133, 139, 189
theory, 6, 7, 48, 52, 54, 84, 114, 123, 166–181
thick concept, 81
Torah, 3, 28, 38
totalitarianism, 106, 108, 114, 189
transcendence, 35, 142, 163, 172

transgression, 13, 17, 21, 29–32, 33, 38, 137, 142, 163, 185
two kingdoms, 149
two swords, 149

union. *See* love
universal, 27, 50, 52, 82, 84–85, 100, 159, 164, 172, 177–178

value pluralism, 170–181
values, 1–6, 9, 43, 46–47, 82–87, *See* freedom, law, love, bipolarity, value pluralism
view from nowhere, 170, 172

vocation, 112, 114
vow, 104, 108, 110

Waldron, Jeremy, 28, 29–30, 47, 50–52
Walzer, Michael, 82, 90, 118, 177
will, 17, 19, 20, 31, 55, 61–62, 65, 67, 69, 71, 73, 75–76, 116, 117–118, 139, 153, 180, *See* General Will
Williams, Bernard, 24, 66, 81–82, 83, 94
Witte, John, 113–114, 116–117, 122–123, 149–150, 151
Wolf, Susan, 187–188
Wolff, R. P., 153